Class, Power and Technology

To Michael, Sarah and Brenda

Class, Power and Technology

Skilled Workers in Britain and America

ROGER PENN

Polity Press

First published 1990 by Polity Press
in association with Basil Blackwell

Editorial office:
Polity Press, 65 Bridge Street,
Cambridge CB2 1UR, UK

Marketing and production:
Basil Blackwell Ltd
108 Cowley Road, Oxford OX4 1JF, UK

British Library Cataloguing in Publication Data

A CIP catalogue record for this book is available from the British
library.

ISBN 0-7456-0141-3

Typeset in 10/12 pt Plantin
by Colset Private Limited, Singapore
Printed in Great Britain by T. J. Press (Padstow) Ltd, Padstow, Cornwall

Contents

List of Figures   vi
List of Tables   vii
Acknowledgements   ix

Part I: The Structure of Skilled Work in Britain and America

1 The Debate about Skilled Workers in Contemporary
  Class Analysis   3
2 Theories of Skilled Work in Contemporary Industrial
  Societies   17
3 Trends in Skilled Labour Since 1940   28
4 Trends in Skilled Work in Contemporary Britain   48
5 Trends in Skilled Work in the United States of America   97

**Part II: The Social Organization of Skilled Work in Britain
and America**

6 Socialization into Skilled Identities   123
7 Skilled Workers in British and American Trade Unions   140
8 The Social Composition of Skilled Workers   150

9 Conclusions   166

Notes   175
Bibliography   182
Index   195

List of Figures

Figure 3.1   A graph of occupational trends in the USA,
1940–1980, for selected craft jobs   35

Figure 3.2   The trajectories of certain skilled occupations
in Britain, 1951–1981   42

Figure 4.1   Example of modern composing work   92

List of Tables

Table 2.1   Hypotheses about trends in skilled work   26
Table 3.1   Occupational change in the USA, 1940–1980
            (percentages)   32
Table 3.2   Trends in craft work in the USA, 1940–1980
            (absolute numbers)   33
Table 3.3   Proportional changes in selected skilled
            manual occupations in the USA, 1940–1980   34
Table 3.4   Trends in skilled work in the United Kingdom,
            1951–1981, with decimal percentage changes   38
Table 3.5   Overall percentage gains or losses of selected
            skilled occupations in Britain, 1951–1981   41
Table 3.6   Trajectories of skilled work in Britain,
            1951–1981   43
Table 4.1   Changing manpower levels at Agecroft Colliery,
            1979–1986   83
Table 5.1   Workers in selected occupations in coal mining
            in the USA, 1967 and 1976   103
Table 5.2   Changes in the levels of skill of manual
            occupations within selected American
            industries since 1965   118
Table 8.1   Gender composition of five selected crafts
            (including apprentices) in the USA in 1890
            and in 1930   151
Table 8.2   Ethnic origins and gender in five selected
            crafts in the USA in 1910   152
Table 8.3   Percentages of males in selected occupational
            aggregates in the USA: 1940   156

Table 8.4   Percentages of blacks and Hispanics in
            selected skilled occupations in the USA,
            1970–1980   158
Table 8.5   Males and females in selected occupations in
            the USA, 1970–1980   160
Table 8.6   Percentage of women in selected crafts in
            Britain, 1951–1981   161
Table 9.1   Skilled workers and party allegiance (percentage
            support), 1970–1987   169

Acknowledgements

My interest in skilled workers in Britain and America was stimulated originally by Dr Gavin Mackenzie, whose *Aristocracy of Labour* (1973) was influential in the development of my own *Skilled Workers in the Class Structure* (1985). The idea of comparative research was planted a long time ago during my MA course at Brown University by Professor D. Rueschemeyer and received further encouragement from Professor Michael Mann, author of *Consciousness and Action Amongst the Western Working Class* (1973).

The present book has emerged from the Skilled Worker Project at Lancaster University. This began as an analysis of skilled workers in contemporary Britain and I have benefited from collaboration with Hilda Scattergood, Rob Simpson and Barry Wigzell on this project. Indeed, I have made extensive use of our joint ventures in chapter 4 of this book. The idea of a British–American comparison was suggested to me by Professor Anthony Giddens in 1984, and I was able to use a sabbatical semester to pursue the American work in 1985. At Berkeley I was greatly helped in my project by Professor George Strauss, Director of the Industrial Relations Institute, and by Ron Rothbart and Rob Wrenn of the Sociology Department. I am particularly indebted to the staff of the Industrial Relations Institute Library for their assistance with the location of secondary literature. Lois West, Steve Stoltenberg, Colin Sampson and Jane Politzer all made important contributions to the overall success of my visit to Berkeley. Professor Sally Hacker of Oregon State University was very helpful in my gaining access to plants in the Corvallis area and in making my visit there so enjoyable. Richard Niemesto and Nancy Foss helped arrange my visits in Michigan and provided invaluable support. I am also grateful to the American workers whom I interviewed during my stays in the USA.

I should like to express my thanks to the Nuffield Foundation, who provided two small grants in 1984 and 1986 to assist with this research and also to the Lancaster University Research Fund for their financial assistance towards my air fare to and from San Francisco in 1985. I should also like to thank Kay Roberts for her excellent work on the production of the various versions of this manuscript. Finally, I should like to express my gratitude to Tony Giddens for his helpful comments on an earlier version of this manuscript and for the kindness and forbearance shown towards a hard-pressed author.

I would also like to acknowledge that some of the material in this book has been published elsewhere. Part of chapter 3 was published by the *British Journal of Sociology* in 1986, and a part of chapter 4 in the same journal in the preceding year (Penn and Scattergood, 1985). In addition, part of chapter 6 was published in 1986 in the *Journal of Interdisciplinary Economics* (Penn, 1986a).

PART I

The Structure of Skilled Work in Britain and America

1

The Debate about Skilled Workers
in Contemporary Class Analysis

A spectre is haunting modern economic sociology: the spectre of the skilled worker. This section of the workforce in modern industrial societies has probably been less understood and more subject to mythology than any other grouping within the division of labour. Skilled workers have become central to contemporary debates within this area of sociological inquiry (see Rose, 1988). The purpose of this book is to present a theoretically based analysis of skilled workers in contemporary Britain and America and thereby to provide an antidote to the confusion that surrounds this area of inquiry. However, this book is more than a comparative analysis of skilled workers. It is also a challenge to contemporary economic sociology and, in particular, to the persistent tendency to approach the issue of skilled work from an *a priori* rather than an empirical stance. This book will provide what is signally lacking in contemporary research within the field of economic sociology: namely, detailed analyses of what modern skilled workers actually do whilst engaged in paid employment. As such these analyses constitute an explicit rejection of the style and procedures of the preceding dominant research tradition.

In this chapter the broad debate about skilled workers in the class structure will be presented. This is followed in the next chapter by an examination of the specific arguments about skilled work within industrial sociology. Such an approach is heuristic since class analysis and industrial sociology are merely differing aspects of modern economic sociology and, as we shall see, both strands of investigation share parallel discursive parameters. The confusion that surrounds the issue of skilled work and the skilled worker can be examined initially in terms of two core debates – the historical and the sociological.

1 The Historical Debate

The issue of skilled workers cannot be divorced from the question of the working class that has so preoccupied social scientists in modern societies (see Goldthorpe, 1979). In Britain there has been an over-whelming view that the working class in synonymous with manual workers. This view is central to both sociological and historical perspectives in Britain. When Thompson (1963), Britain's most famous contemporary social historian, argued that a working class had emerged in Britain by the 1830s, he meant that the British manual working class had developed a shared class consciousness by that time. In other words, a working-class culture centred upon manual work had emerged in Britain as a result of the development of factory production and urban living in the early nineteenth century. A similar perspective is evident in the USA. Form (1985) has recently written a seminal work on 'Working Class Stratification in America', and American social historians such as Montgomery (1976), Brody (1980) and Walkowitz (1981) increasingly talk of 'workers' and 'the working class' in terms that refer exclusively to manual workers.

Such a notion of the working class is still central within contemporary British cultural life. The notion of the working class is still held by most Britons to be synonymous with manual workers. As will be shown later, such a conception is less clear-cut in the USA, but as Jackman and Jackman (1983) and Vanneman and Cannon (1987) have shown, the notion of a manual working class is certainly common in contemporary America. Of course, there are many problems with such a viewpoint. Are the people who work in supermarkets or in hotels or in fast-food restaurants any less working-class than such classic exemplars as coal miners, steelworkers or toolmakers? A whole academic industry has developed on both sides of the Atlantic trying to resolve these boundary questions (see Goldthorpe and Hope, 1974; Wright, 1985; Marshall et al., 1988). Nevertheless, the notion of a traditional working class, centred upon manual work in factories, still holds a central place within contemporary academic and popular images of the class structure.

This academic discourse is based upon a powerful set of texts in Britain. Hoggart (1959) analysed the allegedly tight-knit working-class communities of the inter-war years in Britain. His imagery and parallel versions from Willmott and Young (1957) and Klein (1965) all emphasized the historical existence of a solidaristic, homogeneous, historical British working class. These views flowed into the mainstream of British sociology initially through the writings of Lockwood (1960, 1966) and subsequently through the three volumes of the *Affluent Worker* research (Goldthorpe et al., 1968a, 1968b and 1969). Such images were reinforced by the various writings of the editorial board of the influential *New Left Review* in the mid-1960s (Anderson, 1965, 1966; and Nairn, 1964, 1965). As I have demonstrated in my previous analysis of the development of skilled workers in Britain (1985a), these academic images of the manual working class lack systematic supporting empirical evidence. They are essentially mythical rather than the result of rigorous empirical inquiry. They intersect with popular characterizations of the working class, such as the soap-opera *Coronation Street* and the vogue for Lowry prints. Indeed, it is this symbiosis of academic and popular imagery that explains the powerful hold that this conception of the working class holds in contemporary British sociology. The loss of this key benchmark throws most contemporary British sociologists into a panic and can rarely be sustained. Nevertheless, it remains a distinct possibility that 'the Emperor has no clothes'! Perhaps there never has been a working class in Britain, if by the term we mean an economically unified, politically cohesive, socially distinct and culturally homogeneous entity.

Such a possibility is strengthened by the argument that the manual working class has been divided around the axis of skill since its alleged inception. This viewpoint has been put forward by a large number of both British and American social historians in their analyses of the 'labour aristocracy'. Whilst the concept of a labour aristocracy has acquired a chaotic variety of usages within neo-Marxist approaches to class analysis,[1] it is generally confined within social history to the examination of skilled manual workers. Paradoxically, this was the original thrust of the concept as developed by Engels in the 1880s. He argued (1971) that the failure of Marx's analysis of the proletariat in Britain could be explained by the development – albeit temporary – of a privileged 'aristocracy' within the British working class. These workers, such as carpenters and turners (machinists), constituted a well-paid working-class elite whose economic fortunes were based upon the peculiar monopoly enjoyed by British industry in world markets between 1850 and 1880. In fact, such workers enjoyed relatively high wages mainly as a result of their capacity to unionize, itself a function of the relative scarcity of their new skills which were central to the emergent factory regimes of the later nineteenth century. However, both Marx and

Engels and later Lenin (1971) saw the existence of a well-paid skilled stratum within the manual working class as a purely temporary phenomenon which would be eradicated by the destructive powers of capitalist development.

This image of a skilled working class stratum – economically privileged, highly unionized, socially superior, industrially and politically conservative and ultimately doomed by the march of history – has affected much Marxist social historical analysis. Hobsbawm (1964), Foster (1976) and Gray (1976) have all made use of this imagery for their conjunctural historical analyses of the British working class. Similarly, Aronowitz (1983) has utilized parallel conceptions for his analysis of American labour history. However, Pelling (1968) and later Hinton (1973) in Britain, and Montgomery (1976) and Dawson (1979) in the USA, have shown that this is a distorted view of skilled workers. Pelling demonstrates clearly the anachronistic approach of Marxist social historians like Hobsbawm; he shows that skilled workers were more militant than nonskilled workers in late Victorian Britain and quotes Mayhew (1861), a leading contemporary social investigator, to the effect that:

> The artisans are almost to a man red hot politicians. They are sufficiently educated and thoughtful to have a sense of their importance in the state . . . The unskilled labourers are a different class of people. As yet they are as unpolitical as footmen, and instead of entertaining violent democratic opinions, they appear to have no political opinions whatever; or if they do possess any, they rather tend towards the maintenance of 'things as they are' than towards the ascendancy of the working people.

It is also quite mistaken to characterize late Victorian unions as conservative simply because they had little truck with revolutionary socialism. The whole idea of a trade union was deviant from the *laissez-faire* doctrines of Victorian ideology. A failure to grasp this structural characteristic of unionism is to misunderstand the development of labour politics in this period. Indeed, it is quite asinine to suggest that British trade union leaders in the 1870s and 1880s were 'bourgeois' simply on the basis that they dressed smartly for photographs. Such condescension by well-heeled Marxist social historians has been devastatingly and correctly attacked by Perkin (1978). This depth of misunderstanding can be illustrated by the case of the Cotton Spinners' Union in England during the latter part of the nineteenth century. Its affiliates are usually castigated by radical historians as beyond the pale since many of their officials and members supported the Conservative Party at that time. However, this is scarcely surprising given that most of their employers were Liberals![2] In fact, the Oldham District of the Spinners' Union spent £298,000 between 1871 and 1896 on providing strike pay for its members engaged in local disputes: indeed, between 1883 and 1893, there were 3,005 separate disputes in Oldham. The Oldham District also contributed £320,000 to the Spinners' Amalgamation for supporting more generalized disputes in the spinning industry.[3]

The industrial militancy of skilled workers historically has received considerable attention in recent years. Hinton (1973) analysed the reaction of skilled engineering workers to radical changes in working practices in Britain during the First World War, and Haydu (1984, 1988) has provided a parallel analysis for the USA. However, whilst the notion of the militant craftsman is more accurate than that of a conservative labour aristocracy for an understanding of skilled workers, it still suffers from certain ambiguities. Montgomery (1976) uses the term to refer to the militancy of artisans in factories (such as shoemakers) caused by mechanization itself whereas Hinton (1973) analyses the militant responses of skilled industrial craftsmen to increases in the level of automation in their already highly mechanized work. Furthermore, Montgomery, Hinton and Haydu all display a distinct Marxian pessimism about the long-term viability of mechanized skills in factories. Their analyses represent more a glorification of a Canutean resistance to the inexorable destruction of skilled work under modern conditions. Within this tradition, the skilled worker is seen as an historical relic with little long-term viability within the dynamic processes of capitalist rationalization.

Consequently, we are presented in the field of the social historical analysis of class in Britain and America with a series of historical images of the class structure. The proponents of the notion of the traditional working class suggest the emergence of an homogeneous manual working class, employed predominantly in factories and living in their own communities within the wider urban structure. Many of the leading exponents of this version of the traditional working class suggest that this type of structure is disappearing in the contemporary era. However, running parallel to this framework is an entirely inconsistent model of class relations which emphasizes the historic division between skilled and nonskilled workers within the working class as a whole. For exponents of the thesis of the labour aristocracy, these divisions are conjunctural and entail the superimposition of conservatism upon the 'natural' radicalism of the mass of the manual working class. This latter view is challenged by the image of the militant craftsman, which portrays skilled workers as the vanguard of resistance to the capitalist rationalization of work. However, the militant craftsman is seen as the modern equivalent of the handloom weaver who tried in vain to resist the remorseless tide of capitalist rationalization in the early nineteenth century. Furthermore, a careful reading of this social historical literature reveals a series of fundamental confusions about the precise chronology of when the manual working class was supposed to be homogeneous and when it was held to be riven or structured by a skilled divide.[4]

It was these ambiguities and confusions which prompted my previous work on *Skilled Workers in the Class Structure* (1985). Its central aim was to 'investigate the nature and existence of the working class' and in particular the form and content of the skilled divide within the British manual working class since the 1850s. The research was conducted in Rochdale, Lancashire. Rochdale was one of the earliest centres of industrialization in Britain. It rose to prominence as a centre for textile manufacture and subsequently for the production of metal goods. The research demonstrated that the workforce in both the textile and engineering industries had been organized around the axis of skill throughout the period between 1850 and the mid-1960s (see also Penn, 1983a). The trade union structure solidified this pattern and both wage bargaining and job demarcations were determined by the centrality of 'skill' for relations between employers and workers (Penn, 1982). The research revealed the longevity of stable skilled earnings' differentials in both textiles and engineering: indeed, the proportional difference between skilled and nonskilled workers had not changed significantly in the town since the early 1920s (Penn, 1983b). Far from there being a series of conjunctural changes associated with either increasing homogeneity or with increasing sectionalism in the spheres of work and the labour market, it was clear that the skilled divide had been a continuous and persistent feature of the structure of the manual working class in Britain since the mid-nineteenth century. Such findings suggested that neither a picture of the disappearance of the working class amid increasing sectionalism nor one of increasing homogeneity was consistent with these data. Skilled workers had been a persistent feature of the working class in Rochdale and, by extension, in Britain throughout the period up to the mid-1960s. A central aim of this book will be an examination of whether this skilled divide has changed significantly over the last 50 years or so in Britain and whether there have been similar patterns and developments in the USA over the same period.

2 The Sociological Debate

In Britain the sociological analysis of skilled workers in the class structure is less developed than the social historical debate. On the other hand, the sociological analysis of skilled workers is more developed in the USA than the historical approach there. For heuristic purposes we can characterize the sociological debate as consisting of four distinct conceptual nodes. These four positions can be labelled 'embourgeoisement', 'differentiation', 'proletarianization' and 'stability'.

2.1 The Embourgeoisement of Skilled Workers

The embourgeoisement thesis was propounded in the USA during the 1950s. Mayer (1963) argued that the 'traditional dividing line between manual workers and white-collar employees no longer holds, because large segments of the working class now share a "white collar" style of life and many also accept middle class values and beliefs' (p. 467). In particular, Mayer saw the growth of home ownership and suburban living amongst affluent workers as symbolizing an emergent 'middle class society'. This picture closely followed the imagery of the 'end of ideology' (Bell, 1962) and 'convergence'[5] theorists and seemed to be clinched by the discovery that the pattern of income distribution in the USA had changed from its traditional pyramid profile to a diamond shape. Whyte (1956) went further and argued that the new suburbs in America were the 'second melting pot' where traditional class differences were transcended. Gans' (1962) study of Italians in South Boston also emphasized the new pressures towards middle-class life amongst the new suburbanites. Clearly if the embourgeoisement thesis were to be valid, it should affect skilled manual workers the most, since they have traditionally earned significantly more than the nonskilled, both in America and in Britain.[6]

Indeed, the notion of embourgeoisement remains a central plank of much contemporary US economic sociology. One consequence of this conceptualization is that the working class disappears from sociological view, to be replaced by the analysis of a myriad of disadvantaged groups such as the elderly, non-whites and part-time women workers. Such sociological concern to analyse a kaleidoscopic 'rainbow coalition' parallels the dominant cultural axioms of contemporary America, where individualism is seen as far more significant than class factors in the explanation of societal development.[7]

2.2 Differentiation

Mackenzie (1973) examined the applicability of the embourgeoisement thesis to American society in the 1960s. His research was based on a cross-sectional survey undertaken in Providence, Rhode Island, in 1965. Mackenzie examined whether income differentials between the working class and middle class were collapsing, whether the distinctions between manual and non-manual work were disappearing, whether cultural differences between the working class and middle class were weakening and whether traditional working-class communities were breaking up as workers moved to suburban areas and bought their own homes. His results constitute a partial refutation of the embourgeoisement thesis. His argument is that the class structure of twentieth-century America has become more complex, by which he means that new forms of differentiation have emerged within both the working class *and* the middle class. In particular, Mackenzie emphasizes the systematic differences between skilled and nonskilled workers in his sample. This he characterizes, perhaps unfortunately, in terms of an emergent 'aristocracy of labor'. Nevertheless, Mackenzie's study is both stimulating and provocative. However, his cross-sectional data are not sufficiently powerful to support his historical claims. He is unable to demonstrate that the patterns of differentiation between skilled and nonskilled workers in Providence are anything new. Indeed, the historical material discussed in the previous section should sound a considerable degree of caution here. Nevertheless, Mackenzie's study, influenced as it was by Durkheimian and structural-functionalist notions of differentiation and of the centrality of the division of labour for a sociological understanding of economic inequality, presents a powerful case that skilled workers were distinct from the rest of the working class in America at least by the 1960s.

This viewpoint has received its most powerful theoretical underpinning from Dahrendorf (1959). He argued that there had been a 'decomposition of labour' since 1945, whereby there was a progressive differentiation between routine 'semi-skilled' manual work and new forms of skilled labour associated primarily with the design, operation and maintenance of new forms of production in advanced capitalist societies.[8] This approach can be seen as closely linked conceptually to the notions of 'dualism' developed in the 1970s to explain labour market inequalities in the USA (see Doeringer and Piore, 1971). However, it is worth noting that Mackenzie's and Dahrendorf's conceptualization of duality focuses explicitly on the skilled divide within the manual working class, whereas radical labour market analyses are unclear about the precise sociological contours of polarization within contemporary labour markets. Halle (1984) confirms this differentiation within the American working class. His research showed that skilled mechanics in a New Jersey chemical plant generally enjoyed their work, whereas production workers, who earned considerably more on average than the maintenance mechanics, overwhelmingly disliked their work. Indeed, their dislike was sufficiently strong in many cases to prompt them to utilize their seniority within the plant to 'bump' into apprenticeships at a considerable loss of pay.

Recently, Form (1985) has suggested that there is a five-fold division within the American working class. Form is the foremost analyst[9] of skilled workers within contemporary American sociology and his knowledge of the sociological significance of skill leads him to a model akin to Mackenzie's and Dahrendorf's, but one that is rather more complex. Form defines the working class overall as 'all workers in nonfarm manual and service jobs' (1985:27). Such a definition correctly excludes clerical white-collar workers. Form divides the working class so defined into five strata on the basis of their relationship to property ownership, their level of skill and the economic significance of their sector of employment. In consequence, he distinguishes self-employed manual workers, craft or skilled employees, nonskilled employees in the core sector of the economy, nonskilled employees in the peripheral sector of the economy, and marginally employed groups. Form demonstrates clearly that skilled workers are paid significantly more than the nonskilled and that they are less likely than the nonskilled to see their pay as undeservedly low. He further suggests that the economic and social differences between these strata are becoming wider in modern America. Like Mackenzie and Dahrendorf, Form argues that the structure of the American working class is becoming more differentiated.

2.3 Proletarianization

Mackenzie's, Dahrendorf's and Form's picture of an increasingly distinct upper stratum of skilled manual workers received a major challenge from the work of Braverman (1974). Braverman argued that there was an endemic process of deskilling underway within contemporary capitalist societies whereby skilled labour was being progressively eliminated from production. Braverman seeks to demonstrate that craft workers are robbed of their skill by the progressive implementation of managerial control and the ensuing subdivision and routinization of their traditional work within capitalist societies. This process of subdivision – which Braverman calls the Babbage principle – is the 'underlying force governing all forms of work in capitalist society' (1974:82). According to the theory, every step in the process of work is divorced from specialized knowledge and training and reduced to the simplest possible form. Management is central to this process of deskilling and degradation of craft work.

According to Braverman, management in 'monopoly capitalist' societies is based upon three principles. The first principle entails the 'dissociation of the labour process from the skills of the workers'. Management is involved, through systematic analysis of craft work, in the gathering and monopolization of knowledge hitherto residing in the practices of skilled labour. The second principle involves the separation of conception from execution: as Braverman states, 'all possible brain work should be removed from the shop and centred in the planning and laying out department' (1974:113). Braverman sees this as integral to the progressive dehumanization of the labour process. This is fully achieved by the third principle of modern management: the use of the monopolization of knowledge to control each step of the labour process and its mode of execution. Modern management involves the systematic pre-planning and pre-calculation of all aspects of production: processes which increase the alienation of labour and entail the systematic destruction of craft work. Taylorism and scientific management are seen as both the ideological 'voice' of these developments and the inevitable practice of all modern capitalist managements.

Braverman suggests that developments in automated machinery provide management with the opportunity to achieve control through mechanical means. The main example provided involves the use of numerical control units on machine tools. Prior to the development of electronically based control systems, which are both cheap and reliable, most metalworking had remained within the sphere of skilled machinists. According to Braverman, numerical control leads to the progressive deskilling of machinists as their skills are increasingly embodied in computerized control repertoires that have been produced elsewhere by technical specialists. The skilled machinist is rendered obsolete by the processes of subdivision of work outlined above. Braverman then proceeds to suggest that the same processes have been at work in a range of other occupational milieux which have been the traditional preserve of skilled craft workers – boilermaking, heavy plate construction, sheetmetal shops, construction work, baking, furniture production, meatpacking, clothing and typesetting. Furthermore, computerization also leads to the progressive elimination of maintenance skills with the increasing emergence of self-diagnostic maintenance routines. The net result of all these trends is that there is a decreasing need for either production or maintenance skills amongst manual workers in the USA.

This pessimistic view about skilled work and skilled workers has been very influential within contemporary social science. Clearly the image of deskilling portrayed by Braverman suggests a widespread elimination of skilled work and a concomitant homogenization of the manual working class. It is in stark contrast to the optimistic pictures of Mackenzie and Dahrendorf, who argue that there is a persistent need for skilled workers in modern systems of production,[10] and that such groups are becoming a more distinct stratum within the manual working class.

2.4 Stable Relations between Skilled and Nonskilled Workers

The final possibility is that skilled workers remain a distinct stratum within the contemporary class structures of advanced societies. This is the position of both Goldthorpe (1980) and Wright (1985) who, for quite different theoretical reasons, distinguish and separate the categories of skilled and nonskilled manual workers within their respective models of advanced capitalist societies. However, neither author offers a satisfactory analysis of the contemporary class situation of skilled workers. Goldthorpe, in practice, makes virtually no use of the distinction between skilled and nonskilled manual workers in his analysis of social mobility in Britain in the early 1970s, preferring rather to talk in traditional fashion about the working class. This is surprising given his own data on the differential mobility chances of people born into these categories. However, it is in line with his previous work which consistently conflates the nonskilled stratum of workers with the working class in its entirety.[11]

Wright's work is even less satisfactory. His scholastic Marxism uses the notion of contradiction to explain the stability of capitalist societies.[12] In the face of 'arguments' like that, it is more than likely that

Marx would be a Weberian nowadays! Wright places skilled manual workers outside the working class since he claims that they not only sell their labour power (his definition of a 'pure' worker), but also enjoy jobs that embody the unity of conception and execution. However, he neither explains what the latter precisely means nor can his theory cope with the similarity of many skilled and nonskilled jobs in terms of their autonomy and discretion at work. As I argued in my previous works (1983a, 1983b, 1983c, 1985a, 1985b), the distinction between skilled and nonskilled workers is not determined simply by objective differences in job content. We shall see in later chapters of this book that this is no mere detail, but a central feature of the social organization of work in many industries in modern societies. Marshall et al. (1988), in their own comparison of Goldthorpe and Wright, persist with the weaknesses of both positions and offer little insight into the changing class situation of skilled manual workers in the contemporary period. This is mainly because they follow Goldthorpe and Wright in their divorce of stratification (or class) analysis from the study of work in modern societies. It is a central tenet of the new economic sociology that the findings of industrial sociology are a necessary and vital component of any satisfactory analysis of the structural contours of inequality in modern societies. Such views are also central to the classical tradition within sociology. Both Marx[13] and Weber[14] offer analyses that provide an integration of concerns with the macro-structure of capitalist societies with the micro-details of actual working conditions. It is a strange paradox that Goldthorpe, Britain's leading neo-Weberian sociologist, and Wright, who claims the neo-Marxist crown in the USA, should both restrict class analysis to debates about occupational categorizations. However, as I shall demonstrate, even this restriction of inquiry is self-defeating since neither author has grounded his understanding of occupational differences in rigorous empirical inquiry.

3 Conclusions

It is clear that there is considerable academic confusion surrounding the question of how to approach the analysis of skilled workers in contemporary societies. Within the social historical literature we encounter two contradictory images of the historic working class. The model of the traditional working class suggests that it was homogeneous: unified by a shared economic status, by a common culture and by a unified political mission. The model of the labour aristocracy conversely suggests a perennial division between skilled and nonskilled workers, centred upon economic, political, cultural and social distinctions. Within the overall social historical discourse both images can be utilized. The homogeneous working class of one period can be contrasted with the divided working class of another. The uses of these polar models of the working class is generally *ad hoc*, unsystematic and lacking in rigour. A classic example involves the assessment of class relations in the 1920s and 1930s in Britain. This period is characterized by Foster (1976), Roberts (1971) and Davis and Cousins (1975) as featuring a clear labour aristocracy, whilst Lockwood (1960), Hoggart (1959) and Anderson (1965) see it as a period of working-class homogeneity.

Similar confusions surround the debate about skilled workers in American sociology. For Braverman such industrial dinosaurs are disappearing, whilst for Mackenzie and Form they are fit and doing rather well! There is nothing particularly surprising about these respective states of affairs. Sociology displays a dazzling capacity to produce a plethora of competing models and theoretical orientations, but is rather less impressive in its ability to modify these positions as a result of rigorous empirical inquiry. Nor should we be surprised by the lack of a systematic connection between the sociological and historical debates, although, as can be seen, they display many common properties. Few sociologists have any historical training and vice versa: a situation that sustains rather than eliminates mythologizing about the relationship of the past to the present (see Penn, 1989).

Nevertheless, the historical and sociological debates about skilled workers and skilled work raise a series of important questions for contemporary social science. The first centres, paradoxically, upon how to define the working class itself for sociological analysis. As I have argued elsewhere (Penn, 1982), there is no absolute definition of the working class that can be decided from an *a priori* position. In this book, as with my other research, I utilize the notion of the working class to cover 'all employees in manual and routine service jobs'. This excludes self-employed manual workers since their employment situation makes them significantly different from these other groupings. The self-employed are subject neither to the authority relations inherent in the sale of labour within advanced capitalist societies nor to the standard wage form itself. Within this definition of the working class, it is possible to distinguish a skilled and a nonskilled stratum. Such a definition is heuristic and open to modification. It is, moreover, consistent with the dominant conceptualizations outlined earlier in this chapter. From such a model a series of specific questions about skilled workers and skilled work are suggested which have governed the nature of the empirical research undertaken for this book. Firstly, it is important to establish whether there are any skilled workers in modern societies and if their number is increasing or decreasing. Secondly, it is important to clarify what constitutes a skilled worker and what variant forms of skilled workers there are. Thirdly, it would be interesting to discover whether this stratum sees itself as part of the working class or part of some other social category. Fourthly, it would be valuable to ascertain whether the model of an aristocracy of labour or the militant craftsman best characterizes this group. Fifthly, it is of major importance to know what is happening to skilled unionism and to the social attributes of skilled workers. Historically, skilled unions have tried to restrict skilled work to white, male, adult workers. We need to know whether this remains the pattern under contemporary conditions.

From the previous discussion it becomes clear that any adequate analysis of these issues must be both historical and sociological and must also integrate the rigorous empirical analysis of skilled work with the wider question of skilled workers within the overall class structure. The first part of this book involves an examination of these issues in Britain and America since the Second World War, whereas the second part takes a longer perspective. Such differential chronologies are largely heuristic and contingent upon the questions asked. The first part of the book deals with the question of skilled work in both societies since 1940, whilst the second part addresses the issue of the changing social situation of skilled workers in the two countries during the twentieth century. Clearly, the task set is enormous and I make no claim to have produced a definitive study of these issues. However, I would at least hope that by the end of the text the reader will possess a clearer picture of the situation of skilled workers and skilled work in both countries.

2

Theories of Skilled Work in Contemporary Industrial Societies

While the general debate about skilled workers in the class structure has been characterized by considerable confusion, the debate within industrial sociology in Britain and the USA over skilled work and skilled workers has been determined by a series of precise, if incompatible, general positions. These theories – human capital theory, the neo-Marxist theory of deskilling and the compensatory theory of skill formulated during the Skilled Worker Project at Lancaster University in the mid-1980s – all focus upon the trajectory of skilled work in contemporary industrial societies. However, both human capital theory, which suggests a pervasive enskilling of modern work, and the neo-Marxist theory of deskilling pitch their analyses at a very high level of generality. Braverman talks about the dialectics of capital and labour under conditions of 'monopoly' capitalism and about the nature of the division of labour under the influences of scientific management. Similarly, Fuchs and Bell, the leading exponents of the human capital perspective surrounding skilled work, both present pictures of modern work that have an alleged universal applicability. This book is designed, in part, to scrutinize such universalistic theories of skilled work by means of an examination of two case studies – the USA and Britain. However, before the specific mode of analysis is presented, it is necessary to delineate the central features of each of the three theories that have been developed to describe the central features of changes in skilled work in the contemporary era.

1 Human Capital Theory

The human capital theory of skilled work is associated with notions of post-industrialism and paints a picture of an increasing demand for, and provision of, skilled workers in advanced industrial societies. This secular model will be termed the 'skilling' thesis. The general argument, as found in writers like Bell (1974), Touraine (1969) and, to an extent, Habermas (1976), is that advanced industrial societies require an increasingly educated workforce. Arguments are put forward about the growth of 'knowledge' as a new factor of production and the concomitant growth of knowledge-producing (e.g. universities, research institutes) and knowledge-consuming (e.g. electronics) industries. Indeed, it can be argued with considerable force that post-industrial theories are all primarily theoretical sociological reflections upon empirical work conducted by American labour economists concerned to explain the rapid and dramatic growth there of the service sector of employment. This connection is less obvious in Touraine or Habermas, since their arguments derive more from grand assertions based upon fragmentary and limited evidence than from systematic reflection upon empirical research: but it is quite explicit in Bell (1974), who openly acknowledges his debt to the pioneering work carried out by the American labour economist, Fuchs.

For Fuchs (1968), the major explanatory variable in the growth of the 'service economy' is change associated with the development and implementation of advanced technology. His thesis suggests that the evolution of new advanced technologies – electronics in general, and computers in particular – requires an ever more educated workforce for its development. Emphasis is increasingly put on investment in manpower or the production of 'human' capital. Proponents of human capital theory like Becker (1964) at Chicago, who provide the theoretical basis for Fuchs' work, argue that more and more capital investment takes the form of training and that the workforce becomes increasingly 'valuable' as an input for production. It is the putative effects of, on the one hand, the growth of the 'knowledge-industries' and, on the other, of more and more sophisticated technology that produce a secular 'skilling' of the labour force under advanced industrialism.

Advanced industrial societies *have* witnessed a growth in the sophistication of technology, an expansion of knowledge-producing and knowledge-consuming industries and also a dramatic rise in general levels of education. However, there are certain features of the correlation between extended formal education and expanding knowledge-related industries that should lead to a certain scepticism about the validity of post-industrialist theories of 'skilling'. Firstly, a greater number of years spent at school does not necessarily lead to a greater range of 'skills' in the incumbents. Sources as far apart as the *Black Paper 1977* (Cox and Boyson, 1977) on education and radical sociological research typified by Willis (1977) and Corrigan (1979) cast serious doubt on the likelihood of there being a simple, positive relationship between years of formal education completed and industrial competence. Secondly, for Britain at least, research has suggested that the formal education system is a poor indicator of future occupational attainment since it ignores the crucial role of part-time, post-school education in the accumulation of industrially relevant educational credentials (see Stewart et al., 1980). Without a more complex model of levels of education and training than merely the number of years spent in school, post-industrialist theories remain, at best, conjecture. Thirdly, the undoubted sophistication of the products of advanced electronic technology does not necessarily require the existence of high levels of skill in its routine production. The extensive division of labour and functions within the enormous multinational corporations that produce such commodities as computers, video-recorders and calculators, may well decrease the proportion of technically sophisticated personnel required for research and development and for production within the overall workforce. It is perhaps more likely that there is a decreasing need for skill given the widespread manufacture of such commodities in Taiwan, Hong Kong and South Korea – countries not renowned for their post-industrial structures.

Given the high ratio of capital to labour in such ventures, it would seem difficult to explain the massive increase in the provision of educational services in advanced industrial societies simply in terms of technological exigencies. Indeed, if one examines the expansion of the service sector carefully, it becomes apparent that the fastest growing and largest sectors comprise not technically qualified personnel but clerical and sales-workers, teachers, social workers and medical workers. Nevertheless, there is increasing evidence that new technologies, and particularly micro-electronics, are having a significant effect on the nature of jobs in Britain during the 1980s (for example, Northcott and Rogers, 1984). The skilling thesis, associated with human capital theory and notions of post-industrialism, does therefore constitute a plausible interpretation of occupational change in the modern era. This thesis can be characterized in relation to changes in manual work in the following terms. Firstly, the workforce as a whole is becoming increasingly skilled as the result of technical change. Secondly, both production and maintenance workers are becoming more skilled as the result of the introduction of new technologies, particularly micro-electronics. Finally, a central feature of such increasing skills is a growing level of training throughout the workforces of modern industries. Given their common societal features, such a theory should apply equally in Britain and in the USA with perhaps some marginal differences based upon such factors as the rate of technical innovation, the nature of sectoral employment and the general level of economic dynamism. Clearly, the skilling thesis represents an optimistic version of the inter-relations of technical change and the division of labour in the contemporary period.

2 The Marxist Theory of Deskilling

The seminal work in the new economic sociology is Braverman's *Labor and Monopoly Capital* (1974). Braverman's text embodies a classic integration of general theses concerning broad issues in social stratification with more specific arguments about the changing nature of work. A large number of people from both sides of the Atlantic now attend the annual Labour Process Conferences in England. Researchers from a wide variety of disciplines and perspectives produce work within this area and Braverman's text still stands as the benchmark. Braverman's work, despite its many serious flaws,[1] acts as a linchpin within the contemporary social scientific discourse on work.[2] For example, in 1984 the entire issue of the *New Zealand Journal of Industrial Relations* was devoted to an examination of Braverman's propositions in that country and by early 1985, even the Australian Prime Minister, Mr Bob Hawke, received an official report on *Computer-Related Technologies in the Metal Trades Industry* (Technical Change Committee, 1985) which cited Braverman's conclusions. Nevertheless, I suspect that Braverman's text has become more quoted than read and that few researchers know more than the condensed version of his argument outlined in the previous chapter. This chapter will present his argument in considerable detail, since one of the central thrusts of the ensuing text is a challenge to the adequacy of Braverman's account *in its entirety*.

Braverman argues that the labour process (the process of production whereby power is applied to raw materials and machinery to produce commodities) in modern capitalist economies is determined by capitalist social relations and is not simply the result of technical or organizational imperatives. Braverman, as an orthodox Marxist, assumes that labour creates all value in capitalist economies and that labour processes reflect, in their organizational forms, the antagonistic class relations inherent in such capitalist societies. Since capitalists and their managerial agents cannot rely upon labour to maximize its efforts of its own accord under such a system, they are driven inexorably to maximize their own control over the labour process. Braverman argues that capitalists need to dominate the labour process and weaken the ability of workers to resist. He places great emphasis on the role of scientific management as the quintessential method of achieving this in the twentieth century. For Braverman, scientific management (or Taylorism) is the logical form of modern management and it entails the systematic subdivision of tasks and the incorporation of new technologies that are decreasingly dependent upon the traditional craft skills of the workforce. Such a viewpoint leads to Braverman's most influential conception about the development of modern work – the theory of deskilling.

This theory is aimed directly at the optimistic human capital interpretation of the effects of technological changes upon the division of labour outlined above. Braverman argues that both manual and non-manual work are being deskilled in his analysis of craft work (see especially chapter 9) and clerical work (see chapter 15) in the twentieth century. For Braverman, advanced capitalism is producing a proletarianization of the workforces in such societies and his argument is seen as providing a contemporary vindication of Marx's own historical theory of proletarianization under conditions of competitive capitalism. Braverman's view of modern work is deeply pessimistic, although it provides, in his mind, the objective basis for a socialist transformation of advanced capitalism sometime in the future.

As was shown in the previous chapter, Braverman identifies three principles of modern management. The first involves the 'dissociation of the labour process from the skills of the worker'. This principle involves the incorporation of traditional craft skills into the actual organization of production. The second principle involves the separation of conception from execution within the work situation. Braverman argues that scientific management believes that all possible brain work should be removed from the shop (i.e. factory) floor and centred in the planning and laying out departments. The third principle follows inexorably from the former. Modern managements use a 'monopoly of knowledge to control each step of the labour process and its mode of execution' (p. 199). The main effect of these principles is that the structure of the workforce changes with 'a secular trend toward the incessant lowering of the working class as a whole below its previous conditions of skill and labour' (p. 129). However, the central propositions about the corollaries of these principles upon the nature of modern manual work are to be found in Braverman's famous chapter on 'Machinery', which therefore warrants careful scrutiny.

According to Braverman new forms of technology, and particularly micro-electronics, now make possible the incorporation of control over the worker into the core functions of modern machines. Braverman contrasts the traditional work of the skilled machinist or turner with that of the contemporary operator of a numerically controlled machine tool. In the traditional system of work, small-batch production predominated and the worker had a wide range of tasks to perform. However, with the advent of numerically controlled machine tools, the processes of metal-cutting become 'virtually automatic' (p. 199). According to Braverman, 'Most of the functions of the skilled machinist have been shifted to the parts' programmer' (p. 202). The skilled machinist is reduced to a mere machine attendant with a vast reduction in the scope and variety of his or her job. Braverman then proceeds to argue that the same processes are at work in boilershops, sheetmetal shops, and in the heavy plate con-struction, bread, furniture, construction, meatpacking, clothing and printing industries. Modern industry is seen as entailing a widespread and pervasive deskilling of manual production skills. Furthermore, the advent of self-diagnostic routines on machinery and the use of modular component replacements is having a similar effect on maintenance skills. Braverman's use of evidence becomes increasingly weak at this part of his argument. As a rule, Braverman uses one or two citations to establish a general point but when he gets on to modern maintenance work, instead of providing empirical evidence on the nature of such work in practice, he quotes the president of a firm that manufactures automatic machinery and controls to the effect that 'they require little maintenance'! Such use of evidence is strange from an author who lambastes 'bourgeois' social scientists for listening over much to the managerial apologists of industrial capital!

Nevertheless, despite the problems inherent within Braverman's methodology (in particular his persistent use of one or two examples to confirm a general point arrived at deductively), a series of propositions about the skills involved in modern manual work are evident in his text. Braverman argues that the vast bulk of skilled manual work is being deskilled in modern capitalist industries. Production and maintenance skills are increasingly eliminated by the incorporation of control mecha-nisms within modern machinery. Production workers simply watch machines and maintenance workers come along and change components as indicated by monitors using self-diagnostic routines. Labour becomes ever more homogenized and therefore *interchangeable*. Craft workers are an anachronism under modern conditions, as is training for such mundane occupations. All in all, Braverman paints a bleak picture of modern work and one which has fitted in well with the general mood of pessimism in advanced societies since 1973.

3 The Compensatory Theory of Skill

This theory was developed during the Skilled Worker Project at Lancaster University in the mid-1980s. It was born partly as a result of a dissatisfaction with the dominant styles of research in British sociology concerning the relationships of technical change and the organization of work. The first such style involved surveys of technical change and employment patterns conducted on various samples of firms. These studies, of which Northcott (1985), Northcott and Rogers (1984), Cross (1985) and Daniel (1987) are notable examples, were unsatisfactory for a number of reasons: they are generally atheoretical, they fail to take an historical perspective and they often conflate description with prescription. In particular, these studies are devoid of context and, at best, can only provide interesting snippets of information. Conspicuously, they fail to provide a dynamic model of the relationships between the elements examined – notably technological change, the division of labour and the wider, structural parameters of society. In this style of research there is no attempt to distinguish the wood from the myriad of trees.

The other style of research, on the other hand, finds little difficulty in generalizing and can be seen in its purest and most alarming form at the successive Labour Process Conferences that have taken place annually in England during the 1980s. At these conferences, case studies of technical change and the division of labour within a firm will prefigure a 'weighty' debate about the nature of global capitalism; with set-piece battles between protagonists of Braverman and those who reject such analyses *a priori*. Such a Manichaean situation serves to reproduce a strange combination of theoreticism and positivism within the dominant discourse of much contemporary economic sociology.

In the Skilled Worker Project we have been committed to theoretically driven rigorous empirical inquiry. We see ourselves as operating in the spirit of Merton (1968) and Marshall (1963) in their advocacy of middle-range sociological theories. In particular, we are strongly committed to the development of theoretical generalizations through the medium of empirical analysis. Our overall theoretical orientation can be characterized by the following five core elements.

1 Industrial capitalist society involves a structured conflict between capital and labour. This conflict is fundamentally asymmetric because of the essential characteristic of industrial capitalism: the separation of the producer from the means of production as a result of capitalist ownership rights.
2 These conflicts take various forms. The two most central involve conflicts over wages (the distribution of the surplus) and the organization of the division of labour (the 'managerial prerogative').
3 Such conflicts over wages and the managerial prerogative take place within variable structures. One key element in these variable structures of asymmetric conflict is the nature and structure of the spatial organization of employers and employees.
4 These conflicts over wages and over authority relations are both economic and normative. Issues of legitimacy are central to both sets of relationships.
5 A major factor in the actual relationship between employers and employees is the pattern of collective organization of both parties. Such collective organization can vary both spatially and historically.

These general theoretical principles acted as points of orientation for our analysis of skilled work in contemporary Britain and America. We developed the Compensatory Theory of Skill as our best *first approximation* for an understanding of the relationships between technological change and skilled work in the modern era. The compensatory theory can be outlined initially in terms of five sets of propositions. Unlike Braverman's theory, it is based upon the systematic interplay of theoretical concepts with current empirical research on the nature of skilled work. Firstly, the compensatory theory of skill suggests that technical change is generating processes of *both* skilling and deskilling. Indeed, the *dual* nature of changes in skill is intrinsic to the development of contemporary capitalism. Secondly, in advanced capitalist societies these effects are *international*. Broadly, such internationalization has two aspects – the shift of routine manufacturing from advanced, core economies to less developed, peripheral economies, and the increasing internationalization of the capital goods (machinery) industry. A clear example of the former is the transfer of textile manufacturing from Lancashire in England and from New England and the Southern States of the USA to Third World economies like Singapore, Taiwan, Puerto Rico and Sri Lanka (see Frobel et al., 1980; Lloyd and Shutt, 1983). The capital goods industry is also increasingly international. Much modern machinery in Britain, for instance, is imported from such places as West Germany, Switzerland, France, Finland and Spain.[3] These twin processes have led to the removal of skilled and nonskilled work from Britain to a wide range of alternative geographical locations. The compensatory theory of skill suggests that the dual processes of skilling and deskilling are contained within an international framework and that empirical research must attempt to incorporate this insight. Needless to say, this raises serious difficulties in operationalization but vindicates the pursuit of international comparisons like the one reported here.[4]

A third feature of the theory argues that technological changes tend to deskill *direct productive roles* but put an increased premium on a range of *ancillary skilled tasks* that are associated with the installation, maintenance and programming of automated machinery. This is because modern machinery incorporating micro-electronics tends to simplify many production skills but renders maintenance work far more complex. Fourthly, it is therefore suggested that technological change tends to *advantage* certain occupational groups and to *disadvantage* others. This can be seen both *between* production and maintenance workers, but also within maintenance work itself where there is a far greater need for new electronically based maintenance skills than for traditional mechanical maintenance skills. Finally, the compensatory theory of skill concludes that technical change is affecting traditional forms of the division of labour and therefore poses both threats and opportunities for organized labour in countries like the USA and Britain. Nevertheless, it must be emphasized that the Compensatory Theory is a first approximation and it is *heuristic*. Only rigorous empirical inquiry can determine its validity. Nor should the term 'compensatory' be reified. We are not claiming that skill can be neither created nor destroyed. Our aim is rather to avoid a research strategy that incorporates what Rose (1988) calls a 'confirmation bias'. If the dynamics of skill change are essentially dualistic, then both human capital theory and Marxist theories of deskilling can find *illustrative examples* to support their respective, if incompatible, positions without securing any semblance of an adequate overall analysis.

The Analysis of Skilled Work in Contemporary Britain and America

As can be seen from Table 2.1, a series of competing hypotheses about the contours of skilled work in modern industry can be derived from the theories discussed above. These hypotheses form the propositions to be examined in the first part of this book. However, before the precise form of such an analysis is presented, it is important to state what is meant by skilled work and skilled workers in contemporary societies. This is by no means as straightforward as it might first appear. This research is a discussion of skilled manual work; it looks at skilled manual production workers and skilled manual maintenance workers. Such groups are conventionally described as 'skilled workers' in modern Britain and America. Many, but by no means all, will have served apprenticeships. However, all traditionally will have acquired a skilled status based upon extensive training and experience on the job. As was shown in *Skilled Workers in the Class Structure* (1985), skilled workers have been required historically for both production and maintenance work, and skilled manual work has been a generic feature of traditional British and American industry.[5]

Table 2.1 *Hypotheses about trends in skilled work*

Human Capital Theory	Braverman Theory	Compensatory Theory
1 All forms of skilled work are increasing.	All forms of skilled work are decreasing.	Skilled work is approximately constant – some is increasing and some is decreasing.
2 Production skills and maintenance skills are both increasing.	Production skills and maintenance skills are both decreasing.	Production skills are declining but maintenance skills are increasing.
3 All maintenance skills are increasing.	All maintenance skills are decreasing.	Electronically-based maintenance skills are increasing whereas mechanically based ones are decreasing.

Bearing in mind these points and the nature of the hypotheses to be assessed, the research in the next three chapters will seek to establish what is happening to skilled workers and skilled work in Britain and the USA by a series of empirical 'sweeps'. Firstly, the investigation will seek to discover what has happened to the numbers of skilled workers in both countries since 1940. This will involve an examination of census data from both Britain and the USA. Secondly, the research will assess what is known about the degree of skill involved in these aggregates of skilled workers. This will entail an examination of a wide range of empirical studies into the relationship of skill and technical change in Britain and America.

In Part II, there will be an examination of the social processes involved in contemporary skilled work in Britain and America. This will involve an examination of patterns of socialization into skilled identities, the structure of skilled trade unionism and the changing social composition of skilled workers themselves. Nevertheless, the two Parts are designed to complement each other and, as will be shown, it is impossible to assess fully the changing features of skilled work without recourse to such a multi-faceted approach.

3

Trends in Skilled Labour Since 1940

Braverman's thesis about the deskilling of work in the twentieth century suggests strongly that skilled labour is undergoing a secular decline. According to his model, technical changes are generating an increase in the degree of managerial domination of the labour process and a concomitant deskilling of craft labour. Braverman, like Marx before him, allows some short-term, temporary deviations from this pattern:

> In some exceptional instances . . . the union has been able successfully to insist that the entire job [of working numerically controlled machine tools] including programming and coding, can be handled by the machinist . . . Management is thus sometimes forced to be content to wait until the historical process of devaluation of the worker's skill takes effect over the long run . . . since the only alternative . . . is . . . a bitter battle with the union (Braverman, 1974: 203).

These comments suggest that, from a Bravermanian perspective, we would expect the processes of deskilling to be more advanced in the USA than in Britain since trade unionization is weaker in America[1] and technological change more pervasive and advanced there.[2] This chapter will test such an assumption by examining trends in skilled labour in the USA and in Britain since 1940. However, any examination of broad changes in the division of labour must distinguish between *absolute* and *relative* changes. This is because, for instance, the American labour force has more than doubled since 1940 (see table 3.1). Neither Braverman nor human capital theory normally distinguish these two ways of operationalizing their models. Nevertheless, there can be two tests of the various theses about skilled work during the period since

1940. The first involves an examination of the *relative position* of skilled workers in the occupational system and the other entails an examination of the *absolute numbers* of skilled workers. Whilst Braverman himself fails to distinguish these two components of the thesis, the tone of his analysis often suggests that he is claiming the latter to be the mainspring of contemporary developments. On the other hand, the logic of the compensatory theory of skill is that one would expect a combination of differing relative changes (see table 2.1), some of which may also involve absolute reductions in an era of an expanding overall occupational structure.

There are two methods which can be used to assess the plausibility of these various theories in relation to aggregate numerical changes in the division of labour in Britain and America since 1940. The first would entail the accumulation of a series of intensive, micro-analyses of patterns of occupational changes in either industries, sectors or firms and the development of conclusions from such data. However, such secondary data do not exist in sufficient detail to make this a viable strategy and, as a consequence, the only satisfactory method involves the use of successive US and British census data. This raises the question of how appropriate such data are for an examination of secular developments in levels of skill amongst the workforce.

Census data have a number of problems for social scientists irrespective of the theories and hypotheses addressed. Firstly, occupational data are presented in an aggregated form and the categories used for such aggregations often change from one census to the next. Furthermore, the coding procedures are often obscure, change over time and contain a range of potential but unknowable biases.[3] However, over the period under review there has been only one major revision of the categorization procedures (for the 1980 American Census)[4] and some of the occupations under examination, like electrician or compositor, are less problematic than many others – particularly service workers – since their meaning has changed relatively little over the past 50 years. These points are of particular salience in any examination of skilled workers since both the American and British census authorities have sought to delineate skilled manual workers as a separate stratum within the wider manual working class throughout the twentieth century. In Britain a whole series of consistent mistakes in classification have bedevilled the delineation of skilled workers. As I have shown previously (Penn, 1985a: 127–9), the Registrar-General classified whole industrial sectors as having either entirely skilled or entirely nonskilled manual workforces. This is quite inappropriate for the complex pattern of skills within such industrial sectors. Two examples of this procedure will suffice. According to the Registrar-General,[5] cotton weavers are defined as skilled and mule spinners as semi-skilled in Britain in the twentieth century. This is an exact reversal of the correct picture as shown in *Skilled Workers in the Class Structure* (chapters 6, 7 and 8). The tendency to lump all workers in an industrial sector within an identical class category can also be seen in the paper and board industry. As Penn and Scattergood (1985) have shown, there is a complex internal pattern of stratification within the paper manufacturing industry which is violated by the Registrar-General's assumption that almost all workers in this sector are skilled. As will become apparent later in this chapter, these kinds of errors are not peculiar to Britain – similar errors have been made in the USA over the skilled content of welding. Nevertheless, despite problems of operationalizing precisely the notion of skilled manual work, census data do provide the only satisfactory means of making generalizations about changes in skilled occupations over time currently. Clearly, though, the data reported in this chapter should be treated with due caution.

Are such census data pertinent to the various theories outlined in the previous chapter? Certainly the time span, the period between 1940 and 1980, is central to the three accounts of developments in skilled work. In the case of Braverman, one would expect the processes of deskilling to have been at work between 1940 and 1980 according to the logic of his analysis. Almost all his examples of deskilling in the chapter on 'Machinery' are located in terms of technical changes under way during this era. Furthermore, Braverman uses census data when it suits his argument on changes in clerical work, but in his concluding chapter, ' A Final Note on Skill', he indicates that he does not regard census data as pertinent to a discussion of skill. However, this argument is far from persuasive. Presumably, if production skills are being reduced, we would expect fewer skilled machinists and more nonskilled machine operators; and, further, if craft work is being eliminated we would again expect fewer skilled workers and more nonskilled. The Census certainly permits an assessment of such hypotheses and whilst the results cannot definitively refute Braverman, they do permit greater or lesser degrees of confidence in his account. Similarly, both the skilling thesis and the compensatory theory of skill are focused on changes in the division of labour since the Second World War and it follows that the data presented in this chapter are directly pertinent to such accounts.

1 Trends in the Numbers of Skilled Workers in the USA since 1940

As can be seen from table 3.1 on 'Occupational Change in the USA 1940–1980',[6] the occupational profile of the USA has changed significantly since 1940.[7] The workforce has more than doubled and certain segments within the division of labour have increased whilst others have decreased. The proportion of the labour force engaged in agriculture has declined dramatically since the Second World War – a trend evident both for farmers and for farm labourers. The proportion of domestic servants has also fallen, as have the proportions of industrial labourers and industrial operatives. The latter categories approximate the semi-skilled stratum of the manual (or blue-collar) workforce.[8] The proportions of managers, professional and clerical workers have also expanded but the one category which reveals the *least* change is craft workers, particularly between 1950 and 1980. The slight decline between 1970 and 1980 might appear to be the result of the differences in census category aggregates used at both time periods: in 1970 it was 'Craftsmen and kindred workers', whereas in 1980 it became 'Precision production, craft, and repair occupations'. However, the 1980 table also provides estimates of the 1970 division of labour based upon the new 1980 categorization. According to these figures the proportion of 'Precision production, craft, and repair occupations' in 1970 was 14.1%, which signifies that the small decline between 1970 and 1980 is not an artefact of the changing categories. Nevertheless, the overall impression of the proportion of craftsmen is of a steady-state with a very small but insignificant increase between 1940 and 1950 and an equally small and insignificant decline between 1970 and 1980.

When we examine table 3.2, 'Trends in Craft Work in the USA, 1940–1980', it becomes clear that this apparent structural stability reveals some dramatic differences between specific craft occupations. As becomes apparent both from the figures in tables 3.2 and 3.3, and their graphical representation in figure 3.1, there are some quite dramatic *differences* in trends within craft work in the USA between 1940 and 1980. The numbers of carpenters have almost trebled as have the numbers of plumbers and pipefitters. The figures for electricians and mechanics and repairmen have increased even faster with almost a five-fold increase for the latter and well over 300% for the electricians (see table 3.3). It becomes evident that if one wanted to select occupations to

Table 3.1 Occupational change in the USA, 1940–1980 (percentages)

Occupation	1940 %	1950 %	1960 %	1970 %	1980* %
Professional	7.3	8.5	10.7	11.6	11.8
Managerial	8.2	8.6	7.9	8.1	10.0
Clerical	16.6*	12.1	14.1	17.8	29.6*
Craft workers	11.1	13.8	13.5	13.9	13.0
Operatives	18.2	19.9	18.8	17.9	} 19.2
Labourers	6.9	6.5	5.1	4.8	
Farmers	11.3	7.3	3.7	1.8	} 2.9*
Farm labourers	6.9	4.2	2.4	1.3	
Service workers	6.0	7.6	8.5	11.3	} 13.1
Domestic servants	4.7	2.5	2.6	1.5	
N (millions)	45.1	57.6	64.3	79.7	104

Sources: Decennial Censuses of US Population (see note 6). See note 7 for details of changes in boundaries of categories, especially where there are asterisks.

Table 3.2 *Trends in craft work in the USA, 1940–1980 (absolute numbers)*

Occupation	1940	1950	1960	1970	1980
Carpenters	558,313	985,443	923,837	921,848	1,305,868
Painters: construction and maintenance	322,159	431,109	416,040	359,462	422,470
Machinists		533,726	515,532	390,184	510,699
Millwrights	609,773	60,193	67,876	81,025	134,076
Toolmakers		156,992	186,602	206,775	193,890
Electricians	197,222	324,046	355,522	482,763	625,813
Plumbers and pipefitters	173,915	295,990	331,012	398,159	502,004
Welders	124,741	275,545	386,622	565,505	791,028
Compositors and typesetters	158,072	178,696	182,937	162,504	70,515
Mechanics and repairmen	863,731	1,767,618	2,300,690	2,502,995	3,982,515

Sources: as for table 3.1. See note 7 for a discussion of precise description of occupational categorizations at each Census. The occupations selected are the largest groupings in 1940.

support the deskilling thesis, then the best candidates would be compositors and typesetters and machinists. Indeed, the analysis of these two occupations has been a persistent bias of post-Braverman industrial sociology, in both the USA and Britain (for compositors see Rogers and Friedman, 1980; Zimbalist, 1979; Wallace and Kalleberg, 1982; Cockburn, 1983a; Martin, 1981; and for machinists see Burawoy, 1979; Noble, 1977 and 1984; Jones, 1981; Hartmann et al., 1983; Duhm and Muckenberger, 1983). On the other hand, groups like electricians, pipefitters and plumbers have received virtually no systematic occupational analysis in either country.[9]

Table 3.3 *Proportional changes in selected skilled manual occupations in the USA, 1940–1980*

Occupation	1940	1980
Carpenters	100	233.9
Painters: construction and maintenance	100	131.1
Machinists, millwrights and toolmakers	100	137.5
Electricians	100	317.3
Plumbers and pipefitters	100	288.6
Welders	100	634.1
Compositors and typesetters	100	44.6
Mechanics and repairmen	100	461.1
Labour force	100	230.6

Sources: as for table 3.1

The data also suggest an increase in skilled work consistent with the skilling thesis. However, whilst all the skilled manual occupations examined in tables 3.2 and 3.3 have increased in numbers since 1940, apart from compositors, the pattern of relative change is more complex. Metalworkers (the combined categories of machinists, millwrights and toolmakers) and painters have increased more slowly than the general rate of labour force growth, whilst carpenters have increased at about the same rate as the general increase. Electricians, plumbers and mechanics have all increased far faster than the overall increase of the entire labour force. Welders have witnessed a phenomenal growth relative to all other major crafts since 1940. It is important to point out that welders are *not* categorized as craft workers in US Censuses with the added consequence that they are seen as semi-skilled operatives. Consequently they are not included in the craft category in table 3.1. However, it is by no means clear why this should be so.

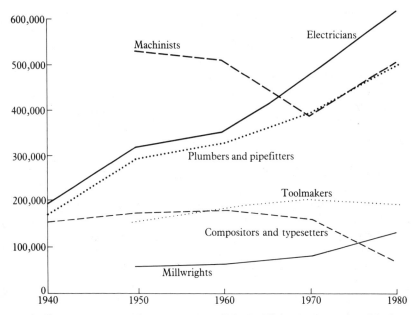

Figure 3.1 *A graph of occupational trends in the USA, 1940–1980, for selected craft jobs*

Welding[10] involves the joining together of separate pieces of metal. Examples of its use include pipes, locomotives, boilers, ships, gear cases and storage tanks – all of which are fabricated from metal. The growth of metal construction is the motor behind the emergence of the occupation of the welder. There are, broadly, two kinds of welder – the skilled welder who constructs metal fabrications and the welding machine operator who uses an automatic welding machine. The problem for social scientific analysis of welding is the systematic conflation of these two kinds of work within census categories in the USA.

The nature of electric arc welding is highly skilled. In this type of welding the pieces of metal to be welded are brought together at a very high temperature by the heat liberated at the arc terminals. Two of the skills involved in such welding are dexterity and patience. The welder must maintain the electrode at a correct distance from the base metal and draw it along at a speed adequate to form an acceptably strong weld. This has to be performed with a face shield to protect the face and eyes, and often involves cramped and difficult positions. Other aspects of the skill of the welder involve knowledge of the different types of joints used in welding (butt, fillet, lap, edge or plug), the ability to read drawings and the ability to produce work that can pass various kinds of testing (such as X-rays). In the USA these tests are conducted by the ASME (American Society of Mechanical Engineers) or by the API (American Petroleum Institute), depending upon the industrial sector in which the welding takes place. In Britain, these tests are performed by Lloyds or the AOTC (Associated Offices Technical Committee). A central feature of welding skills involves an understanding of the weldability of different metals and alloys, a knowledge of pressure lines within metals and a grasp of the relationships between variations in electrical currents and the quality of welds. Welding has to be continuously self-monitored. A welder must identify and correct faulty welds which can be caused by a variety of factors, such as a too short (or too long) arc and a too fast (or too slow) speed of travel. Modern welding is becoming more complex as the variety of alloys increases and the need for high quality welds is enhanced in the fabrication of high-pressure chambers and containers of dangerous substances, such as chemicals, petrol or radio-active materials.

It is possible that welders in the USA have been classified as nonskilled because they tend not to complete formal apprenticeships. However, Strauss (1965) has shown in his classic article on training patterns in the USA that this has been a traditional pattern within metalworking in American industry throughout the twentieth century. A study of skilled workers in St Louis[11] in 1957 revealed that welders and flame cutters constituted the second largest skilled group in the local metalworking industries and that none of the workers being trained within this category at the time were registered as apprentices.[12] Nor, for that matter, was there significant apprenticeship training in the vast majority of the other skilled metalworking trades in St Louis. Clearly the lack of apprenticeship schemes is insufficient to categorize a worker as nonskilled in the USA.

Welders are regarded as skilled by other occupational groups in America. The International Union of Electrical, Radio and Machine Workers (IUE) recognizes[13] welding as an apprenticeable skilled trade on a par with equivalent occupations such as electrician, toolmaker or millwright. Clearly the central problem becomes how to assess the likely proportion of skilled welders and nonskilled welding operatives within the overall category of welders in the US Census. This is not directly possible from existing data. However, evidence from Britain suggests that no more than 20% of all welders are involved in the operation of welding machines.[14] This would seem a reasonable estimate for the USA as well and, if accepted, it suggests that there has been a massive increase in skilled welders since 1940. Consequently, there are good reasons to suggest that the occupational groups included in the craft category in table 3.1 actually *underestimate* the numbers of skilled manual workers in the USA rather than the opposite.

These American data strongly suggest the plausibility of the compensatory theory of skill. The US Census does not permit the separation of production and maintenance skills, but the occupations analysed in tables 3.2 and 3.3 with the highest rates of increase are precisely those where one would anticipate the highest proportions of maintenance workers – mechanics and repairmen, plumbers and electricians. The skilled production occupations of compositors and of toolmakers reveal respectively a dramatic decline and small fall over the period up to 1980.

It is clear from the data presented above that there is no general support for Braverman's theory of deskilling. Certain skilled manual occupations – notably compositors – have suffered an absolute decline since 1940 and others, like toolmakers, have suffered a relative decline. However, these specific occupational changes have been compensated for by the increase of other skilled occupations. Furthermore, when we examine the balance of decline and growth, it would appear that occupational groupings containing strong elements of maintenance work have expanded relatively fast, whereas production skills have remained relatively static, or in some instances, actually declined. Such findings are consistent with the compensatory theory of skill outlined earlier. There is also a certain degree of confirmation for the skilling thesis since the proportion of skilled workers within the overall manual working class has increased since 1940. However, the skilling thesis provides little insight into such counter-tendencies as composing and machining.

What accounts for the patterns uncovered in the numbers of skilled workers in the USA in the last 50 years? The most striking feature of developments in the American labour force is its rapid expansion. Clearly immigration and natural increase have sustained this expansion, as have the increasing numbers of women within the labour force. Skilled occupations have increased at a similar pace to this overall burgeoning of the labour force. The movement from wooden to metal fabrication in modern industry and construction has produced a secular shift towards metalworking occupations. The use of electricity, and now electronics, for the power and control of modern machinery has enhanced the demand for skilled electrical and electronics workers.

Table 3.4 *Trends in skilled work in the United Kingdom, 1951–1981, with decimal percentage changes*

Occupation	1951	1961	% change	1971	% change	1981	% change
Carpenters, joiners, cabinet-makers	314,500	327,710	+ 4.2	318,270	– 2.9	298,510	– 6.2
Carpenters, joiners	282,300	300,590	+ 6.5	294,120	– 2.2	273,830	– 6.9
Cabinet-makers	32,200	27,120	– 15.8	24,150	– 11.0	24,680	+ 2.2
Painters, decorators	280,900	335,850	+ 19.6	241,050	– 28.2	206,540	– 14.3
Sheetmetal workers	87,400	91,820	+ 5.1	85,870	– 6.5	132,950	+ 54.8
Fitters, machine erectors	—	731,940	—	599,360	– 17.8	516,510	– 14.1
Toolmakers	223,500	87,010	– 61.1	92,250	+ 6.0	74,480	– 19.3
Welders	70,800	117,830	+ 66.4	139,390	+ 18.3	150,940	+ 8.3
Turners	82,400	—	—	67,930	—	49,670	– 26.9
Machine tool setters and setter operators	119,600	—	—	185,700	—	75,310	– 59.4
Machine tool setters	—	—	—	—	—	55,230	—
Machine tool setter operators	—	—	—	—	—	20,180	—
Turners, machine tool setters and setter operators [total]	202,000	254,800	+ 26.1	253,630	– 0.5	124,980	– 50.7
Electricians	139,800	260,680	+ 86.5	293,100	+ 12.4	—	—
Electrical fitters	101,500	42,650	– 58.0	55,400	+ 29.9	—	—
Electricians *and* electrical fitters [total]	241,300	303,330	+ 25.7	348,500	+ 14.9	267,420	– 23.3
Plumbers and pipefitters	147,300	167,870	+ 14.0	201,650	+ 20.1	177,570	– 11.9
Compositors	39,800	43,360	+ 8.9	36,570	– 15.7	26,350	– 27.9
Motor mechanics	164,900	—	—	192,380	—	246,950	+ 28.4
Precision instrument makers and repairers	27,900	53,780	+ 92.8	52,990	– 1.5	32,020	– 39.6
Economically active (including unemployed)	22,578,500	24,014,320	+ 6.4	25,021,430	+ 4.2	25,405,590	+ 1.5
Economically active (excluding unemployed)	22,133,300	23,338,700	+ 5.4	25,733,320	+ 1.7	22,916,190	– 3.4

Sources: Decennial UK Censuses of Population, 1951–1981

Braverman ignores these features of modern work in the USA and, whilst his analysis is consistent with the experience of compositors (typesetters), such experiences are neither typical nor normal. The expansion of the American labour force and the growth of many skilled occupations since 1940 has led to the development of the skilling thesis. However, this is an oversimplified theory which ignores both the asymmetries of increases and the counter-tendencies to such general increases. The data so far in this chapter are clearly far more consistent with the compensatory theory of skill than with either the skilling or deskilling theses. The question therefore remains as to the nature of developments in skilled work in Britain over the same period.

2 Trends in the Numbers of Skilled Workers in Britain since 1951

This section presents data on skilled occupations in Britain between 1951 and 1981 from successive British Censuses. It is not an exact comparison with the American material presented in the previous section since there was no Census of Population in Britain in 1941, as a result of the Second World War. The same heuristic problems surround the interpretation of these British data, particularly the difficulties associated with changing occupational categorizations.[15] Furthermore, the British Censuses since 1945 have employed somewhat more refined occupational divisions within the manual workforce and the picture concerning trajectories of skilled occupations becomes, therefore, more complex. Nevertheless, it is possible to compare a range of specific occupations like carpenter, toolmaker, welder and electrician with similar aggregate data from the USA. This section will explore the British data and then compare them with those from America.

As is evident from table 3.4, the British labour force did not expand greatly between 1951 and 1981. In particular, if the unemployed are not included, the numbers in the labour force have only risen from 22.1 million in 1951 to 22.9 million in 1981. This is quite different from the dramatic increase in the American labour force which rose from 45.1 million to 104 million between 1940 and 1980. None the less, as is evident in table 3.4, this general stability in the labour force masks some significant differences in the trajectories of specific skilled manual occupations. As is evident from table 3.4, welders have more than doubled whereas turners and tool setters nearly halved over the period under review.

2.1 The General Trajectory of Skilled Occupations in Britain since 1951

The data in table 3.4 on skilled occupations in Britain since 1951 reveal that none of the hypotheses about the trajectory of skilled work as outlined in chapter 2 is strictly confirmed. The majority of skilled trades examined have experienced relative decline since 1951, but this is not the case with sheetmetal workers, welders, plumbers, electricians, precision instrument-makers or motor mechanics (see table 3.5). Nor are the trajectories of increase and decrease consistent over the 30-year period. From table 3.4 it is evident that both precision instrument-makers and repairers and electricians and electrical fitters have increased proportionately between 1951 and 1981, but experienced relative decline over the final decade between 1971 and 1981. This is a different pattern from the accelerating decline of compositors and the gentle reduction of carpenters, joiners and cabinet-makers (see figure 3.2). Clearly all forms of skilled work are not decreasing in modern Britain, if by that it is meant that skilled workers are progressively disappearing across the spectrum of skilled activities. The compensatory theory of skill is closer to the mark, certainly between 1951 and 1971. Some skills appear to be increasing under modern conditions, whereas others are being eliminated. However, since 1971 more skilled occupations have witnessed relative decline than have moved in the opposite direction. There does not appear to be a strict balancing of enskilling and deskilling, rather a shift towards smaller numbers of skilled workers across a wide spectrum of activities.

2.2 The Relationship between Production Skills and Maintenance Skills

Again it proved difficult to separate production and maintenance skills within these Census occupational aggregates. However, it is possible to suggest that there are various broad categories of the occupations presented in table 3.4 in terms of the conjunction of production (p), construction (c) and maintenance skills (m). In table 3.6 these are presented in terms of pure types and mixed types, with the dominant type being presented first. Consequently electricians and electrical fitters are labelled (mp) since it is assumed that the bulk of these occupations are involved in broadly maintenance activities. This procedure involves a range of simplifications and is presented as a heuristic device. Only more detailed research can corroborate or disconfirm these categorizations.

Table 3.5 *Overall percentage gains or losses of selected skilled occupations in Britain, 1951–1981*

Occupation	%
Carpenters, joiners, cabinet-makers	− 5.1★
Carpenters, joiners	− 3.0★
Cabinet-makers	− 23.3
Painters, decorators	− 26.5★
Sheetmetal workers	+ 52.1
Fitters, machine erectors (1961–1981)	− 29.4★
Toolmakers	− 66.7★
Welders	+ 113.2
Turners	− 39.7★
Machine tool setters and setter operators	− 37.0★
Turners, machine tool setters and setter operators [total]	− 38.1★
Electricians and electrical fitters	+ 10.8★
Plumbers	+ 20.5★
Compositors	− 33.8★
Motor mechanics	+ 49.8
Precision instrument-makers and repairers	+ 14.8★

★ signifies a decline between 1971 and 1981, where known.
Source: Table 3.4

Nevertheless, despite its limitations, table 3.6 does reveal an interesting pattern. All the occupations that are decreasing the fastest (toolmakers, compositors and turners) are in traditional production skills. The two fastest increases (welders and sheetmetal workers) are also in longstanding metal trades – although, as was indicated earlier, both have been subject to a range of changes since 1945. This suggests a conclusion that rivals all the hypotheses suggested earlier in chapter 2: namely that *some skills are becoming relatively more important in modern production, whereas others are declining.* Of course, it is possible to argue that welding and sheetmetal working skills are being rationalized in the modern era. However, the evidence from Swords-Isherwood and Senker (1980) and various publications by the Engineering Industry Training Board[16] suggest that this is far from being the case.

When the balance between production and maintenance skills is examined, it becomes clear that the bulk of the occupations that have increased proportionally (like plumbers and electricians) since 1951 *do* contain significant numbers of maintenance workers, and conversely

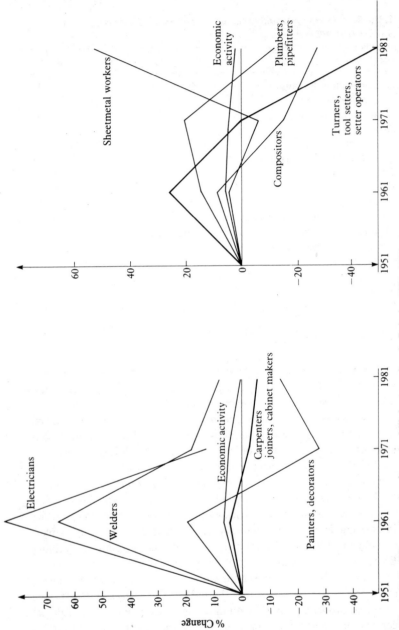

Figure 3.2 *The trajectories of certain skilled occupations in Britain, 1951–1981*

Table 3.6 *Trajectories of skilled work in Britain, 1951–1981*

A *Proportional increases* (greatest ranked at top)	
Welders	pmc
Sheetmetal workers	p
Motor mechanics	m
Plumbers	mpc
Precision instrument-makers and repairers	pm
Electricians and electrical fitters	mp
B *Slow porportional decrease* (less than 10%)	
Carpenters	cm
C *Fast proportional decreases* (greatest ranked at bottom)	
Painters, decorators	cm
Fitters, machine erectors	pm
Compositors	p
Machine tool setters and setter operators	p
Turners, machine tool setters and setter operators [total]	p
Turners	p
Toolmakers	p

c = construction skills
p = production skills
m = maintenance skills
Source: Table 3.4

those declining the fastest (such as toolmakers and compositors) are those that are purely production skills. There is an evident danger of inferential errors given the absence of more than one purely maintenance occupation in the data (motor mechanic), but the hypothesis that there has been a greater resilience of maintenance skills in the modern era *is* consistent with the data.

2.3 The Relationship within Maintenance Skills

These data are not consistent with Braverman's idea that all maintenance skills are decreasing. The number of motor mechanics has increased substantially since 1951. This is scarcely surprising given the increased volume of cars in use in contemporary Britain, but it is important to remember that more workers are employed fixing cars than in directly manufacturing them. Such mechanics are subject to increasing levels of training and retraining which are necessitated by the increasing sophistication of the technologies which they encounter. However, the data are not sufficiently differentiated to make any sensible inferences about the balance between different kinds of maintenance skills in modern Britain. Maintenance electricians, maintenance fitters and instrument mechanics – the main categories of maintenance workers – cannot be discerned from the broad aggregates in which they are placed by recent Censuses. Only in 1951 is there sufficient information and the ensuing absences of data make any positive conclusions, beyond the rejection of Braverman's simple deskilling hypothesis, impossible.

3 Skilled Occupations in Britain and America in the Modern Era

It is apparent that there are some broad similarities in the patterns of occupational change amongst skilled workers in Britain and America. In both countries there is evidence of a strong decline of compositors which is associated with the demise of hot-metal typesetting in the modern printing industry (see Rogers and Friedman, 1980, for the USA; and Cockburn, 1983a, for Britain). However, compositors have taken on the same status for modern sociologists that handloom weavers have held for pessimistic interpretations of the Industrial Revolution (see Bythell, 1969). It is a strange paradox that the demise of handloom weaving should be directly linked to the rise of the metal craftsman so admired by Braverman a century later. These very same craftsmen constructed the machinery that facilitated the automation of weaving in nineteenth-century Britain (see Penn, 1985a). It remains a possibility that the introduction of new technologies into modern printing is also associated with similar kinds of processes. The loss of the skills of the compositor is connected with the growth of skills amongst maintenance electricians and also amongst the technicians who provide support services for the new machinery. Furthermore, evidence from Goss – the Preston-based printing machinery suppliers now owned by Rockwell International – indicates that the new technologies utilized to manufacture electronic printing presses do indeed require a considerable expansion of production skills for their construction (see Holden, 1985).

In both America and Britain, there is evidence of a reduction in the importance of machinists and turners. It becomes apparent that if one wanted to select occupations to support the deskilling thesis, then the best candidates would be compositors and turners (or machinists, as they are called in the USA). As has been demonstrated earlier, the analysis of these two occupations has been a persistent bias of recent industrial sociology in both countries. Indeed, they form the centrepiece of Braverman's own analysis. On the other hand, groups like welders, sheetmetal workers, electricians, pipefitters and plumbers have received virtually no systematic occupational analysis in either country. Such distortions severely handicap the development of an adequate contemporary economic sociology.

Nevertheless, in both America and Britain, there is considerable evidence for the parallel relative expansion of several occupations. The three areas which stand out in this respect are the occupations associated with metal fabrication, vehicle repair and electrical maintenance and installation. All three areas of skill represent significant aspects of the changing nature of modern work. Welders and sheetmetal workers are involved both in the construction of industrial plant and of much of the equipment produced in the heavy engineering industries (see Penn, 1986). Similarly, the role of the electrician has increased as the use of electrical power and, recently, of electronics in the control units of modern machinery has proliferated.[17] The centrality of the skills of the motor mechanic should be evident to any car owner. Whilst some routine vehicle servicing has been simplified, the complexity of the systems within modern motor cars and their rapid changes mean that the knowledge required to undertake car repair work has expanded considerably since 1945, both in America and in Britain.[18]

There is an evident difference in the buoyancy of skills between Britain and American, which is strongly associated with the relative dynamism of the two economic systems. If we examine the rate of expansion of skilled occupations in the period up to 1961, which parallels the post-War boom, it is evident that the general rate of increase was more sluggish in Britain than in America. When we come to the period after 1971, which is associated with more general economic recession, the contrasts become more acute. In Britain most skilled occupations declined relatively between 1971 and 1981, whereas most of the American ones experienced considerable relative expansion. Such results are contrary to the social scientific orthodoxy in Britain[19] and require further analysis. The picture will become clearer in the next sections, but the provisional explanation concerns broad developments in the relative industrial structures of the two societies.

Each industry has, at any time, a different proportion of skilled workers. Some industries, mainly in the area of personal consumer products, utilize predominantly nonskilled workforces on assembly lines to provide for mass markets. Examples of such industries are motor cars, tyres and footwear. Other industries have greater proportions of skilled workers, since they produce non-standard, capital goods. Examples here would be the firms that construct printing presses or paper manufacturing machinery. Britain has witnessed a significant relative decline in these skill-intensive industries, especially when compared with America. The collapse of Alfred Herbert, Britain's largest machine tool company, in Coventry in the mid-1970s is a graphic illustration of these processes. At present, Britain possesses two of the seven leading world textile producers (Courtaulds and Vantona Coats) but the textile machinery industry – which began in Britain in the nineteenth century – is in dire straits (see Lloyd and Shutt, 1983) and an increasing proportion of new equipment is supplied from abroad, notably from Switzerland, West Germany and Italy. Similar points can be made concerning the paper industry. In Britain, considerable use is made of Finnish, West German and American equipment (see Penn and Scattergood, 1985), whilst in the paper mills I visited in Oregon in 1985[20] and in the factories of Michigan visited in 1987, there was no evidence of any capital inputs from outside the USA. The data presented in this chapter are consistent with the thesis that there has been a broad decline in the skill-intensive, capital-goods (or machinery) industries in Britain but not in the USA.

4 The Three Theories of Skilled Occupations Reconsidered

The overall results suggest that Braverman's image of the destruction of all forms of skilled work is misconceived with regard to both America and Britain. There is more support for this thesis in Britain, particularly in recent years, than in the USA. However, when looked at overall, his theory seems to be pertinent for only a limited number of atypical occupations. There is more support for the skilling thesis in America than in Britain, but the compensatory theory of skill does seem to offer the better account of the dissimilarities and divergences of development within the variety of skilled occupations in both countries. In both Britain and America there is limited evidence of deskilling (compositors) and of enskilling (welders), but also a range of nationally specific variations.

It proved impossible to say anything about the balance between electronic and mechanical maintenance skills due to the limitations of census data in both countries, and difficult to draw firm conclusions about the balance between production and maintenance skills. There was evidence both in America and in Britain for enhanced relative gains amongst maintenance work when compared with *some*, but by no means all, production tasks. Perhaps one of the most interesting conclusions from these data is that the balance of modern production skills is changing away from toolmaking and turning (machining in the USA) towards sheetmetal working and welding.

The data in this chapter concern the numbers of skilled occupations in Britain and America. It could be argued, and indeed has been, that such data are not convincing since workers' resistance can lead to skilled workers performing what is increasingly in fact nonskilled work at skilled rates of pay. In other words, the category of skilled workers contains an ever-expanding proportion of people engaged in nonskilled work. Braverman himself allows for such a short-run deviation from his theory, as was shown at the beginning of this chapter, but recent authors seem unclear about the durability of such a situation. In many ways these arguments look like classic, last-ditch rescue attempts for a collapsing theory (see Holmwood and Stewart, 1983, for an elaboration of this theme), but they do suggest that any adequate account of modern skilled workers must include an analysis of the nature of modern work and particularly that performed by skilled workers like welders, electricians and toolmakers. Such an analysis will be attempted in the next two chapters. However, the only method possible in such an area of inquiry is a combination of case studies with related secondary data. As the latter are sparse in both Britain and America, reliance on case studies becomes crucial and problems of typicality and representativeness become severe. Nevertheless, the aim is to link the materials on the nature of work performed by skilled workers with the evidence on the trajectories of skilled occupations in both countries that has been presented in this chapter.

4

Trends in Skilled Work in Contemporary Britain

The previous chapter established that there had been an expansion in the numbers of a range of skilled occupations in Britain and America since 1940 and a decline in some others, such as compositors and machinists. The purpose of this and the following chapter is to examine developments in the *content* of the work undertaken within a range of skilled occupations in order to assess whether the patterns uncovered within the census data are paralleled by similar developments in the content of the work performed by a range of skilled workers. This has been achieved by means of an examination of a series of industries such as paper, printing, metalworking and coal mining. These industries were selected partly because they are key reference points in the debate on skilled work in contemporary industrial sociology on both sides of the Atlantic, and partly because they embody considerable variations in the types of skilled occupations present within such industries. As far as possible, the same industries have been examined in the USA as in Britain. The British data are presented first since most of the British fieldwork was undertaken prior to my research in the USA and, to a considerable degree, the British results affected the way the American material was approached. The British fieldwork was undertaken as part of the Skilled Worker Project at Lancaster University and involved collaboration between myself and Scattergood, Simpson and Wigzell. These collaborative ventures were all informed by the broad principles of economic sociology outlined earlier, and the preferred method of research involved detailed examination of changes in the division of labour at establishment[1] (plant) level. The emphasis was more on depth rather than breadth since many of the questions about developments in the content of skilled work can be identified satisfactorily only at the micro-level.

1 Developments in Skilled Work in the Paper Industry

This research was conducted by Hilda Scattergood in conjunction with myself. It included two phases: the first involved the study of technological change in three paper mills employing 408, 250 and 670 people respectively in the summer of 1984. The second phase involved our return to two of the three mills in the autumn of 1985 to investigate subsequent technical changes and developments in the division of labour. We examined the effects of technical changes on the division of labour, with special reference to skilled work, since 1970. Our research involved a series of visits to the factories concerned and discussions with directors, personnel managers, senior shop stewards, various production and ancillary manual workers, laboratory workers and supervisory personnel. Our method of inquiry involved open-ended interviews with an underlying basic schedule of questions about technical change and the division of labour (see Penn and Scattergood, 1985, for this schedule). Attention has been concentrated on the paper-making parts of the mills since this is the main area where computerization has been installed.

1.1 James Cropper plc

Cropper's is a specialist paper-making firm, located near Kendal, which employed 408 people in 1984. This represents a considerable fall from 1970 when the firm employed 650 people. Like many medium-sized firms in Britain today, Cropper's survive in the market by concentrating on certain specialized, high-quality products. Their main specialism is coloured card and they dominate the market for dark-coloured card products in the UK. Consequently, reliability and quality of colour are of prime importance in the production system at Cropper's and the beatermen, who are responsible for the addition of dyes and colour matching, are traditionally regarded as particularly skilled workers at this firm.

Paper at Cropper's is made from imported pulp and from waste paper. The two main processes within production involve colour mixing of the liquidized pulp, and paper-making which involves the successive drying, heating and stretching of this liquidized pulp. The first process is controlled by beatermen and the second by machinemen. There were four paper-making machines at Cropper's in the summer of 1984, of which three had undergone varying degrees of computerization since

1970. Two machines involved computer monitoring of production, whilst the third had complete computer control. The fourth machine – the smallest – had no computerization at all. All three machines that had been computerized were supposed to be fully automatic. However, this had proved impossible to achieve in practice as a result of the engineering difficulties involved in monitoring and controlling the production of high quality card on traditional machinery. As will be seen, this has had significant effects on the levels of skill *actually* in operation within the plant.

In the pre-computer era, the machineman and his two assistants would tear out a piece of card, examine it and then modify the equipment where necessary. The introduction of computer monitoring has led to a change in the kinds of skill required but no apparent large change in the degree of skill exercised by the machinemen and their assistants. The monitors provide continuous information on the state of the paper being produced (weight, wetness and thickness) but any changes have to be made manually by the adjustment of operating valves. The knowledge of what to do in any given circumstance is a matter of judgement based primarily on experience, and neither machinemen nor management regard the changes resulting from computer monitoring as anything other than marginal.

There were interesting changes involved in the work surrounding the fully automatic paper-making machine. Here the division of labour was identical to the other machines in that a machineman supervised the machinery helped by two assistants. This job required far less manual activity and it would appear as if the retention of a skilled worker to supervise the machinery was based upon three sets of inter-related factors. First, management still had three machines operating under the traditional division of labour, and as Penn (1983b, 1985a) has shown in the engineering industry, this poses certain constraints on management in the creation of a new division of labour. Trade unions and workers expect to 'follow the work' and consequently machinemen at Cropper's expected to work alongside the new machinery. Management had little option but to accede to this expectation. Furthermore, the new computer-controlled machinery required somebody to interpret and check the dials on the new control units. As we have indicated, computerization of paper-making has proved difficult and lengthy and consequently, in this period of 'teething trouble', it made economic sense to retain the machinemen anyway. As is well known, once a working practice becomes established it acquires a considerable force in its own right as a customary set of expectations of the workforce. The final aspect involves the fact that computerization had not, in practice, led to automatic production. The machineman is still required to act upon information supplied by the computer. Now he presses buttons rather than turning valves, but nonetheless his actions still presuppose knowledge and experience of paper manufacturing in order to make a correct judgement of the appropriate action to be taken. The machinemen, and the management, at Cropper's regarded computerization as creating additional knowledge rather than as eliminating skill. These three sets of factors all appear to have interacted in the emergence of the working practices on the newer processes at Cropper's. Consequently, we can see that the computerization of paper-making at Cropper's has had little effect on the formal division of labour in this area of production work, and not much effect on the nature of specific job tasks. The numbers employed in paper-making have also changed little since 1970. Each machine continues to be run for three eight-hour shifts with a team of three workers associated with each machine (36 workers in all). The decline in employment at Cropper's does not seem, *prima facie*, to be the result of computerization of card production.

The other main area where there has been computerization at Cropper's is in the colour-blending processes. The computer in use provides a reading on a sample of colourized pulp mixture from the beating vat which is compared with a sample provided by the technical department. The computer does not give any instructions to the beaterman, merely a comparison of the two colours. The choice of the amount and kind of dye to be added if there is a significant mis-match is still made by the beaterman and is affected by the kind of pulp mixture, the nature of any additives already present and also by variation in the colouration of the dyes themselves. The beaterman is *assisted* by the computer rather than *controlled* by it. Essentially, the computer eliminates vagaries of lighting conditions which can affect any visual matching by the human eye. Again, the skill of beatermen is a matter of experience. It takes at least four years, and often considerably longer, as a beaterman's assistant before anyone is considered for promotion to the rank of beaterman. City and Guilds examinations are available, but they are not a formal requirement for becoming a beaterman. The introduction of computer-assisted colour blending has not affected the numbers employed in this area of the plant. Four beatermen and two beatermen's assistants are employed per shift and these numbers have remained constant since 1970. It seems clear that computerization in the area of colour-blending has not affected the division of labour or job tasks significantly: a viewpoint shared by management and by the beatermen themselves.

Overall, computerization of the two main production processes at Cropper's has not led to a reduction of skills nor to any great enhancement. Some skills have changed from intuition based on learned experience to the interpretation of consoles and VDUs. The more wide-ranging diagnostic skills of the pre-computer machinemen are replaced by those of alertness and the finer accuracy of the computer-aided man, but overall there seems to have been little change in the division of labour or job skills in the main production processes at Cropper's.

The main sphere of changing skills at Cropper's since 1970 is in the area of maintenance work. In 1970 there was one mechanic and one electrician employed in production maintenance per shift at Cropper's – a total of six maintenance craftsmen. By 1984, there were two mechanics, one electrician, one instrumenter and one maintenance supervisor per shift, and in addition there was one engineer and one instrumenter working on a separate day-shift, which gave a total of 17 maintenance workers. The reason for this expansion in maintenance work is two-fold. First, there is the computerization of production which accounts for much of the maintenance work of the instrumenters, electricians, and the day-shift engineer. However, since 1970 many areas of the plant outside direct production have been mechanized notably storage of pulp and the transmission of pulp by conveyors to the blending vats. There has also been mechanization in the finishing and packing areas with the introduction of forklift trucks and the palletizing of orders for dispatch. These inter-related processes have led to the widespread elimination of labouring tasks and have accounted for 60 redundancies in recent years. Here we can see an interesting paradox. Although computerization and reduction in employment have occurred simultaneously, they are not causally related. Indeed, the number of direct workers involved in production processes that have been computerized has not changed, whilst the number of maintenance workers has more or less trebled. The main job losses at Cropper's have involved the elimination of much routine nonskilled manual work as a result of the mechanization of ancillary parts of the plant. Beatermen, machinemen, and maintenance fitters and electricians are all regarded as skilled workers and they all regard themselves as more or less equivalent in terms of their common skilled status. This is marked within the industry by the fact that all four skilled occupations receive similar rates of pay.

1.2 Henry Cooke

Henry Cooke Ltd is a smaller plant than Cropper's, employing 250 people at a mill nine miles south of Kendal. The two paper-producing machines are quite old, having been built in 1945 and 1954 from second-hand machines. However, Cooke's have installed computer controls on to these machines since 1970. They have utilized computers which are produced by the Measurex Company of San Francisco, who are among the world's leading producers of computerized control systems for paper manufacture. Computerization has had no effect on manning levels in direct production. A team of three workers headed by a machineman is employed on both machines for each eight-hour shift and this has not changed over the last 15 years. No extra maintenance men are employed either, which appeared surprising given the experience at Cropper's. However, there are additional maintenance functions generated by the new computerized machines at Cooke's but these do not appear at Cooke's as employees. This is because Cooke's have a service agreement with Measurex whereby a computer technician is permanently installed at the plant but is part of Measurex's labour force. Furthermore, this technician is primarily concerned with the hardware and his primary tasks involve the diagnosis and replacement of faulty micro-circuitry. He is also able to perform minor software tasks, but generally these kinds of problems require the attendance of a software engineer or programmer from Measurex's regional office in Warrington. This indicates that the relationship of computerization and maintenance can become quite complex and can involve extensive sub-contracting relationships. In many cases, where the machinery is more costly and more complicated, these relationships become international as the machine producers are based at considerable distances from the machine users.

When computerization was introduced in the 1970s there were considerable anxieties amongst workers and managers about possible effects on the degree of job satisfaction for machinemen. However, the experiences reported to us by the machinemen suggested that they had not undergone significant reductions in the skill of their jobs. The computer was seen as giving the machineman more information than hitherto and as requiring him to learn how to interpret its readings and manipulate the paper-making process. One machineman saw the introduction of computerization as enabling him to exercise tighter control over the machinery. Clearly these remarks are subjective but they are nonetheless significant. First, the deskilling theory as elaborated by Braverman is about the putative effects of deskilling upon workers' consciousness. The evidence from machinemen at Cooke's suggests that these effects have not occurred and that *pari passu* the underlying process is not occurring either. This is an important point to make since many contemporary neo-Marxist Bravermaniacs seem to have forgotten this connection and simply talk about 'objective processes', independently of any subjective effects. Second, these comments from the machinemen indicate that the question of skill at work and how it might be changing is a complicated process about which participants have a view. We believe these views are important resources for contemporary sociology. These points will be examined in greater detail in chapter 6.

1.3 Thames Board

At the time of the research Thames Board were a part of Unilever, manufacturing strong, glossy cartonboard – the kind of material used for packaging cornflakes and soap powder. The mill at Workington was built in 1967 and has been extended and modernized in recent years at a cost of around £100 million. The plant originally produced 60,000 tonnes per annum, but since modernization it has increased its capacity to 150,000 tonnes. Thames Board are thought to produce between one-quarter and one-third of British consumption of packaging cartonboard, and the Workington mill is amongst the largest in Western Europe.

There are two machines producing board at Workington. There is an original 1967 machine that retains pneumatic instrumentation, although it has also recently acquired an overhead monitoring system which gives a digital reading on caliper and uniformity. This machine is like the computer-monitored machines at Cropper's. However, the second machine is fully automated and is controlled by a Honeywell TDC 2000. This computer was developed originally for the petro-chemical industry but has been adapted for paper production. All processes are fully automated from pulping through board production to coating the paper. Coating is controlled by a French sub-system created by Cellier and Company, whilst the finishing process is controlled by another sub-system developed by the Management Decisions Development Corporation of Cincinnati especially for Thames Board. As becomes evident, the automated systems at the Workington plant involve a wide range of international inputs. Computerization is also taken into the warehouse where the floor is divided, like a chess board, into 'bin spots' and each order is automatically labelled, sealed and delivered to its 'bin spot' for despatch. Modernization of the warehouse has led to the total elimination of all labouring work in the Workington mill and all manual workers are now either skilled or semi-skilled.

It would appear as if the introduction of automated machinery into production has had little effect on the formal division of labour. A team of five work on both machines. There are two skilled workers, a dryerman and a wet-end attendant, and two semi-skilled dry-end assistants (effectively dryermen's assistants). These four workers are under the direction of a machine tender – who, despite the name, is a foreman. The wet-end attendant repairs the wire mesh on to which the pulp mixture is pumped for the drying process. The dryerman monitors the drying and extrusion processes on the machines. Interestingly, the teams are interchangeable at Thames Board. This means that all workers must be able to transfer from pneumatic to computer-controlled systems and this has meant that production workers have had to undergo extensive retraining in order to comprehend the new computer-controlled production system. The reason for this specific form of the division of labour derives from three sets of inter-related processes. First, the workforce, and in particular the dryermen, have sought to extend the scope of their jobs. Second, there are considerable economic advantages for management in the flexibility of their work crews, particularly since there is very little labour turnover in production. Underlying these processes is the fact that newer and older forms of producing co-exist in the same plant, which constrains management and enhances the relative power of the workforce – particularly skilled manual workers whose experience is still critical for the effective running of the paper machines. This is because, even on the newest computerized machines, actions are required both in emergencies and when routine problems arise which presuppose considerable knowledge of what is actually happening within the machine. Both management and production workers strongly believe that the computerized machinery extends the range of skills and knowledge rather than reducing them. This pattern repeats the experience at Cropper's and is, in all likelihood, a general feature of the modern paper industry.

Flexibility and interchangeability are also features of maintenance work. Around 20% (120) of the entire workforce at Thames Board are involved in maintenance work in a broad sense. Ninety of these are 'breakdown men' – skilled maintenance craftsmen (mechanical fitters, power station fitters, electricians and instrument mechanics). These numbers have risen since 1979 by about 7%. Each shift has two instrument mechanics, two electricians and two technicians. During the day there are also six instrument mechanics, six electricians and three technicians also involved in the maintenance of the plant who work five days out of seven (either Tuesday to Saturday or Sunday to Thursday). Between Tuesday and Thursday both day shifts overlap and it is during this period that major maintenance work is done. This means that on Tuesday, Wednesday and Thursday there will be 36 maintenance workers available if required. Nor in the case of Thames Board is this offset by a reduction in the skills of production workers as the result of computerization. All production workers have been trained for both machines at Thames Board. This training, undertaken partly by Thames Board and partly by Honeywell, is aimed at providing a thorough understanding of how the machines work. For while computerized machines are running smoothly, it might appear as if jobs have been routinized, but once they start to go wrong, swift action is required which presupposes a wide knowledge of how the automated processes actually work.

1.4 Conclusions

In all paper mills examined there has been considerable technical change since the early 1970s involving varying degrees of computerization of production. The main motivation appears to be the challenge presented by the fierce competitive situation in the British paper and board industry, where EEC (European Economic Community), EFTA (European Free Trade Association) and Commonwealth production challenge British manufacturers in their domestic market. However, in the firms examined there have been few redundancies and those identified at Cropper's seem to have been due to advanced mechanical methods such as conveyor belts and forklift trucks replacing labourers. It is more likely that *lack* of automation causes redundancies in general, rather than its presence – a viewpoint supported by the experiences of the British cotton, motor cycle, motor car and shipbuilding industries (amongst others).

Overall there seems little evidence of deskilling. In production there appeared to be less reliance on the intuitive skills of beatermen at Cropper's in colour-matching, but the changes appeared marginal to the overall degree of skill required. Deskilling did not apply to production workers at Thames Board since the men working on the computer-controlled machine and the older, pneumatically controlled machine were interchangeable. One conclusion is that perhaps Braverman's theory of deskilling may have some application in large assembly plants, but it is a poor guide for changes in industries like the paper and board industry where the product is manufactured in one large, continuous process. Such a viewpoint is supported by Halle's (1984) recent research at a New Jersey petro-chemical plant.

There is perhaps more support for the skilling thesis in the area of production. Production workers at Cropper's and at Thames Board have acquired new forms of knowledge as a result of computerization without losing the bulk of their former skills. Training has been increased and many managers and production workers with whom we talked felt that training was still inadequate. In particular, it was often suggested that the process production worker needed greater engineering skills in order to deal with problems involving the functioning of the machinery.

The most dramatic changes in the mills examined lay in the area of maintenance skills. There is no doubt that changes in maintenance skills are taking place and that the numbers of maintenance workers are increasing, and the general level of their training makes these workers undoubtedly more skilled. At Cropper's there was a large increase in the number of maintenance workers and some of the skills are relatively new, particularly in the area of instrumentation. Instrumenters at Cropper's were trained on a block-release scheme after the finish of traditional engineering craft apprenticeships as machine fitters. However, recently new instrumenters have started taking technician apprenticeships at Cropper's. Similarly, instrumenters are in considerable demand at Thames Board and they had to be recruited on a national basis from the petro-chemical industry where they exist in relatively large numbers. Clearly, as workforces remain static or decline in absolute terms, these developments mean that skilled workers are becoming a larger proportion of the overall workforce.

Skilled manual work remains a general feature of paper production. Occupations are still organized around the identity of skill. Beatermen, machinemen and dryermen are regarded as skilled and have fought to maintain their position amongst the manual workforce. They retain the same skilled grade as maintenance craftsmen in all the plants despite their lack of formal apprenticeships. At Cropper's and at Thames Board the introduction of new automated machinery in parts of the plant did not significantly change the form of the division of labour. Such conclusions support the historical arguments put forward by Penn (1983a, 1983b and 1983c) which suggested that the social determination of skill is very much the effect of local labour markets and, in particular, the relative power of skilled manual workers within plants.

Nonetheless, occupations are structured around notions of 'skill' within the paper and board industry. This is hardly surprising within the maintenance areas which can be seen as a part of the wider engineering industry, but it was also clear in the area of paper production itself. Skilled paper workers like beatermen, machinemen and dryermen acquire their skilled status as a result of a long period of practical 'learning'. They guard their skill jealously, and through their strong presence in their union – SOGAT '82 – they maintain a position of parity with skilled craft engineering workers. Such findings are consistent with the arguments of Turner (1962), Savage (1982) and Penn (1983a, 1983c), all of whom have emphasized the crucial role of trade unionism in the battle for skill amongst manual workers in Britain. These issues will be further examined in chapters 6 and 7.

What, then, of the compensatory theory of skill? We found that technical change did generate positive effects on skill, but not much in the way of deskilling. We certainly identified international effects *within* the plants examined. All three firms had varying relations with a range of foreign producers of computerized equipment and systems. However, insufficient is known as yet about the detailed divisions of labour within these foreign firms to permit firm conclusions. Nevertheless, this a productive area for future research and the experience at Cooke's suggests the dangers of trying to identify changes in skill simply at the level of employees of a specific company. At Cooke's, like many smallish firms that are automating, maintenance functions are sub-contracted on to other firms – usually the vendors of the automated equipment. Penn and Scattergood (1985) hypothesized that these firms employ highly skilled workers both for production and for installation, maintenance and support, and that, in consequence, computerization in the paper and board industry is producing an international skilling process. However, this remains an open question. In these case studies of the paper industry there is little evidence of differences between the areas of production and maintenance of the kind initially suggested by the compensatory model. Whilst maintenance skills had increased, production skills had remained more or less constant. Nor was there evidence of significant differences between electrical and mechanical skilled trades as suggested by the compensatory theory.

As was indicated earlier, Scattergood and Penn returned to Cropper's and Thames Board in the autumn of 1985 to investigate further developments at these two plants. At Thames Board there had been some changes in the paper manufacturing machinery. The No. 1 machine had received by this time Measurex monitoring equipment which provided greater information to the paper workers on the machine. This new equipment had not resulted in any significant increase in production but had improved quality markedly. Nonetheless, it requires reiteration that the Measurex system provided digital information that the operators had to *interpret* based upon their pre-existing knowledge of the paper-making process. The work crews remained interchangeable between both the paper-making machines in the plant.

Nevertheless, there had been some marked developments in the division of labour that were unrelated to technical changes. As a result of increasing holiday entitlements of the workforce, which had risen from two weeks to five recently, and also of the reduction in the basic working week from 42 hours to 39 hours, the plant had changed from a four-crew to a five-crew shift system. Under the former system, four crews were required to operate the plant. In the autumn of 1985, in an attempt to reduce high levels of overtime payment and to alleviate problems of providing cover for absent workers, an extra crew had to be employed. Thames Board had sought to rationalize the former work crews to reduce the cost impact of such a change. In the area of paper production, instead of four crews of 80, they employed five crews of 65 – a net increase of five production workers. However, in the area of maintenance, no reduction in the size of teams proved possible and so Thames Board had to increase their maintenance workforce by 25%. This is an interesting example of how reducing the working year can generate more jobs, although this process has significantly differential impact upon different groups within the manual workforce. It also indicates that technological change is only one factor in the development of the division of labour in modern industry and that the balance of specific causal factors requires detailed empirical analysis on the ground – a fact that also vindicates the research strategy adopted by the Skilled Worker Project.

Nevertheless, it is clear that in the contemporary paper industry technological changes are advantaging skilled workers in general within the plants, and skilled maintenance workers more than skilled production workers. The groups most clearly disadvantaged in these paper mills are nonskilled manual workers of various kinds. It is significant that when Thames Board rationalized their production crews between 1984 and 1985 it was in the areas of nonskilled rather than skilled production tasks that they made their reductions. Such a picture of skilled work in capitally intensive process plants stands in sharp contrast to the older imagery portrayed by Nichols and Armstrong (1976). They focused on nonskilled, labouring work in such plants. As we have shown earlier, such work is fast disappearing in the modern paper industry. Our findings are more consistent with Halle's (1984) account of contemporary process work in the USA which demonstrates the wide range of skills required for such production activities.

2 Maintenance Work in Modern Britain

The evidence from the research into the paper industry suggested that technical change is having a significant positive effect upon the skills of maintenance workers. The second piece of research within the Skilled Worker Project (undertaken in collaboration with B. Wigzell) was an explicit attempt to probe these issues in greater detail. Generally, relatively little is known by contemporary social scientists about modern maintenance work. Dubois (1981), in his comparison of British and French maintenance workers in seven plants, has shown that in Britain one witnesses 'the virtually exclusive allocation of maintenance tasks to skilled workers who have passed their apprenticeship' (p. 352). Dubois goes on to argue that 'there exists in Great Britain a more subdivided breakdown of work among the trades most commonly engaged in maintenance; on the other hand, there is no role for versatile skilled workers' (Dubois, 1981: 353). In France, on the other hand, the employer 'remains entirely free to do . . . as he chooses, including creating a body of multiskilled workers by resorting to such possibilities as he has for training on the job' (Dubois, 1981: 353). Dubois illustrates his points by the example of two fibre-glass factories – one in France and the other in Britain. He states that

> in France the maintenance workers on shift are practically all electrician-mechanics who can deal with both electrical and mechanical faults; they are expected to be able to repair a majority of the breakdowns. In Great Britain, in contrast, the maintenance shifts are composed of fitters, plumbers and electricians. In France there are separate trades but there is no fundamental

problem in creating, in the workplace itself, a versatile grade like an electrician-mechanic. In the British factory, as in Great Britain generally, there are not and cannot be any multiskilled jobs because of the demarcation rules. Thus in order to perform the jobs done by French electrician-mechanics there has to be a team of three men: electrician/plumber/fitter. In effect, the function of mechanic is subdivided into two. There is also a similar subdivision in the English canning factory. The demarcation between trades is very precise; each new task is at once allocated to a trade and in case of argument about the allocation a new grade is created defining a separate sphere of competence and work. The pipe-fitter is thus the worker authorized to do mechanical maintenance work at the level of the furnace. In the event of a breakdown, there can be a succession of workers on the job, the electrician before the fitter, the fitter before the plumber, and if there is an overlap with the work of another trade, the foreman must seek the goodwill of the foreman whose trade territory is being encroached upon (Dubois, 1981: 353–4).

Dubois concludes, as far as British factories are concerned, that 'maintenance work is reserved for craftsmen (production workers and mates are not allowed to do maintenance), there is a sharp demarcation between trades (and no multiple skills), that work is reserved for the firms' permanent employees' (p. 358). Dubois' view of maintenance work in Britain is clear. It is dominated by the traditional craft ethos and entails strict demarcation between adjacent crafts within the division of labour. However, such a situation is not seen as insurmountable, as it is but a contingent feature of British industrial relations and there are possibilities for change, although Dubois is not particularly sanguine about their likelihood in the immediate future.

Scarborough (1984) has shown how difficult it can be to extract major changes in maintenance work in Britain, in his study on the introduction of new technology associated with the Mini Metro production lines at BL's Longbridge plant between 1978 and 1981. Maintenance at Longbridge traditionally involved seven crafts – millwrights, pipefitters, machine tool fitters, jig and tool fitters, maintenance fitters, toolmakers and electricians. According to Scarborough,

each trade was jealous of its own job rights and their demarcations were rigidly applied to maintenance and repair work on the production line. As a result, 'on-line' repair jobs might involve any one or more of five different trades groups. The trades' dominance of the maintenance function was further reflected in their careful defence of practices which supported their operational autonomy – refusing to respond to any requests except those channelled through their maintenance supervision, for instance, and refusing to carry out the logging of maintenance tasks (p. 11).

On balance, the evidence from BL – a firm famous during this period for a combative management seeking to change existing working practices radically – suggests that multi-skilling is perhaps more of a chimera than a practical possibility in present British industry.

This view is strongly challenged by Cross's research on the Flexible Craftsman. This study, conducted at the Technical Change Centre in London, examined the work of maintenance engineering craftsmen in British process plants. Cross claims that there is already a merging of electrical and mechanical craft jobs in 'brewing, toiletries, pharmaceutical, food processing, cigarette-making, plastic processing, glass container manufacturing and tyre making' (Cross, 1985: xiv). However, caution should be taken before accepting Cross's conclusions. His evidence comes only from 55 large firms located predominantly in process industries, and his text often conflates existing changes with possible developments. As will become evident, discussions about multi-skilling in a firm, or even trade union support for its development, do not guarantee its actual emergence on the shop floor. Cross's research findings are overwhelmingly derived from interviews or self-completion questionnaires with various managerial personnel. He did talk with 23 craftsmen and seven shop stewards, but this has to be balanced against 750 interviews with management. Nevertheless, his research is at least empirically based and, whilst one might be sceptical about the typicality of his results, he certainly does establish the case that there are changes under way in the organization of maintenance work in some modern British process industries. Of considerable interest to this analysis, and particularly to the compensatory theory of skill, is his claim that much of the multi-skilling involves merging of electrical and mechanical crafts (Cross, 1985: 156). However, he admits considerable union resistance to these issues and suggests that the AUEW-E and EETPU[2] should merge to solve them! As will become apparent, demarcation disputes can be just as significant a problem within unions which represent differing crafts as they evidently are between different craft unions.

Senker et al. (1981) present a different picture from Cross in their research on 'Maintenance Skills in the Engineering Industry'. They indicate that maintenance work is becoming more complicated and more important as a result of technical changes, particularly those associated with micro-electronics. Their conclusions about the use of automatic diagnostics are rather different from Braverman's! 'So far, automatic diagnostics are very limited in terms of the functions they cover; and not, according to the users we interviewed, very effective yet in aiding quick diagnosis' (Senker et al. 1981: 33). Senker et al. also suggest that the 'demarcation between mechanical craftsmen and electricians is much more rigid. Most managements prefer not to run the risk of mounting a serious challenge to these demarcation lines' (p. 33). Both Senker et al. and Cross agree on the desirability of multi-skilling from the perspective of managerial demands for increased efficiency. However, they differ in their estimates of its generality in Britain in the 1980s. For Cross, evidence from process industries suggests its development, whereas Senker et al.'s analysis of the engineering sector suggests that it is hardly occurring at all.

The issues concerning the nature of modern maintenance are, there-fore, these. Firstly, to what extent are traditional craft demarcations breaking down? How far, in other words, is there an emergence of dual or multi-skilling? Secondly, are some occupational groups gaining a greater share of these new forms of maintenance whether or not these involve processes of skill combination? Finally, are issues of demarca-tion made easier when there is no inter-union jurisdictional dispute? It was with these questions in mind that Wigzell (1984) undertook his research into the nature of changes in maintenance work since 1979 within the seven largest plants in Cumbria. As will become apparent, these plants cover a wide range of technologies and product markets.

For many, Cumbria conjures images of the Lake District and the tourist industry. However, around the perimeter of Cumbria are a series of traditional industrial centres like Barrow, Workington and Carlisle which contain some very large establishments. Cumbria as a whole has witnessed the full impact of the current economic depression. Unemployment more than doubled between 1980 and 1984, but never-theless the country has lost jobs at a slower rate than nationally whilst new jobs have been appearing faster. Since 1980 unemployment has been running regularly at around 1% less than the national average.

The choice of large plants for research was determined partly by the greater likelihood of major technological innovations in such plants, and

partly by the concentration of relatively large numbers of skilled maintenance workers, particularly those in the areas of electronic and traditional forms of maintenance work. Eight establishments were selected
for research, of which seven were able to cooperate with our survey.
These were Bowater-Scott, British Cellophane and British Shipbuilders
(all Barrow-in-Furness); Pirelli (Carlisle); Albright and Wilson
(Whitehaven); British Gypsum (Kirkby Thore); and British Nuclear
Fuels (Sellafield). The main method for collecting data centred upon
interviews with EETPU shop stewards, although where possible ordi-
nary EETPU members were also interviewed. Wigzell's original plan
was also to interview relevant managerial personnel, but various constraints made this generally impossible. Whilst recognizing the possible
dangers of such a research strategy, the results are of sufficient interest
to justify it. The interviews conducted were semi-structured and
open-ended. They were based upon a schedule of questions about the
impact of technical changes (particularly automation) upon maintenance skill levels with particular focus on maintenance electricians and
instrumenters.

3 The Case Studies

3.1 Bowater-Scott

Bowater-Scott Ltd is a multinational with joint UK and US parents[3].
The Barrow plant produces mainly soft tissues, such as 'Andrex', and
had 1,500 employees in 1984. It was a closed shop. The largest union,
GMBATU,[4] represents production workers; ASTMS[5] represents
managerial staff; the AUEW-E[6] represents fitters; SOGAT'82[7] specialist
production workers (like embossers); and the EETPU electricians on
machine commissioning and maintenance. The workforce had been
reduced by over 120 in 1984, but these had been mainly amongst workers represented by SOGAT '82. The numbers in the EETPU in 1984
(33) had not changed significantly over the last ten years. There had
been only limited automation in the plant, but it was felt by the EETPU
representative that skill levels had increased for maintenance electricians as the result of the new knowledge acquired. There was
considerable tension between electricians and instrumenters. The instrumenters were represented by EESA,[8] an autonomous staff association
within the EETPU. Their numbers had decreased over the last few

years as a result of the introduction of dual-skilling. This term referred to the acquisition of instrumentation skills by maintenance electricians in the plant. This is a clear example of intra-union conflict between different skilled occupational groups. Training for the maintenance of the new machinery was haphazard. The vast bulk of training was 'on-the-job' and devised by management. The company was prepared to pay course fees for electricians to attend evening classes in their own time, but as there was a continuous shift pattern of working this was not really a practical proposition and was rarely used. New machinery had come from Finland, West Germany, Italy and the USA, but little formal instruction had been provided. The maintenance staff relied upon past experience and collective knowledge. Perhaps not surprisingly, dissatisfaction with training provision at the site was expressed by the EETPU representative.

3.2 British Cellophane

British Cellophane produces cellophane wrappings used in packaging various commodities like cigarettes and crisps. The Barrow plant employed 400 workers. It was a closed shop and the unions were the TGWU[9] (production workers), AUEW-E (fitters), EETPU (commissioning and maintenance electricians) and UCATT[10] (construction workers). Automation within the factory was almost complete and there had been considerable job losses (mainly amongst production workers) since 1979 (200). This was partly a function of automation and partly a reduction in overall plant capacity of 20%. There were 16 EETPU members – eight electricians and eight instrumenters – and there had been a reduction in the total of two over the last five years. Nevertheless, it was felt that extra skills were being required from both electricians and instrumenters which necessitated greater levels of training for such workers. Management, in general, seemed reluctant to provide training courses for EETPU members. The general pattern was for management to receive maintenance knowledge and then impart it in an *ad hoc* fashion to maintenance craftsmen. Very occasionally outside firms like Foxborough Instruments and Kent Instruments had provided training, but the general managerial view was that formal training in technical advances was an individual responsibility. Shift-working patterns, however, made attendance at such courses very difficult in practice for maintenance workers.

3.3 British Shipbuilders (Vickers)

Despite the presence of Bowater-Scott and British Cellophane, Vickers employ about 50% of Barrow's current working population. They specialize in the production of nuclear-powered submarines under Ministry of Defence contracts. In 1984 Vickers employed approximately 12,500 and the plant was a closed shop. The main unions on site are GMBATU (production workers and boilermakers), AUEW-E (fitters and related engineering crafts), EETPU (commissioning and maintenance of machinery), TASS[11] (draughtsmen), APEX[12] (clerks) and UCATT (building maintenance workers). There had been substantial reductions in the numbers employed at Vickers since it had been nationalized in 1977, but most of these were concentrated amongst nonskilled production workers represented by GMBATU. The numbers in the EETPU at Vickers were approximately 800, which included those in EESA. There had been no losses of electricians or instrumenters but a large drop (around 70 in the previous two years) in the numbers of plumbers employed. This was the result of the introduction of new precision pipe-bending machinery. Maintenance and repair of new and existing machinery was considered by the EETPU as within their traditional orbit of work. However, Vickers were increasingly taking out maintenance contracts with the suppliers of new machinery, which had generated considerable dissatisfaction amongst EETPU members in the plant. Nevertheless, it was felt by the EETPU representative that higher skill levels were now required from their maintenance workers as the result of the increasing use of electronics within new machinery. This upgrading of maintenance skills had led to friction with the technicians' unions, ASTMS and TASS. This was because as electricians gained greater skills – particularly of a formal kind – they were being regraded as technicians and claimed as members by these two white-collar unions. The loss of members by this enskilling process is a serious problem for the EETPU at the plant but is strongly resisted.

The process of enskilling was also leading to a dichotomous structure within the maintenance crews themselves. Vickers had set up a squad of eight electricians with sophisticated electronics expertise who received an extra 8% pay when engaged in work that other crews could not handle. This 'super' crew was tending to monopolize electronics skills at the expense of other maintenance electricians. The new machinery installed recently came from many sources (Switzerland, West Germany and Austria and the UK). The new machinery was normally installed by the manufacturers' technicians who provided on-the-spot training to maintenance and production operatives. British Shipbuilders also provided classroom training within the plant during normal working hours. Nevertheless, there was a considerable amount of 'on-the-job' training whereby knowledge and experience were passed from person to person on an *ad hoc* basis. Furthermore, on certain machines, considerable maintenance was handled by outside contractors. Overall, maintenance skills were seen as increasing, but these were offset by the elimination of much craft expertise associated with the pipe work performed by plumbers.

3.4 Pirelli

Pirelli Ltd (an Italian-based multinational) in 1984 employed around 900 at its Carlisle plant in the manufacture of tyres, footwear and car seat inners. The plant is a closed shop and the unions there are the TGWU (production workers), ASTMS (management and technicians), AUEW-E (fitters) and the EETPU (machine commissioning and maintenance). There had been considerable automation in the plant and also substantial job losses over the last few years. The bulk of these losses were amongst production workers, but since 1977 almost 50% of the EETPU membership had disappeared. This has led to an increased workload for the remaining 30 maintenance craftsmen, which had been associated with the introduction of a new pay incentive scheme. The new machinery at Carlisle had been largely imported from Pirelli factories in Italy and the USA. This meant that managerial staff were sent to these locations for initial training and then returned to Britain to train their own maintenance teams. Training and retraining were regarded by the company as important and considerable use was made of Carlisle Technical College. In addition, specialist courses on instrumentation were provided at Pirelli's own technical school. Pirelli were also moving towards what they termed 'multi-skilling'. This involved the interchange of electricians' and instrumenters' skills, and also an increase on the normal craftsman's pay rate. It was felt that the content of the maintenance work had become more skilled and involved increased responsibilities. However, despite the higher level of skills required for maintenance work, it was also felt that the fewer breakdowns associated with the new machinery and the use of preventative maintenance had increased the possibilities of boredom amongst maintenance workers.

These findings parallel the conclusions of Penn and Scattergood's (1985) research on the changing skills of production workers in the paper industry where evidence of enhanced skills used less frequently was also to be found.

3.5 British Gypsum

British Gypsum is a part of British Plaster Board Industries. In 1984 the Kirkby Thore plant employed 700 workers in a closed shop producing plaster and plasterboard. The unions in the plant were GMBATU (production workers), AUEW-E (fitters), ASTMS (office staff and supervisors), EETPU (machine commissioning and maintenance) and UCATT (construction maintenance). There had been increasing automation within the factory over the last few years. Whilst numbers of production workers had been falling steadily – several hundred in the last decade – the numbers of EETPU maintenance workers had remained constant. The new machinery had necessitated increased training but this was haphazard and *ad hoc*. On one occasion the installation plans and maintenance manuals were written in Spanish! Fortunately, one of the factory operatives was of Spanish descent and was able to assist with translations. There had been discussions about multi-skilling which, in this instance, meant the combination of fitters' and electricians' roles. However, the AUEW was wary of this because they thought that fitters might find it difficult to retrain adequately on all aspects of electricians' work, and that consequently it would provide an opportunity for electricians to perform fitters' work but not vice versa. As a result, the AUEW – the larger union on the site – had blocked moves in this direction.

3.6 Albright and Wilson

Albright and Wilson Ltd at Whitehaven manufacture raw materials such as tripolyphosphates for use in detergents, shampoos and washing powders. This subsidiary of an American chemicals multinational employed 2,000 people in a closed shop in 1984. The unions operating in the plant are GMBATU (production workers), AUEW-E (fitters), ASTMS (technical and supervisory staff), EETPU (machine commissioning and maintenance) and UCATT (building maintenance). There had been a dramatic reduction in employment in the plant since 1979: almost 3,000 employees had been shed. The biggest losses were amongst production workers but the AUEW had lost 60 jobs over the period. There were now 143 EETPU members – 63 electricians, 60 plumbers and 20 instrumenters. There were also four instrumenters in the AUEW, a reduction of ten since 1981. EETPU jobs had fallen by 12 since 1979, which represented a loss of 7.7%. This has to be contrasted with an overall loss of 60% within the entire workforce. It was felt that the automation programme at the plant had enhanced the jobs of both electricians and instrumenters and that both occupations remained more or less on a par in terms of relative skill. Training had been provided initially 'on-the-job' by the suppliers of the new machinery installed, some of which was from Spain and West Germany. Again, examples were given of service manuals being provided in Spanish. There had been considerable discussion about multi-skilling within the establishment but this had been opposed by the AUEW who feared that it might accelerate the decline in their numbers. Nevertheless, it was evident that traditional mechanical maintenance tasks such as hydraulics and pneumatics were being progressively displaced by electronically based tasks. Given the *impasse* with the AUEW, the EETPU on site were seeking technician status for their maintenance workers with a view to amalgamating the electrician and instrumenter roles.

3.7 British Nuclear Fuels Ltd

BNF at Sellafield employed 6,000 people in 1984, most of whom are engaged in the processing of nuclear fuels. Sellafield was a closed shop with GMBATU representing production workers, the AUEW-E representing fitters and related engineering crafts, ASTMS the management and technical staff, EETPU maintenance electricians and instrumenters, UCATT building maintenance workers and Tass the sheetmetal workers engaged on internal fabrications. BNF were the only company in the survey not to report significant job losses over the last few years. Membership of the EETPU had risen by 20% since 1980 to its present 600. The interviews at Sellafield were more comprehensive than elsewhere, since we were able to interview the senior EETPU representative (along with a member of management) and also two other EETPU representatives – an electrician and an instrumenter.

The first interview centred mainly around the deskilling thesis and it was felt that the introduction, commissioning and maintenance of new machinery in the plant necessitated greater levels of skills from EETPU members. However, the second interview produced a view that skills had changed rather than increased. The reality at Sellafield seemed a compound of both views. For almost all EETPU members there was a process of acquiring additional skills. For some, these new skills were the sum of their new jobs which led to a view that skills had simply changed, whereas for others the newer skills and a process of enskilling was apparent. Such findings suggest the complex relations between new skilled tasks and overall subjective awareness of skill by craftsmen in the present era.

There has been considerable discussion within the plant about multi-skilling. Indeed, the EETPU, who favoured such a change, had balloted its members at Sellafield about the desirability of such a development. In this context, multi-skilling signified the combination of electricians' and instrument mechanics' roles. The instrumenters in the union felt that this would leave themselves vulnerable to job losses and despite an overall 'yes' vote to the principle of multi-skilling by EETPU members, the strong specific opposition of instrumenters had led to the proposal being shelved. Training seemed to have declined since 1980. Before then there had been considerable use of 'in house' classroom tuition, and also BNF had used the EETPU's own training facilities at Cudham Hall. (These facilities are outlined at length in Penn and Wigzell, 1987.) Since 1980 it was far more common for companies supplying new machinery to provide *ad hoc*, on-the-job training. If it were necessary to visit the factories of machine suppliers, this would be undertaken by managerial staff who would disseminate the information piecemeal to their own maintenance workforces upon their return.

3.8 Conclusions

The main focus of this section is upon the effects of technical change upon skilled maintenance work. In all seven plants examined in Cumbria there had been substantial technical change over the last few years with considerable substitution of capital for labour. This had produced differential effects on various parts of the workforce. With the exception of British Nuclear Fuels, all had witnessed sharp reductions in the numbers of nonskilled production workers employed. However, the picture for skilled electrical and electronics maintenance workers was more complex. At Bowater-Scott and British Gypsum numbers were constant, whereas at British Cellophane and Albright and Wilson there had been a slight fall. At Vickers the numbers of such maintenance workers had remained more or less static, but there had been a large elimination of skilled production workers – notably plumbers involved in precision pipe-bending. Pirelli had seen a significant fall in maintenance workers, whereas British Nuclear Fuels had seen a large increase in this category. However, if we set aside the experience of BNF, since it does not operate under anything like market constraints, the general picture is of a wholesale reduction of nonskilled production work and a relative preservation of skilled maintenance work. Trade unions like GMBATU and the TGWU appear to be under greater pressure in the contemporary period than do unions like the EETPU. We shall return to the effects of this pattern in chapter 7. The relative strength of the EETPU is due to the general increase in skills required of maintenance workers, especially in the areas of instrumentation and electronics. This was the belief of all our respondents with the exception of two junior EETPU representatives at BNF who suggested that skills were changing but not necessarily increasing.

Nevertheless, the changing technical requirements of skilled maintenance jobs were having considerable effects on the relationships between contiguous occupations within plants. The relationship between instrumenters and electricians – both traditional skilled crafts – was particularly complicated. Historically, electricians have dealt with the supply of electricity to and within control units, whilst instrument mechanics have maintained the dials located in such units. As micro-electronics develop, these demarcations become less and less clear-cut. At Bowater-Scott the two occupations were in the same union but within separate sections. The introduction of dual-skilling had led to a relative decline of instrumenters when compared with electricians at the plant. It was fear that this might happen that lay behind the rejection of the combination of the two crafts at BNF by instrumenters there. In this case both crafts were members of the EETPU main craft section, but none the less the inter-craft conflict was still a serious problem. At Albright and Wilson these issues were compounded by the fact that some instrumenters were members of the EETPU and others were in the AUEW. Most of the reduction in the numbers of instrumenters was amongst AUEW members, whilst electricians in the EETPU had experienced increasing skill content in their maintenance jobs.

The other contiguous craft relation to be subject to considerable strain was between fitters and electricians. At both British Gypsum and Albright and Wilson attempts to combine these occupations into a 'multi-skilled, maintenance craftsman had floundered upon opposition by the AUEW. The central factor in this tension was the evident differential impact of micro- electronics upon the two crafts. The introduction of micro-electronics means that there are far fewer moving or mechanical controls associated with new machinery and that the balance of maintenance requirements is moving from mechanical to electronically based skills. As a consequence, in the case studies reported here, the balance of advantages seemed to be with the EETPU rather than the AUEW.

The evidence on training for skilled maintenance work is that it is generally haphazard and *ad hoc*. There were certainly variations between the plants examined. Training seemed extensive at Vickers and BNF (both state-owned enterprises). There was a general managerial belief that formal acquisition of new skills by existing craftsmen was the personal responsibility of such individuals and that their role, as management, was to provide on-the-job, specific and informal forms of extra training. In several cases management received a more thorough grounding in maintenance skills than craft workers with the concomitant feature that management was frequently engaged in maintenance activities such as fault diagnosis. There were several reasons for this. One central feature was the fear management had of the putative impact of extensive knowledge of maintenance by their craftsmen. This was seen as a strategic danger since it would provide such workers with tremendous leverage within the plant. In consequence, management attempted to restrict generalized maintenance knowledge and to retain active involvement within it. This combination of low trust relations between managers and workforce and a perceived threat to managerial authority is a classic expression of latent class antagonisms within the plants investigated. Whether it is a satisfactory or efficient form of organization remains an open question. To a great extent training provision generates contradictory impulses for any firm in Britain. Given the generally low levels of state provision, the voluntarist system means that as a firm provides increasingly trained workers, other employers (who often save this expense) can poach such workers. A counter-strategy to this involves the incorporation of such trained workers into the enterprise – either by high pay rates or by the provision of additional benefits. However, our research suggests that these are not the main considerations of the managements in the plants examined. Rather, crisis-management and short-term considerations meant that training was not given a high priority. Only further research can reveal the wider economic and social implications of this structural pattern.

It becomes evident from the research findings in these seven plants that Dubois' (1981) picture of maintenance work rather than Cross's (1985) is the more typical. Despite considerable talk of dual and multi-skilling, such developments have not occurred to any great extent in the plants under consideration. On balance, electricians seem to be bene-fiting more than other skilled groups involved in maintenance, and this has led to demarcation issues with fitters and instrument mechanics. At Thames Board, another large plant in Cumbria, there was evidence of an internal conflict within the EETPU between electricians and instru-ment mechanics which was only resolved by a detailed agreement that each occupation would cover a stipulated set of tasks. Despite a manage-ment desire at Thames Board to eliminate trade demarcations, talks with the various trade unions concerned had led to no changes by October 1985.

Clearly, these issues are not resolved simply by membership of the contending groups within the same trade union. At Bowater-Scott there was considerable antagonism between instrumenters and electricians, who were both within the EETPU. Likewise the opposition of instru-menters at BNF at Sellafield to multi-skilling had dissuaded the EETPU from agreeing it with management despite an overall majority in its favour expressed by union members at the site. Whilst an amalgamation of the EETPU and the AUEW might be desirable, it should not be seen as a panacea for demarcation difficulties intrinsic to changes in the nature of modern maintenance work.

What, then, of the theories outlined at the beginning of this book? Some support was found for the deskilling thesis. Certainly plumbing skills had been eliminated by automation at Vickers and the demand for skills of fitters and instrumenters was in flux. None the less, nonskilled production work was being eliminated in large amounts which parallels the earlier findings about the paper industry, whilst maintenance work was increasing in terms of skill requirements and remaining generally constant in terms of numbers. Certainly the proportion of skilled main-tenance workers had increased in all the plants examined, which strongly challenges Braverman's dismissal of their significance in mod-ern factories. This also, therefore, gives considerable support for the skilling thesis. However, it is more important to emphasize the *duality* of skilling and deskilling processes outlined in the compensatory theory of skill. It is evident that *contemporary technical change generates both skilling and deskilling*. Within the limits of the data, we would argue that the experiences in Cumbria suggest that *skilling affects maintenance workers whereas deskilling is concentrated amongst some types of production workers* (although this is complicated by the low levels of skill of many production workers already). The data reported here suggest that the balance of advantages and disadvantages between occupational groups is complex. There are important issues of *demarcation* between contiguous skilled craft maintenance occupations. This means that the form of new technologies, which are increasingly reliant on micro- electronics, advantages groups that can lay claim to such knowledge over those who cannot. Nevertheless, in Wigzell's case studies little evidence was found of systematic use of EETPU training courses – rather there was a slow process of accretion by electricians into the new electronically based technologies. This process requires further attention. Clearly, at one level it involves 'following the work' – a time-honoured strategy of craft workers. At another level it involves the allocation of new forms of work to pre-existing groups within the division of labour. Nevertheless, these results suggest that *the compensatory theory of skill best characterizes trends in maintenance work in contemporary Britain.*

4 Skilled Work in Contemporary Engineering

4.1 Computer Numerically Controlled Machine Tools

As was shown in the first two chapters of this book, the question of the likely effects of the introduction of numerically controlled (NC) and computer numerically controlled (CNC) machinery on the division of labour, and particularly upon skilled machining work, was a central plank in Braverman's original deskilling thesis. At least five projects have examined these issues in modern British industry. These will be analysed in this section whilst the subsequent section will report on research conducted by the Skilled Worker Project on the effects of technical change upon skilled work in an electrical engineering assembly plant.

The central study of NC machinery in Britain is Jones' (1981) investigation of five engineering firms in the late 1970s. Jones investigated the effects of the introduction of NC machinery on the distribution of skills in a series of firms that specialized in small-batch production. Of particular interest was the division of the skills of programming and metal-machining between the occupations of turner and programmer within the plants. Jones criticizes Braverman's image of the 'double deskilling' involved in these developments and argues that 'some tool knowledge is required on the shop floor during machining operations and metal-working experience is required in advance of machining by part-programmers' (p. 189). Jones reveals that the machine operators systematically use buttons to override the programmes and to work manually on the components in the traditional fashion. He also shows that in other cases, the work was finished off on conventional machines. Furthermore, Jones demonstrates that machine operators must be able to detect tool wear from the noise of the machine turning and that this skill tends to advantage apprentice-served traditional craftsmen who have had experience on conventional machine tools. The new machinery produced a 'grey area' between machine operators and programmers which centred on the checking and modification of the tapes that instruct NC machine tools. The actual division of these tasks in each of the firms was a function of 'product and labour markets, organizational structures and trade union positions' (p. 198). As Jones concludes, emphatically: 'There is nothing "inherent" in the hardware of NC or its concept that would allow for the deskilling and control and surveillance assumed by both theorists of the labour process and publicists for NC installation' (p. 198).

Wilkinson (1983a, 1983b), in his studies of the shop floor politics of new technology, comes to similar conclusions, although he claims that deskilling is more typical than the emergence of what he terms the 'computer-aided craftsman'. Wilkinson explored the social and political processes involved in the introduction of new technologies in the West Midlands between 1979 and 1981. Like Jones, Wilkinson avoids assembly plants and focuses instead upon batch production; he also shows the variability of the division of labour in the plants examined, particularly between operators and programmers. The most interesting and extensive of the four main case studies involved an examination of a machine tool manufacturer. In this firm, 70% of production was in small batches, mostly to customer specifications. Eight of the nine CNC machines used in production were designed with the explicit intention that programming should be carried out away from the shop floor. However, the AUEW-E which represented machinists had insisted that CNC work be done by skilled craftsmen who had been accustomed to carrying out setting and operating on conventional machines. Wilkinson reveals that almost all the machinists (turners) had become involved in some degree of programming or tape editing despite these design intentions: this had occurred because the turners had obtained the keys to the control cabinets on the CNC machines which unlocked the tape editing facilities.

Such developments had resulted in considerable conflict with TASS, the union representing the programmers, which had sought to exclude craftsmen from this role.

Jones also noted tension between technicians and craftsmen over the introduction of new machinery in his case studies. There was a very similar pattern evident at Goss, the printing machinery manufacturers in Preston, when I conducted research there in 1986. There was considerable friction between CNC operators, who were fully apprenticed turners and programmers, over the modification of the computerized control recipes in the machines. This was exacerbated by the fact that most programmers were former turners who now entered the shop floor wearing the traditional regalia of management – jackets and ties!

Fincham (1983) discovered similar variations in the division of labour in his analysis of four engineering plants in Edinburgh, although he offers no explanation for these differences. At two large engineering plants, CNC working had become routinized nonskilled work, whereas at another (a marine engineering firm), Fincham states that 'the company had agreed to employ skilled men on the CNC equipment . . . since very considerable skills were still required to operate this machinery'. Wilson's (1985) research is able to throw further light on this area. In her study of a company manufacturing rotors for turbine generators at an establisment of around 2,000 employees, she shows that there is a polarization between different kinds of CNC operators. Fifteen CNC machines had been introduced in the firm. The programmers were all former craftsmen and had become members of TASS, whereas the CNC operators were all craftsmen who had worked on conventional machines and remained in the Engineering Union (AUEW-E). Tapes could be edited at all the machines by the operators but not all operators had received the same training. As Wilson states, 'some of the operators have been trained to program machines, and others have not. Levels of training differ' (p. 15). Given that some of the CNC machines are used for large batch work whilst others are used for a variety of machining tasks, it would seem likely that there is a polarization amongst the machinists between those who have received minimal training and do mostly repetitive machining of large batches and those who have undertaken greater training and perform the more varied machining tasks. Nevertheless, Wilson shows clearly that all CNC operators need to use their pre-existing machining skills acquired on conventional machinery to monitor, check and modify CNC machining processes.

Hartmann et al. (1983) also emphasize the variable effects of the introduction of CNC machinery in their comparison of British and West German manufacturing industry. They argue that 'all our data lead us to stress the extreme malleability of CNC technology' (1983: 230). Hartmann et al. demonstrate that planning by operators was more pervasive in West German small batch machining whilst 'British plans still followed the more traditional NC organizational view where programmes are made in the programming department and proved on the shop floor by the programmer and the operator' (1983: 227). Of particular interest is their analysis of the interaction between the supply of skilled labour, the design of CNC systems and the management of its development on the shop floor. In West Germany around half the workforce in manufacturing industry had completed a formal apprenticeship at the time of their research, which is a far higher proportion than in Britain. This supply of skilled craft labour strongly influenced the design of CNC systems for use in West German industry and the industrial culture of craft skill predisposed management to incorporate it into its routine use. Indeed, given the accelerating divergence of apprenticeship training programmes between the two countries since this research, one would hypothesize that these differences have increased since Hartmann et al. completed their research.

There is little discussion in this corpus of research on NC and CNC machine tools about the effects of their introduction upon maintenance skills. This is mainly because most of the authors have concerned themselves with criticizing Braverman's analysis of the deskilling of machinists, without noticing his parallel arguments about the concomitant deskilling of maintenance work. In July 1984, I visited Flexibox in Manchester to investigate these issues. The company, a part of the Burmah group, originally made components for pumps in oil refineries but now make a range of metal seals and metal couplings for various heavy industrial uses. Flexibox is a multisite firm in the UK, with a plant at Wythenshawe in Manchester and at Ballymena in Northern Ireland, and an administrative headquarters at Trafford Park in Manchester. Like the firm reported by Wilson (1985), all the CNC operators at the firm had been upgraded from the role of skilled turners. The company had installed four CNC lathes and two CNC machining centres in its Manchester plant to complement around 60 conventional production machines. The machines were both British and Japanese and the machine tool companies supplied on-site training lasting approximately one month. Turners so trained were given an extra payment for their 'multi-skilling'. The work at Manchester was of very high quality and there seemed to be no evidence of deskilling. However, the maintenance workers traditionally employed at Wythenshawe were exclusively mechanical fitters: there were no electricians employed as maintenance workers and consequently the firm had little choice but to rely on the manufacturers for electronics servicing. The general feeling of managers and operators with whom I spoke was that the CNC equipment in use and the high specifications of the components being turned or milled had enhanced rather than reduced the level of skills attached to metalworking. Management were emphatic that maintenance skills were becoming far more complex.

It is evident from these various research projects into the effects of CNC machinery on the nature of skilled work that Braverman's deskilling thesis is totally inadequate. All the research projects examined demonstrate some examples of the introduction of CNC machinery and constant, if not enhanced, operator skills. Indeed, the path from NC to CNC machinery, far from increasing the pressure towards deskilling, has produced the opposite effect: CNC machinery makes it easier for skilled turners (machinists) to enhance the skilled content of their jobs by adding programming skills to their traditional knowledge of turning metals. Whilst this is not a universal feature, as the skilling thesis would suggest, it is sufficiently generalized as to render Braverman's prognoses most implausible. Production skills *can* increase with the advent of micro-electronically controlled machine tools, which parallels the findings about the production skills of beatermen and machinemen in the paper manufacturing industry. This is a major qualification to the compensatory theory of skill as formulated in chapter 2. Nevertheless, despite the lack of attention given to the effects of the introduction of CNC machinery upon maintenance skills, the evidence to hand (from Flexibox) *does* suggest that maintenance functions are increasingly significant and that the skills of maintenance workers are both increasing and in short supply. These findings confirm the compensatory theory of skill and complement the findings in the previous two sections of this chapter.

4.2 Electrical Engineering

The research reported here was undertaken at MK Electric in Edmonton, London. It involved a visit in the summer of 1981 and a return visit in early 1984. The 1981 research was conducted in the earliest phases of the Skilled Worker Project and much of it involved observation and interviews with various people in order to orient myself to the details of modern technological developments. The second visit was undertaken to investigate the effects of automation upon the assembly of some of the firm's highest volume products – plugs and sockets. This second visit involved interviews with senior management, middle management, supervisory personnel, representatives of the manual workforce and a selection of manual workers.

In 1979 senior management in the firm received information about electrical components newly produced in the Far East that might challenge their dominant position in the British market. A team was despatched to Japan, China, South Korea and Taiwan to investigate these claims and returned with samples of electrical components that revealed the existence of such a potential threat. In particular, Far Eastern producers were manufacturing items very similar to the high-volume components being produced by the firm in Britain. Senior management then decided upon a major programme of automation of the high-volume assembly lines in 1980. Considerable effort was made to ensure the cooperation – indeed , the positive response – of the manual workforce to these changes in production. One major factor in the success of the automation programme was the guarantee by the firm that it would not make any workers redundant as a result of automation if this could possibly be avoided. In the economic climate of 1980 and 1981 this was a highly significant undertaking and involved a gamble by management that they could lose any excess labour through natural wastage. Manning of the new automated lines was to take place from within the plants being automated in so far as this was practical.

Two points can be made about this strategy. Firstly, the immense cost of the new machinery (involving millions of pounds in investment) meant that management needed to gain a positive response from its workforce – without this, the new technology could have been an expensive white elephant. Secondly, the firm in question had been a relatively progressive employer over a long-term period and, consequently, its previous behaviour meant that representatives of the workforce were inclined to trust the undertakings given (which always had a moral rather than a legal force) and that workers were predisposed to cooperate with technical change. The importance of beliefs about technological change in the determination of responses to innovation will be dealt with at greater length in chapter 6, but suffice it to say that fear of foreign competition and particularly the dramatic rapid collapse of other electrical engineering companies, such as Gestetner, in the immediate vicinity were dominant elements of a generalized belief system within the firm. Secondly, the axiomatic belief amongst Marxist schools of industrial sociology that the relationships between capital and labour are always antagonistic fails to illuminate the real processes underlying the dynamics of change in the firm being considered. Certainly the firm displayed the normal range of industrial conflict between management and workers. However, it was the general realization that without automation the firm itself was threatened that is central to the processes of change. Furthermore, it is important to grasp the symbiotic relationship between high-volume and low-volume assembly lines. Only 20% of the firm's production was in batches sufficiently large to make automation an economic possibility. These high-volume assembly lines were the most vulnerable to foreign competition and without them it was held to be unlikely that the firm could continue to sustain the sales of other – far more profitable – specialized (complex) components. One part of the range guaranteed the viability of the others. Indeed, depending upon the nature of growth in the demand for products, it can be seen that automation of high-volume items could reduce their relative costs and help sustain a growth in the low-volume, hand-assembled items.

The cost and strategic significance of the new machines meant that maintenance became even more vital. Instead of one general maintenance electrician and one fitter to cover a large area of the plant, it became necessary to utilize one electrician and one fitter per shift (the new machines were being used for two eight-hour shifts) exclusively for the automated machinery. The electricians were retrained by the manufacturers of the machinery with courses on electronics and microprocessors and renamed 'electronic engineers'. Supervisors also had to be trained in the new technology, along with the routine machine minders. Instead of about 150 hand-assemblers, with one supervisor and two (shared) maintenance men, the new automated production involved two teams of 12, each of which included a supervisor, an electronic engineer and a fitter. The impact of automation upon the division of labour and skills is clear in this instance. The new automated machinery led to the elimination of over one hundred routine manual jobs in hand-assembly and the generation of a small number of skilled maintenance jobs. Overall, the impact of automation in this instance produced a 'skilling' of the manual workforce by the elimination of a considerable number of routine nonskilled manual jobs.

Almost all the new automated machinery at MK Electric had been built in Switzerland and West Germany. This has a significant effect upon the overall impact of new technologies on the issues of skill and the division of labour. As was shown by Wilkinson (1983a) in his study of a machine tool company, machinery manufacture involves very highly skilled manual and non-manual workers. Usually the machines are cus-tom-built, but even those purchased 'off the rack' require a massive input of skilled labour. If, as was the case in the earlier phases of industrial innovation, the bulk of such machines were designed and manufactured in Britain, then the overall effects of automation on skilled manual work *and* on the overall level of employment would be all the greater within Britain itself.

5 Skilled Maintenance Work in the Coal Mining Industry

This research was undertaken by Penn and Simpson in 1985 and 1986. It involved an examination of changing patterns of work in the Lancashire coalfield, and in particular within the pits at Agecroft (in Salford) and the Bickershaw complex (near Leigh). The research included interviews with management, methods engineers, pit deputies, trade unionists and a wide range of mineworkers themselves. In addi-tion, we were given access to confidential manpower data at each of the pits and to the detailed contracts of work of various face-teams. The authors made two underground visits together and these were supple-mented by additional underground visits by one of the authors (Simpson) on his own. Our main focus was on the differing trajectories of change in skilled maintenance work within the coalfield since the mid-1970s; this entailed a comparison of both production and mainte-nance workers and of surface and below-ground activities. This differs from previous research on coal mining in Britain (Dennis et al., 1956; Burns et al., 1983, 1985) which gives the impression that coal face workers are the predominant group in mining. This is a myth. At Agecroft in August, 1986, there were only 42 workers engaged directly in facework out of a total workforce of 650. A coal mine is a complex social and technical environment with extensive operations both above and below ground. In order to assess the changing patterns of skilled maintenance work in coal mining, it is necessary to investigate its development in all areas of operation. For the purposes of analysis this account will distinguish surface and underground operations and within the latter it will separate coal cutting (facework), development work and transportation and haulage. Surface operations will be further sub-divided into the control room and other maintenance work.

5.1 The Changing Nature of Underground Maintenance Work

5.1a Facework and development work In order to understand the expansion of maintenance work underground, it is crucial to understand the broad changes in the production systems of mining since 1945. In the pre-mechanized phase of mining, which lasted in Lancashire until nationalization, coal cutting was undertaken by powered tools and fill-ing of tubs by hand. It was the advent of machinery on to the face that generated the need for fitters and electricians to install, maintain and repair the equipment. This normally entailed one fitter and one elec-trician per shift during this phase of early mechanization. The main increases in maintenance workers have occurred more recently as a result of changes in the methods of mining. In particular, there has been a shift from advance to retreat mining and also there is now more sophisticated equipment involved in coal cutting and roof support. Nowadays there will be one electrician, two or three fitters and one specialist in chock (mechanical roof supports) maintenance per face team and also one fitter and one electrician in each development team. The development teams are engaged in boring the tunnels that are the basis of retreat mining with the use of road-headers (powerful drilling and excavating equipment). Tunnels are advanced prior to coal cutting which is performed back towards the main shafts (hence the term 'retreat mining'). The data in table 4.1 confirm the existence of such trends. The proportion of mechanics and electricians underground had increased from 13.2% of the entire pit workforce in 1979 to 15.9% in 1986. This parallelled a simultaneous increase in the proportion of face and development workers from 27.2% to 31.2% over the same period. These changes have taken place as the number of faces actually opera-tional fell from four in 1979 to only one in 1986, and as Agecroft had changed from advance to retreat mining. This was paralleled by devel-opments at the Bickershaw complex where there had been eight faces in 1970 producing 1.3 million tonnes but only four faces by 1986, although with a similar level of aggregate output. It is within this overall pattern of decline that the asymmetries of manpower have to be located. For example, at Agecroft the overall workforce has fallen from around 1,700 in 1976 to 651 in 1986.

Table 4.1 *Changing manpower levels at Agecroft Colliery, 1979–1986*

	1979		%	1986	%
Undergound					
Faceworkers	156 ⎱	230	27.2	203	31.2
Development workers	74 ⎰				
Mechanics	58		6.9	55	8.4
Electricians	53		6.3	49	7.5
Officials	65		7.7	65	10.0
Coal transport	78 ⎱				
Materials transport	82	239	28.3	150	23.0
Salvage	18				
Roadway repairs	61 ⎰				
Weekly paid industrial staff	21		2.5	15	2.3
	666		78.9	537	82.4
Surface					
Winding and banking	23		2.7	8	1.2
Mechanical ⎱				12	1.8
Electrical	57		6.7	1	0.2
Other crafts ⎰				23	3.5
Weekly paid industrial staff	10		1.2	7	1.1
Others	89		10.5	63	9.7
	179		21.1	114	17.5
Total	845		− 23.0	651	

Source: British Coal Manpower figures

Unfortunately the aggregate manpower data did not permit the disentangling of the numbers of fitters and electricians at various sites underground. However, our interviews at Agecroft confirmed that the proportions had increased at the face and in development work, whilst they had fallen in the areas of diesel, shaft and conveyor maintenance. In 1964, there were 22 fitters engaged in various forms of mechanical maintenance in areas away from the face and development headings whereas by 1986 there were only six. This had been achieved as the result of subcontracting (for example, English Electric now service the diesels underground whereas previously this had been done by Coal Board fitters), the elimination of spare capacity, a reduction of maintenance actually done underground and an intensification of the work of those fitters actually employed away from the face and development headings.

Overall, it was clear that new technologies have produced a change in the content of skilled electrical maintenance work underground. There is an increasing range of equipment underground requiring electrical and electronic maintenance. Coal-cutting machines, conveyor belts and environmental safety monitoring equipment are increasing, in both scale and complexity. This necessitates a wide range of theoretical and practical skills amongst electricians underground. However, whilst it was normal 20 years ago for electricians to dismantle and repair faulty components themselves, nowadays they simply replace them and their repair is undertaken either at the British Coal repair centre at Stoke or by the machinery suppliers themselves. For example, in the 1960s, electricians would trace the more obscure faults by using circuitry and wiring diagrams and drawings. This would often entail tracing a fault through a lengthy system. Nowadays, on the other hand, if there is a fault within an electronic component on the conveyor belts, for instance, the electrician will simply replace the faulty unit in its entirety. Nevertheless, we encountered no evidence in any of the pits under investigation of the advent of self-diagnostics, fault specification by machines themselves nor any signal as to who should repair the fault. Our questioning in this area generated much amusement and there was great scepticism amongst senior managers, maintenance workers and local union officials as to the likelihood of such developments. What was evident was not the disappearance of electrical maintenance craftsmen as a result of automation, but an increasing number of supervisory and managerial personnel devoted to the supervision of such activities. At Golborne, near Leigh in Lancashire, which is a part of the Bickershaw complex, there were 54 electricians below ground and ten chargemen electricians (first-line supervisors), five assistant electrical engineers, two deputy engineers and one unit (chief) electrical engineer. This expansion paralleled the expansion of this function relative to others amongst the manual workforce.

Overall these data support the view that underground electrical maintenance in mining is changing and is probably becoming more skilled. It is certainly not becoming deskilled. The introduction of modular removal of components does not, in itself, simplify the work. The electrician has to understand these modules, their interaction and their location within the wider systems of production and monitoring. This increase in knowledge has not been achieved in the main through massive changes to the training system. For the most part, electricians have acquired these new forms of knowledge in a piecemeal, *ad hoc* fashion.

Indeed, this lack of systematic retraining was perceived by many electricians to reflect a persistent tendency by management to underestimate the range of new skills required for the electrical and electronic maintenance of modern coal extraction systems. Our data show clearly that there is an increasing range of equipment underground that maintenance electricians have to understand. These twin factors led us to conclude that the work of underground maintenance electricians is becoming more complex and more skilled in the present era.

The changes associated with mechanical fitters are similar and equally complex. The coal-cutting equipment is now easier to dismantle but more complex overall. The number of fitters in each face team has increased from one in the mid-1970s to two or three in 1986. Such fitters are required to tend to the motors and gearboxes on the shearers and on the conveyor systems around the face. They are also engaged in chock maintenance where there has been a great increase in the complexity of the internal hydraulic systems that power the chocks. Elsewhere underground there have been even more dramatic changes in the division of labour. The transportation of coal and some equipment now takes place on conveyor belts controlled by electronic sensors. This has increased the number of maintenance electricians required to maintain this system. The recent introduction of FSV (Free Steered Vehicles) for haulage work has led to an increasing need for mechanics able to maintain the diesel engines that power them, whilst reducing the need for fitters who maintained the conventional haulage engines.

5.1b Surface work   In the immediate period after nationalization there was a wide range of maintenance craft skills needed in surface work. In the boilerhouse at Agecroft, three or four fitters were needed in 1964, whilst by 1986 there were none required. Nowadays, the collieries receive much of their energy from the CEGB and the maintenance of the boilers at Agecroft is sub-contracted on to the manufacturers themselves. Other craftsmen, like blacksmiths, welders, joiners, platers and turners were used in the surface workshops preparing chock supports, scaffolding, rails, piping and other materials for production. With the increasing levels of mechanization much of this work has been eliminated and there is also a powerful tendency to buy in completed subsystems for production. Overall, there are significantly fewer craftsmen engaged in surface work today. At Agecroft there were 57 craftsmen above ground in 1979, whereas in 1986 this had been sharply reduced to

36. This represented a proportional fall from 6.7% in 1979 to only 5.5% of the entire labour force in 1986.

On the other hand, the advent of computerized coal production, transportation and safety monitoring has greatly increased the range of skills required for the maintenance of the hardware and software of the control-room where these computers are centred above ground. Training for these new systems has been provided by British Coal research and development staff from Bretby, where the FIDO (Face Information Digest Online) has been developed. British Coal have not sent their maintenance workers to the suppliers of the new equipment (at Agecroft they included DEC and BICC), unlike many other contemporary British employers (see Penn, 1987). There was considerable dissatisfaction that the Coal Board and the National Union of Mineworkers (NUM) had not negotiated a New Technology agreement around such changes and maintenance workers complained bitterly that they received neither adequate retraining nor extra payments for new skills acquired, unlike their colleagues in other industries in the North West.

It is clear that the proportion of skilled maintenance workers has increased overall in the pits under consideration. At Agecroft, they had risen from 19.9% in 1979 to 21.4% in 1986. However, this masks quite different trajectories above and below ground. Traditionally coal mines had extensive maintenance workshops above ground where a wide range of maintenance craftsmen were employed. These activities have been severely curtailed as British Coal has sought to maximize its workforce engaged in direct production. The use of sub-contractors and the effects of new forms of production and technology have reduced substantially the demand for such skilled maintenance work in British pits. It is important to emphasize these points since most sociological analyses of coal mining have ignored surface activities and the complex division of labour involved in coal production. However, these changes on the surface contrast strongly with the expansion of machine maintenance tasks below ground, particularly in the development headings and at the face. Here we encounter an expansion in the numbers of skilled maintenance workers and an increasing complexity to such work, despite the advent of modular construction. The latter has reduced the amount of dismantling of components underground but the overall expansion of the variety of production equipment has led to an increase in the levels of skill of both mechanical and electrical-electronic maintenance workers underground. Nevertheless, there are counter-tendencies to these dominant patterns both above and below ground. On the surface the job of the control room maintenance worker has become very complex as the result of the introduction of new computerized systems, whereas below ground the tasks of the maintenance workers engaged in ensuring the functioning of the conveyors has become intensified and simplified to some degree.

These changes are clearly connected to the introduction of a wide range of new technologies in the contemporary British coal mining industry. Job skills are changing and overall they have increased, although there are some important exceptions. Much skilled work has also been transferred to outside firms – both machine suppliers and various sub-contractors. Training for new maintenance skills appeared haphazard and *ad hoc*. As we saw earlier, this is very much the common pattern in contemporary British industry. There has been little effect on demarcation lines although British Coal have recently modified their traditional apprenticeship system to develop multi-skilled maintenance workers in their ten regional maintenance works. The new programme will involve training in mechanical, electrical and welding skills. It will come as little surprise to discover that this new scheme has not been agreed formally by either the NUM or the Union of Democratic Mineworkers (UDM).

There is substantial support from our data for the view that these inter-related sets of changes have led to maintenance workers becoming more distinct as an element within the workforce. Maintenance electricians and fitters have traditionally been members of the NUM in a form of industrial unionism unique in Britain. The NUM has been dominated traditionally by faceworkers who constituted the elite of the mining workforce. This traditional hold upon the union by faceworkers is partly based upon their position as the most skilled group underground, standing at the apex of the internal career trajectory of manual mining work, and it also reflects the numerical strength of mineworkers as a whole. As Turner (1964) has shown, trade union leaders generally reflect the interests and concerns of the majority of the rank-and-file. In the case of the NUM, this has always entailed a very powerful position for faceworkers in the union. Nevertheless, various groupings have sought historically to achieve a degree of separate representation within the NUM. The Durham Mechanics and the Winders are clear examples of this process. Within the Lancashire coalfield, the Leigh Craftsmen represented maintenance workers traditionally at the Bickershaw complex, whilst at Agecroft there was a separate branch for craftsmen and another for colliers.

These potential cleavages have been exacerbated recently by the twin pressures of industrial and political divergences within the workforce in the Lancashire coalfield. At present up to 70% of maintenance workers at Agecroft have joined the UDM and the Leigh Craftsmen have joined it in their entirety. This is partly because many craftsmen continued to work during the Miners' Strike of 1984 and 1985, but it is fuelled additionally by intense dissatisfaction over the failure (in their eyes) of the NUM to represent the interests of skilled maintenance workers. This receives its strongest expression around the issues of differentials in earnings between faceworkers and maintenance workers, both on the coalface and in the development headings.

What, then, of the various theories of changes in maintenance work outlined earlier? The first point to note is the complexity of the changes and the wide variety of developments in different parts of the coal-mining system of production. There is evidence of the elimination of craft maintenance skills above ground as the result of new forms of working, and of the loss of skilled maintenance workers from pits as the result of the general reduction in manpower, itself largely determined by the policy of concentrating output at the most productive seams. Never-theless, there is no general evidence to support Braverman's view that the introduction of computerized controls or monitors will destroy the skills of maintenance workers. Neither in the control room nor on the coalface nor in the development headings was there evidence of simplification, intensification or loss of skill. There was some evidence of such developments away from the face, particularly in connection with the computerized conveyor systems. However, there is no general evidence to support the deskilling thesis in relation to maintenance work in the contemporary British coal industry.

There is far more support for the skilling thesis: there is much more evidence of enskilling than of its reverse. We did find some evidence that there was an increasing asymmetry in the developments of traditional mechanical and electrical maintenance work as suggested by the com-pensatory theory of skill. The coal-cutting machines (shearers) had become more simple for mechanical maintenance with the advent of modular construction. In former days fitters would attempt to repair motors or gearboxes on the coal face; now they simply replace faulty components. However, the skills of maintenance mechanics have expanded in other directions with the introduction of more complex chocks on the face, the increasing size of the roadheaders and the recent advent of FSVs (Free Steered Vehicles). The compensatory theory of skill postulated an increasing asymmetry between electrical and mechanical maintenance skills: our data provide some evidence of such developments.

Nevertheless, the compensatory theory of skill also alerted us to the potential conflict between production and maintenance workers and to the inter-firm aspects of technical change and skill. We did find evidence of an increasing removal of skilled work from the pits themselves. The growing use of manufacturers' facilities to service and repair machines and the rising tendency to send faulty equipment to British Coal regional repair centres represented a continued narrowing of the *base* of skilled jobs, even if those that remained were generally becoming ever-more skilled. These twin processes have facilitated a growing tension between skilled production workers (faceworkers and development workers) and maintenance workers. There was a very strong feeling amongst the latter that the NUM was an unsatisfactory vehicle for their interests. As we shall see in chapter 7, this is a common feature of industrial unionism, particularly in the USA. Maintenance workers are increasingly flexing their muscle in the contemporary coal industry, particularly over the vexed issue of bonus payments, and this is largely due to their expansion in the underground heartlands of British coal mining.

6 The Printing Industry

The effects of changes in technology upon the nature of skilled work in the British printing industry have been of major interest to sociologists over the last decade. Martin (1981) investigated the attempts by *The Times*, *The Financial Times* and the *Daily Mirror* to introduce modern technology in the late 1970s, and Cockburn (1983a) has made a powerful case to support the view that the skills of the compositor have been subject to massive erosion in London's Fleet Street. McGoldrick and McEwan's (1986) examination of these issues in the British provincial press, as we shall see later, comes to a rather more complex conclusion. None the less, the well publicized disputes at *The Times* in 1980 and between News International and the main print unions in 1986 have placed the relationship of technical change and skilled work at the centre of the media stage in recent years. It is the contention of this section of the book that much of the discussion of these issues is confused and ignores both the *variety* of occupations within the printing industry and also the new skills associated with composing upon a computer screen.

However, in order to establish this thesis – which is controversial to say the least – it is important to grasp both what the traditional skills of compositors were, and what the new tasks entail following the advent of computerized printing.

McGoldrick and McEwan (1986) present an excellent summary of the traditional pattern of skills associated with the pre-computerized linotype process of production. My own research on these issues at the *Geelong Advertiser* and the Melbourne *Sun-Herald* in Australia in the autumn of 1984 confirms their account. McGoldrick and McEwan state that:

> the linotype system created a new range of skills. Typesetters retained responsibility for the quality of their work and added the maintenance and care of the machinery to their spelling and judgmental skills . . . The other set of printers' skills, namely composition, involved three distinct stages. First of all the compositors operated . . . the 'mark up' of the job . . . they would note the distinctive features of the job; the size of margins, the width of columns, the face and size of the type characters to be used (e.g. capitals, bold type, headlines) and they would leave these as a set of instructions, in a special printers' code, for the typesetters. After the type was set, the compositor would then collect the 'galleys' or trays of type and order them in the correct page sequence for printing. The final stage of composition was known as 'working the stone' whereby the galleys of type were levelled off on a work surface and adjusted to ensure that all the margins and spacings were correct and to incorporate any illustrative blocks of photographs (McGoldrick and McEwan, 1986).

The tasks of compositors were not only highly skilled but also performed at high speed. Compositors had to be able to react swiftly and competently to rapid changes in format with the arrival of late stories for inclusion in the paper.

The new computerized technologies in printing, often referred to as photocomposition or 'cold metal' (in contrast to the previous 'hot metal' system), have altered these production processes quite dramatically. Photocomposition involves the production of a photographic negative as the printing plate rather than the mass of lead type produced under the linotype method. In the new computerized systems the text can be typed on to a VDU or screen and rearranged in a fashion similar to word processing. Once complete the text will be printed on to photographic copy paper, trimmed and 'pasted up' on to a page. It is often assumed that this has eliminated the skills of printing workers in general and compositors in particular. It is claimed (see Cockburn, 1983a) that the work has been deskilled, degraded and can be done by any qualified typist. The reason for this is that the keyboard now used is that of the standard QWERTY typewriter and all that is required is for someone to type it in. Indeed, much of the industrial conflict in contemporary British printing appears to take this form. The National Graphical Association (NGA), which is the compositors' craft union, objects both to 'tele-ad' girls and journalists producing text directly for the 'paste-up' page. However, the conflict is not simply about deskilling, but about the appropriate division of labour to be associated with the new system of production.

There is more to modern composing work than simply typing on a keyboard. Each newspaper has a series of different styles for differing kinds of headline and for different sections of the paper. For their effective use, the keyboard operative requires considerable knowledge and experience of these 'house' systems. In certain areas, it is possible to develop standardized formats with specialist software. This is a constant tendency in the areas of advertising. It is also possible for clients to provide their own formats for larger advertisements. In the main areas of news and editorials, it is possible for journalists to learn the 'house' styles or to have much of it formated for them. Clearly there is a serious danger that the new electronic technologies in newspaper production could produce a double 'squeeze' on the traditional pattern of skilled work in the composing room. This could come from both journalists and 'tele-ad' girls simultaneously and severely reduce the need for compositors in the production process.

Nevertheless, despite such possibilities, there has been no such elimination at the most advanced contemporary British printing plant – the *Daily Telegraph* presses in Manchester. Journalists continue to supply crude copy to the compositors who then type it on to the screens according to the traditional 'house' codes. The compositors also arrange the page layout of the photographic copy produced on the screens. When I visited this plant in 1986, it was apparent that the compositors preferred the new system of working and did not regard computerization as degrading their jobs. The most significant problem from their point of view had been not deskilling but redundancies, since the new technologies required fewer compositors than hitherto. However, much of this was not connected with the new keyboards *per se*, but with the transmission of much of the completed paper directly from the main plant in London.

It is interesting to note the example in figure 4.1. This was performed by the author but rejected by the compositors after printing, not because of ardent Republicanism, but because the headline words were both too far apart and too close to the main text to be appropriate for such a story. It is one of the weaknesses of much contemporary industrial sociology on printing that it has failed to penetrate into the details of the jobs now present in modern plants. In particular, whilst there has been much discussion about the advent of QWERTY keyboards, there has been virtually no analysis of the software systems actually used and how they affect the jobs in printing plants. The example in the figure demonstrates that proficiency in typing is insufficient for an adequate knowledge of how to compose a news story on a computer screen. Of course, such codes and aesthetic judgements could be learned by journalists or typists, but it is highly significant that in this case this expertise was retained by the compositors. We will return to the factors that lay behind this outcome later in this section.

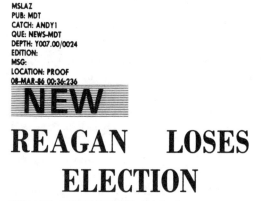

Figure 4.1   *Example of modern composing work*

There is a much more serious bias in much of the literature on printing which reflects the tendency to pick upon one occupation to fit a preconceived theoretical stance. Such a combination of abstract theorizing and the odd anecdote is one of the most pernicious legacies of the 'Methodenstreit' of the 1970s within the social sciences and particularly within sociology. The problem, in a nutshell, is that there were many skilled occupations in the pre-computerized printing industry, almost all of which have been transformed by the newer computerized technologies. Almost all the texts on technical change and occupational structures in modern printing are silent on this issue. Just as Marx saw the handloom weaver as the embodiment of the tendencies inherent within early industrial capitalism, the compositor is seen as the archetype for twenty-first century working patterns by many contemporary commentators. Such a viewpoint is based upon a highly selective method of analysis and upon a disastrous combination of 'theoreticism' and the crudest positivism.

The best examples with which to challenge this simplified picture are the machinemen who run the newly computerized printing presses and the maintenance workers who maintain them. The new *Daily Telegraph* printing press at Manchester was designed by Goss at their nearby works in Preston to reduce the traditional autonomy and discretion of the machinemen. Under the traditional system of production, the machinemen were required to alter the flow of ink across the press and to adjust various aspects of the running of the machine by the use of valves. Like the machinemen in paper manufacture, they would examine a printed page at a glance and assess the changes needed to be made. Like the coal miners discussed in the previous section, they worked in entirely autonomous work groups, with virtually no supervision and with a very strong predisposition to stop the presses if management entered the machine room. The design team at Goss were well aware of these traditional relationships and particularly the wide discretion that machinemen enjoyed. Serious efforts were made to programme many of these decisions into the software systems designed to control production. The Goss design engineers were acting in the way expected from Braverman's account of the exigencies of capitalist management. However, within a matter of weeks of opening the new plant in Manchester, it was clear that the machinemen were altering the machine from their control room by means of a wide array of buttons, basing their actions upon a visual inspection of the page combined with computerized information supplied by a series of monitors within the machine. The *Daily*

Telegraph management were rarely seen in this critical area of the plant.

The reasons for this continuity in the occupational discretion of the machinemen are both interesting and indicative of the simplicity of Braverman's view of the social relationships surrounding skilled work in modern computerized workplaces. The failure to transform the work of the machinemen was based upon three sets of inter-related factors. Firstly, the Goss design team experienced a wide range of technical difficulties in the development of their control software. These parallel the difficulties encountered in the paper plants discussed earlier in this chapter. Secondly, the *Daily Telegraph* management had neither the knowledge, experience nor inclination to ensure the maximization of control over their machinemen. Finally, the machinemen themselves had a strong desire to maintain their traditional autonomy by restricting the degree of automation within the control software. This triangular matrix of forces produced the outcomes described above, and provides a more balanced and more contingent view of the relationship of technological change and the division of labour than that found in much contemporary literature.

Compositors and machinemen are the core skilled groups within the NGA. There is a strong presumption that the need to ensure cooperation from the machinemen had an effect upon management's arrangements in the composing room. Whilst they could have tried to minimize the utilization of compositors by retraining journalists and/or typists, management would have increased resentment and mistrust within the machine room at the very moment when they had to rely upon these machinemen to operate the new presses. In this context, it is highly significant that News International spent many months training an entirely new workforce at their new plant in Wapping in 1985 before they closed their old plants in Fleet Street and excluded the traditional print unions and most of their members from the new site.

It is also strange that none of the analyses of contemporary printing has anything to say about the effects of computerization upon maintenance work within the industry. This is partly because the trade unions that represent machine maintenance workers – the EETPU and AEU – are not greatly liked by those who romanticize about trade unions in contemporary Britain.[13] Indeed, there is a view shared by some socialist and feminist 'groupuscles' and influential amongst certain tendencies in sociology that skilled workers are the 'enemy within' the contemporary British labour movement. Whilst it is undoubtedly the case that both the union leaderships and the bulk of the membership of these unions are no longer staunch supporters of socialism, this constitutes no reason why their working environments should be ignored. It is the proper role of sociology to face the realities of modern Britain and not to engage in escapist fantasies.

The role of machine maintenance has become enhanced with the advent of new equipment in printing. The presses are expensive and complex machines which have a variety of international inputs and a wide array of hydraulic and electronic sub-systems. Such developments have necessitated extensive retraining by the machine suppliers and have strengthened the relative position of such groups within modern plants. These patterns are consistent with those found in the contemporary paper manufacturing and coal mining industries and with the overall tendencies within maintenance work described above.

7 Conclusions

The data in this chapter are consistent with the findings in the previous chapter. There is little empirical support for Braverman's deskilling thesis. It is far too simple and mechanistic for an adequate understanding of the changing nature of skilled work in Britain. The deskilling argument, with its reliance on abstract reasoning and occasional anecdotal evidence, has been shown to be false. It is a remarkable fact that so many academics still believe the tenets of the deskilling thesis. None the less, it is essentially a myth.

The skilling thesis, whilst closer to the mark, is also far too simple. The experiences of compositors and plumbers are indeed aspects of the realities of modern industrial capitalism, but the skilling thesis obscures the differential nature of changes in skilled work and, in particular, the asymmetries of maintenance and production skills. Nor can it grasp the international flows in skilled work associated with the relative success or failure of capital goods industries in different countries. The compensatory theory of skill was undoubtedly closest to the realities of developments in skilled work in Britain since 1945. However, whilst there is a clear asymmetry in the trajectories of production and maintenance skills, it is also clear that there are wider variations within production work itself. In paper manufacture, production skills have increased in recent years, whilst those in mining have simply changed. In the engineering industry there is some evidence of reductions in levels of production skills associated with newer forms of machinery. This was perhaps strongest during the dominance of NC lathes as the new form of technology. However, as CNC machinery has increasingly superseded NC equipment, it appears likely that most production skills are in the process of enhancement, although by no means in every case. In printing there have been serious efforts to deskill the work of compositors and machinemen, yet the evidence from Britain's newest and technologically most advanced plant in Manchester reveals the general failure of this strategy.

5

Trends in Skilled Work in the United States of America

This chapter will focus upon contemporary developments in skilled work in America. Unlike the previous chapter, it is based less upon personal primary empirical research, and more on data distilled from a variety of secondary sources. This creates significant problems for analysis and interpretation since the USA is more akin to a continent than a country like Britain. There are very wide differences in economic, political and social structures between regions in the USA (see Issel, 1985: 39) which are probably more like the differences between Britain and other Western European countries than the differences within Britain. Furthermore, the secondary sources mainly used are reports produced by the US Federal Government rather than by American industrial sociology. The latter has more or less collapsed in the 1980s, and in particular there is little plant-based industrial sociology in contemporary America. This is partly due to a greater degree of wariness towards sociological inquiry by American industrial managers. This means that there is a certain discursive asymmetry within the argument in this chapter when compared with the previous one. With such caution in mind, it should be pointed out that the industries included for discussion in this chapter were selected with the view, firstly, of providing a comparison with the material in the previous chapter and, secondly, of providing evidence on the wide diversity of skilled work in modern societies.

1 The Coal Mining Industry

The US coal industry has been subject to considerable sociological research in the last decade.[1] However, most of this research has been either historical or about coal mining *communities*: there is little research from sociologists about the nature of modern mining work.[2] Nevertheless, there has been considerable mechanization in the US coal mining industry throughout the twentieth century. In 1925, some 588,000 miners produced 520 million tons of coal, almost entirely from underground seams. By 1981, output had increased to 774 million tons, but required only 208,000 miners to extract it.[3] Furthermore, 482 million tons were produced by 72,000 miners in the Western open-cut mines (62% of the total output produced by 35% of the mining workforce). This bifurcated structure of US coal mining requires that the effects of technical change be examined in both sectors separately.

1.1 Surface Mining

Surface mining[4] generally involves the removal of earth and rock from above the coal and the subsequent cutting and excavation of the coal from surface seams. After this, the rock and earth must be replaced nowadays to restore the physical environment. The main equipment involves earth-moving machinery, particularly bulldozers, draglines, excavators and power shovels. The labour process in surface mining is similar to road construction, although the firing of oblique seams of coal is similar to deep-mined techniques. The main developments in this sector involve the increasing size and capacity of the equipment and increasing efforts to improve its reliability.[5] Equipment monitors and the increased use of diagnostic tools have been introduced to this end. However, this has led to a growing proportion of maintenance craftsmen employed in this sector. I shall return to this issue in greater detail later. A major frustration in the analysis of this sector in the American coal industry is that, despite its rapidly increasing salience, little research has been carried out on the nature of the work involved in it. Yarrow (1979), in his discussion of the 'labour process in coal mining', devotes merely one paragraph to overground mining and other secondary literature adopts a similar line (see, for example, Marovelli and Karhnak, 1982). It is assumed that everyone knows what the division of labour in road construction might be and that attention should be focused on deep mining as it is both more esoteric and romantic. This is reinforced by the fact that the deep mining areas are the stronghold of unionization and militancy historically in American society (e.g. Bernstein, 1960). Such traditions attract social historians and contemporary analysts alike. We shall return to surface mining, therefore, after a consideration of deep mining.

1.2 Underground Mining

The first phase of mechanization underground involved the introduction of electrically powered hand-held machinery, notably drills and cutters. By 1945, 90% of coal mined in America was undercut by machine, but much of it was still hand-got by the classic room-and-pillar mining system (see Penn and Simpson, 1987, for details). However, since 1945 there has been considerable mechanization underground. This has involved several stages of mechanization of the conventional room-and-pillar method and also the belated advent of the longwall system.[6]

1.2a Room-and-pillar method (early mechanized stage), 1945–1960 A room-and-pillar method of mining is similar in lay-out to the chess board system in Britain during the hand-got era which preceded the advent of longwall mining. However, in America the room-and-pillar method has been extensively mechanized since 1945. The rooms are areas from where coal has been removed and the pillars comprise columns of coal left to support the roof. The columns are removed when the seam has been worked out, allowing the roof to fall in. Five machines are sent to each face in rotation. The first is the cutting machine which cuts a hole beneath the coal seam with a long cutter bar. It is controlled by an operator who has to decide how many cuts to make, depending upon the hardness of the coal and the nature of the materials above. He is assisted by a helper who moves cables and performs various ancillary tasks. Next a face-drilling machine operator drills a series of holes into the face, which are then packed with explosives by a shooter who detonates these charges to cause the coal to fall. Then a loading machine conveys the broken coal into a shuttle car which hauls the coal to a belt conveyor somewhere behind the face. The conveyor transports the coal to the main haulage line (either a line of rail cars or another conveyor) for removal from the mine. Finally, a roof bolting machine inserts steel bolts into the roof near the face in order to bind the overhead layers of shale into a strong laminate (see Marovelli and Karhnak, 1982). This is the most dangerous job in the sequence. As Yarrow relates: 'The operator must know what length bolt to use to reach through the cracks . . . A skilled operator can divine the roof conditions by the look and sound of the top and the amount of pressure needed to drill the holes. The safety of the whole crew depends upon his knowledge and care . . .' (1979:

177–8). Once this has been done, the sequence of activities is repeated. Nevertheless, there were wide regional differences in the extent to which this method of mining continued untransformed into the 1960s. In 1967, 46% of US underground coal was extracted using this method, but in Kentucky, 82% of the coal was obtained this way, whilst in Alabama, 98% was garnered by such conventional coal-cutting machinery. On the other hand, in Pennsylvania, only 19% of coal extraction involved such a system in 1967.[7]

1.2b Room-and-pillar (continuous mining machines) The continuous mining machine replaced the first three machines used in the previous method – the cutter, the driller and the loader. The machine fractures coal from the coal face and loads it on to a conveyor in one continuous process. The standard machine has a rotating drum with cutting edges that rip off the coal. The drum starts at the top of the seam and cuts downwards whilst arms beneath push the fractured coal on to a conveyor belt that moves the coal on to the haulage system behind the face. After the continuous mining machine has cut about 20 feet it is withdrawn and transferred to another face whilst the roof bolter secures the roof. Continuous mining machines were widely adopted in the 1960s and 1970s, so that by 1976, 74% of all coal mined underground in America was obtained using this method. Nevertheless, in that year there remained marked regional disparities between different fields – Pennsylvania and Illinois obtained over 90% of their coal using this system, whereas Kentucky gathered only 40% of its coal by continuous mining, and in Alabama it accounted for only 34%.[8] Indeed, in Alabama, almost half the coal mined underground in 1976 was got using the classic early twentieth-century mining methods described earlier.

The job of the continuous mining machine operator is highly skilled. When the cutting bits strike rock they generate a cascade of sparks that can easily ignite an explosion. Considerable care must be taken in the use of the machinery, and experience of underground conditions is a vital resource. The job of bolter remains unaffected by the introduction of continuous miners, and both the continuous mining machine operator and the bolter are responsible for the creation of safe passageways – in itself a task which requires considerable knowledge and skill. Both room-and-pillar methods remove pillars of coal in reverse sequence and allow the roof to collapse, which is also a highly skilled and dangerous operation performed by the continuous mining machine operator. The continuous mining machine operator is the linchpin of this type of mining system. He sets the pace, determines safety conditions and leads the facework crews.

1.2c Longwall mining Longwall mining uses a continuous mining machine that cuts coal from the face using a shearer. The cutting machine cuts coal from the face of a block perhaps 500 feet wide and up to a mile in length. It travels backwards and forwards across the face and the fractured coal falls on to a continuous conveyor below the face. The mine no longer uses the room-and-pillar system since the roof adjacent to the face is supported by hydraulic props that advance automatically as the face moves forward. The roof behind the supports is permitted to cave in. Longwall mining has not been adopted widely in the US. In 1981 only 6.2%[9] of underground production was obtained from longwall faces. The reasons for this are various.

Longwall shearers are, in Yarrow's words, 'costly and temperamental' (1979: 181), and require seams with less than five degree rolls along the face. Traditionally, they have been subject to considerable down-time as the result of machine malfunctions and this tends to halt all production. Given that most US mining companies have commercial contracts to supply a customer *regularly* with a given output, a break in supply can lead to the customer moving to another supplier, unlike the situation in Britain, where the state-owned National Coal Board (now renamed British Coal) monopolizes the domestic production of coal. The capital investment needed to develop a longwall face of 500 feet can cost between $5 million and $7 million (Marovelli and Karhnak, 1982: 98). To add a series of faces to ensure continuity of production would be even more expensive for mine owners. Finally, longwall mining requires standardized coal seams, whereas the continuous mining machinery can accommodate greater variations in conditions (Marovelli and Karhnak, 1982). Nevertheless, there has been a significant increase in the number of longwall faces in the USA during the 1980s. This is a function of the price of coal and the increasing reliability and sophistication of the longwall machinery in American mines, much of which now originates from Europe.[10]

This leads to an interesting contrast between the British and American deep-mined coal industries. Lord[11] has shown that the least mechanized longwall faces in Britain are more productive than the most mechanized and has suggested that the goal of the fully automated pit is probably a chimera. In Britain, massive investment in machinery by the state-owned Coal Board has increased output per man-year, but the overall return on capital invested by 1980 was zero. Fettweis[12] found likewise that mechanization can be counter-productive in mines since 'machines up to now have always proved less able to adapt to difficult or changing conditions than people working manually'.[13] In addition, the more sophisticated and complex the machinery, the more prone it is to break down in the rugged underground environment.

In the USA, on the other hand, there are thousands of privately owned coal companies. Many are quite small: 80% of US mines produce less than 100,000 tons per annum, although the mines producing over 500,000 tons per annum produce half of total national output, despite being only 5% of the total number of mines (Bureau of Labor Statistics, 1981: 1). The US coal industry is competitive in structure and receives little state assistance financially. In such a situation, massive technological change has not proved viable economically and mechanization has not developed as far in America as in Britain. Here we witness the paradox that attempts to use technical change to reduce the control of skilled faceworkers over their work in coal mining has been more marked in Britain – which has a state-owned coal industry – than in the USA, where market constraints are far greater. It is also interesting to note the persistence of a wide range of coal extractive technologies in the USA which contrasts with the increasing homogeneity of these technologies in Britain. Such conclusions strongly challenge the assumption of much contemporary neo-Marxist economic sociology which assumes that managerial control over workers, particularly skilled craftsmen, is necessarily *maximized* under conditions of capitalist ownership.

What, then, of developments in maintenance work in the American mining industry? Table 5.1 provides details of changes in selected occupations in both the underground and overground sectors. In surface mining the proportion of maintenance workers increased from 11.1% in 1967 to 14.6% in 1976, whilst underground they increased from 8.9% to 10.3% over the same period. However, there are marked variations between maintenance crafts in the two sectors. Electricians remained constant as a proportion of the surface labour force, but increased by 72% in absolute terms underground and by a full 1% as a proportion of all workers underground. On the other hand, mechanics and welders both increased fast as proportions of the surface workforce, whilst mechanics only increased slowly in relative terms in underground mines. Such variations are a function of the technologies in use where electricity, electric motors and (increasingly) electronics predominate underground, whereas large machines undertaking rugged work are the norm in open-cast, surface mining. These increases in maintenance workers are paralleled by swiftly rising groups of skilled production workers. Continuous mining machine operators and roof bolters both almost doubled as a proportion of underground workers, as did bulldozer operators overground.

Table 5.1 *Workers in selected occupations in coal mining in the USA, 1967 and 1976*

Occupation	1967	(%)	1976	(%)
All underground mines	72,644		94,411	
Continuous mining				
machine operators	2,807	(3.8)	5,851	(6.2)
Cutting machine operators	2,598	(3.6)	1,480	(1.6)
Drillers, machine	1,333	(1.8)	1,122	(1.2)
Electricians, maintenance	2,117	(2.9)	3,640	(3.9)
Mechanics, maintenance	4,360	(6.0)	6,014	(6.4)
Roof bolters	5,039	(6.9)	11,287	(12.0)
All surface mines	14,866		33,979	
Bulldozer operators	1,862	(12.5)	7,484	(22.0)
Drillers, machine	779	(5.2)	1,504	(4.4)
Electricians, maintenance	197	(1.3)	441	(1.3)
Mechanics, maintenance	703	(4.7)	2,320	(6.8)
Power shovel operators	2,439	(16.4)	3,377	(9.9)
Welders, maintenance	755	(5.1)	2,219	(6.5)

Source: 'Technology, Productivity, and Labor in the Bituminous Coal Industry, 1950–1979', US Department of Labor, Bureau of Labor Statistics, February 1981, *Bulletin 2072*

How do these findings compare with the situation in the British coal industry? Answers to this question are complicated by the fact that the US coal industry is more heterogeneous than that in Britain. Not only do we encounter significant surface extraction[14] in America, but also a wider range of deep-mined systems. Nevertheless, the picture is broadly similar for Britain and America. In both countries the nature of the work environment requires skilled faceworkers. Changing geological conditions and omnipresent danger have precluded the development of factory-style rationalization or subdivision of face-working tasks. Similarly, technological advances have increased the proportions of maintenance craft workers. This has gone further in Britain than in the USA, but in all cases they have increased significantly since 1960. Such findings are consistent with the compensatory theory of skill. In underground mining it was found that the numbers of electricians are rising faster than those of mechanics, but this was not the case in overground sites. However, the discovery that production skills were also generally expanding is more consistent with the skilling thesis. Little evidence of deskilling was encountered. Yarrow (1979) suggests that the longwall system may deskill faceworkers in the USA at some future date, yet Burns et al. (1983), Dennis et al. (1956) and Douglass and Krieger (1983) suggest that such an outcome has not occurred in Britain, which has had considerable experience of such systems since 1945. Indeed, these were the findings of recent British Coal reports on the social organization of American underground mining.[15] It is difficult to adopt Adam Smith-type, pin-factory specialization underground. Nor is supervisory surveillance of much use – at least as far as up to the present period is concerned. Faceworkers still retain their knowledge of the interface between machinery and geological conditions. Without this knowledge or their meticulous use of it, machinery would be damaged and the work environment would become extremely hazardous.

2 The Paper Industry

The US paper industry has been developing technologically throughout the post-war period. In the mid-1960s continuous digesters in pulp manufacture, improved materials handling systems such as highly mechanized paper roll transfer systems and an increasing use of instrumentation, were having the consequence that, according to a Bureau of Labor Statistics (BLS) report in 1966, 'more skilled workers will be needed' (p. 161). The report also showed that employment of skilled workers overall was increasing swiftly at the expense of helpers and labourers. The increasing complexity of paper-making equipment required greater numbers of skilled maintenance and repair craftsmen.

By 1975 a second BLS report showed that mechanization had become even more pervasive. Wood handling was now increasingly mechanized with conveyors reducing manual handling. Computer-controlled equipment was becoming more common, which was leading to operators having to do less manual manipulation of control devices and more monitoring of machine functions. The report states that 'At one large mill which introduced computer control of paper-making machine operations . . . the computer sets production variables such as temperature, pressure, and flow rates; before computer control they were set by the machine tender. The machine tender still performs some control and monitoring duties and is available in cases of emergency' (p. 8). Such information suggests that the machines are semi-automatic and that the machine tender is required to alter the controls based upon the interpretation of dials on computer consoles, as is the case in Britain.

These conclusions are supported by data collected by myself during a visit to the James River Paper Mill at Halsey, Oregon, in May 1985. This plant was part of the James River Corporation, a multi-site US paper-making company with establishments in places like Kalamazoo, Michigan; Green Bay, Wisconsin and Pennington, Alabama. The main products were tissues and toilet paper. In the paper-making section, dyes were introduced to colour the paper. A computer provided information on the degree of colour matching, but like the equipment at Cropper's in England, it provided no information to operatives on how to modify the colour mix. Computerization assisted operatives but they still had to interpret the information and use their skills and knowledge to amend the colour mix. The overall paper-making machine – a Beloit – was controlled by Measurex computer systems and there was a Measurex technician permanently on site to deal with both the hardware and software on the control system. Again, this pattern replicates the sub-contracting system of maintenance at Cooke's in England, detailed in the previous chapter. Operators in the digester room and on the main paper-making machines regarded the new computerized instrumentation as a bonus, providing more information about the processes that they were required to interpret and act upon. Interestingly, machine tenders were paid $21 per hour, whilst maintenance crafts received $17.50 per hour. This is in contrast to British paper mills where all skilled workers are paid at the same rate. I shall return to the significance of these differences in chapter 7.

There were 100 maintenance workers at the plant out of a total of 600 employees (of these 120 were staff). There were four maintenance crafts: electricians, pipefitters, instrument mechanics and millwrights. All these groups did welding which constituted a form of 'multi-skilling'. There was considerable tension between electricians and instrument mechanics over job demarcations associated with the new microelectronic technologies in various control systems. This was despite the fact that all these craft workers were members of the UPIU (United

Paperworkers International Union) (see Kleinsorge and Kerby, 1966). These occupational conflicts were exacerbated by the fact that electricians were licensed in the State of Oregon to perform electrical work, whereas the instrumenters were not so licensed. However, within the new control boxes it was not easy to decide precise points of cut-off between the two occupations. Management tried a formula that gave 'on–off' work to electricians and 'continuous' work to instrumenters, but this did not succeed in practice. Management then instituted a programme that aimed at flexible multi-skilling, whereby both occupations could do everything pertaining to micro-electronic maintenance; but this had not worked out either, since neither occupation was willing to jettison its exclusive claim to its basic sphere of work. Nor had the UPIU been able to devise a solution to this issue. It is of considerable interest that precisely these same issues of demarcation have occurred in recent years at Thames Board in Workington and at Australian Paper Mills in Botany Bay, Australia (see Penn and Scattergood, 1988). I shall return to these issues in chapter 7.

In broad terms the effects of technical change on skilled work in the American paper industry were similar to those in Britain. Skilled maintenance had increased, nonskilled work had been heavily reduced and production skills had been changed and, in the view of the participants, enhanced in both countries. Demarcation disputes between adjacent maintenance trades were of a broadly similar form, despite the fact that in Oregon all production and maintenance workers were in the same trade union. Such findings again shed doubt on the assumption held by many contemporary British advocates of union merger and 'multi-skilling', like Cross, that issues of inter-craft conflict can be dissolved by industrial unionism.

3 Iron-Ore Mining

Iron-ore mining is similar to surface coal mining in terms of the main operations of production. In 1987, I visited the Empire Mine in Palmer, Michigan, in order to examine the effects of technical change upon the division of labour there. In the pit large rotary drills were used to drill blast holes in the rock. These holes were filled with explosives and blasted to loosen the earth, and then excavators would drop the materials into enormous trucks. The rock was then crushed and the crude ore ground to a powder-fine consistency. Finally, the iron ore was processed at very high temperatures to produce small pellets which were destined for the steel mills of Gary and elsewhere on the lower Great Lakes.

The focus of my visit was upon the process plant where the pellets were fired. The machinery in use (grinders, crushers, sieves and kilns) all involved computer control systems. These computerized systems required over 80 electricians for maintenance. These men had either served a four-year journeyman apprenticeship or a six-year Master apprenticeship and wore distinctive coloured helmets to mark them off from both production workers and management. These electricians had been trained by the suppliers of the new equipment during the installation phase and were required to consult blueprints in each area of the plant. Nevertheless, despite the increasing complexity of their work, there were considerable periods during which they would be sitting around. This raises the possibility that modern machine maintenance work may be both skilled *and* tedious. This is a situation not foreseen by Braverman, whose romanticized historical image of the skilled craftsman is exclusively located in traditional production activities.

The control room operators were not regarded as skilled workers. This is because they did not require a long period of training to learn their job and they relied heavily on supervisors when difficulties arose. This was in sharp contrast to the maintenance electricians who enjoyed considerable autonomy and discretion in their activities. The control room operators progressed to their job via an internal promotion ladder, but unlike the situation in the paper industry they were not regarded as skilled. We may hypothesize, therefore, that internal career ladders lead to skilled work in conditions where operators are required to exercise considerable discretion in the monitoring of equipment and need to understand the complex interaction of multi-factored processes. In iron ore pellet processing, there are few variables involved and hence little need for wide-ranging operator expertise. In the paper industry, on the other hand, there can be up to 120 differing variables within the manufacturing process and consequently considerable experience and training is required.

From this evidence it is clear that the computerization of production had not led to the elimination of maintenance workers. Rather their levels of skill had been increasing, although their use at work was intermittent. There was little evidence of enskilling of control room operators since, unlike the situation in paper manufacture, there were few opportunities for complex judgements to be made within routine production activities. This latter finding suggests strongly that the relationship of computerization to production skills is a complicated matter in the modern era, and contemporary social science has only begun to scratch the surface of these phenomena.

4 Metalworking Machinery

The metalworking industry in the USA, like that in other advanced industrial societies, is highly complex. There were 371,500 workers employed in the US metalworking machinery industry in 1980 (Bureau of Labor Statistics, 1982). Despite the images of large engineering plants in much recent industrial sociological literature (cf. Braverman, 1974; Noble, 1977, 1984), most employment in the metalworking machinery industry is concentrated in small plants. Further, it is estimated that three-quarters of the industry's output is in batches of less than 50 items (Bureau of Labor Statistics, 1982). This size factor is of crucial importance for an understanding of the significance of contemporary changes in metalworking machine technology. Indeed, it is easy to form a distorted picture of the contemporary American metalworking industry from an analysis of large assembly plants. However, at the medium-sized ASC plant in Detroit which I visited in April 1987, there was extensive computerization in the design and draughting areas, but virtually none on the shop floor. Rather, there was a continued reliance on a range of traditional manual craft skills.[16]

There is, nevertheless, a range of technical changes under way in the American metal industry. The most sophisticated machinery is computer numerically controlled (CNC). This involves the transmission of information from a computer of some sort to control units on a machine. Slightly less sophisticated are numerically controlled (NC) machine tools where the tool is controlled by instructions generally received from a tape or a set of punched cards. In addition there are also what are termed 'intermediate technologies' such as digital readout (DRO) and manual-data-input controls (MDI) which are not as sophisticated as NC machines. Digital readout is a device which enables a machinist to position the tool more accurately, and it is held to decrease positioning times by up to 80%. Manual-data-input controls enable the machinist to change the machine's position automatically, whereas on DRO the operator must watch the display panel and make any necessary adjustments manually.

However, the relationship between these new types of control systems and the skills of machinists can vary significantly. In the case of NC machinery someone is required to produce the tapes, and also the operator must have sufficient knowledge of the processes under way so as to be able to override the tape. There are a variety of possible difficulties. Firstly, the tape may have internal flaws that require manual intervention. Secondly, the machine–tape interface may vary if a fault emerges; and finally, tapes may only be able to achieve certain tolerances and then manually controlled finishing is required. Similar problems are encountered with DRO and MDI control systems. These factors often mean that the new jobs associated with the new control systems often devolve on to skilled machinists. However, this is by no means universally the case. Under certain conditions, particularly where there is large-batch production, a programmer and a nonskilled operative may perform the new tasks. However, given the small-batch nature of much production in the metal industry, most of the new machines are manned by skilled machinists, who will over time acquire new skills. Of critical importance here would be systematic data on the relationship between traditional metalworking skills and the practical requirements of the newer kinds of control systems. Evidence from the British plants discussed in the previous chapter suggests that considerable knowledge and experience of metalworking processes *is* a general requirement of most contemporary machine operators.

What is clear, however, is that the development of CNC and NC machinery does generate a range of new skills. In the case of CNC machines, the incorporation of microprocessor technologies into control units does require maintenance workers with electronically based skills. NC and CNC machines both require programmers, and as Jones (1981), for example, has shown in the engineering industry in the South West of Britain, there is considerable variation in who, in practice, acquires these programming skills. Indeed, even in the high-volume General Electric aircraft engine plant in Lynn, Massachusetts, analysed by Noble (1984), it is clear that machinists on NC machines exercised sufficient leverage on the shop floor to force GE to concede to them a high degree of autonomous control over their work. Noble demonstrates clearly the power of these machinists when he concludes that the attempts by management to increase their control over machinists through the implementation of NC machinery attacked 'the very people upon whose knowledge and goodwill the optimum utilization, and the cost effectiveness, of NC ultimately depended' (1984: 269). In particular, 'unanticipated machine reliability problems' enabled the GE machinists to obtain a working system that preserved their discretionary control over their machinery. Whilst Noble himself locates these data within a quasi-Bravermanian framework, there seems no reason to force the data into such an explanatory mould. Rather, it suggests that the evidence from America on the effects of technical change upon the skills of machinists is entirely consistent with the data and interpretations outlined in the previous chapter on Britain.

5 The Printing Industry

The printing industry, and particularly the changing nature of the compositor's work as the result of technical changes, has received considerable attention in the US (McLaughlin, 1979; Rothbart, 1981; Wallace, 1985; Eisen, 1986). This is partly because the printer was long regarded as the exemplar of non-alienated labour. Blauner (1964) described the printer as 'almost the prototype of the non-alienated worker in modern industry', and Braverman (1974) extolled the craft pride of the typesetter. As American pundits became more interested in the quality of working life in the 1970s (*Work in America*, 1973), changes in the nature of the work of typesetters seemed to demonstrate the irrefutability of the pessimists' case. For if typesetting, the archetypical manual craft skill, was being deskilled and degraded, what possible grounds for anything other than dismay could there be? The subsequent work of Zimbalist (1979), Rogers and Friedman (1980) and Wallace and Kalleberg (1982) seemed to drive the nail well and truly home. However, as we have already seen, this narrow focus on typesetters has misled commentators and provided a distorted image of general trends in skilled work in the modern printing industry. In Britain, the print unions have looked at the experiences of American print workers and assumed that the de-unionization of much printing work has been the result of technical changes (SOGAT, 1985). Such a viewpoint has been sustained by extensive media coverage in Britain as well. A careful examination of these issues will reveal that technical change and de-unionization, whilst coetaneous, are not causally related.

The printing industry in the USA has seen pervasive and continuous technical change over the last 20 years. The computerization of typesetting with the use of video display terminals (VDTs) is perhaps the area most are aware of, but the presses themselves have also witnessed the application of micro-electronics. The introduction of electronic composition has led, after bitter industrial conflict, to the shifting of much of the typesetting away from the traditional composing room to reporters and the clerical workers who take advertisements over the telephone ('tele-ad girls'). This has had a dramatic effect on the numbers of compositors in the USA, as was revealed in chapter 3. For despite a series of prolonged strikes in New York and Washington in the 1970s, the main printing union, the International Typographical Union, has been declining in membership throughout the period. Its membership, according to its Vice-President, R. Wattinger, had fallen from 107,000 to 42,000 between 1964 and 1984.

However, the introduction of web-offset printing has, according to the BLS (1982: 1), 'increased the demand for lithographic craft workers and decreased employment in some letterpress-related occupations'. These printing machines themselves are becoming more complex with the introduction of computerized monitoring systems which has enhanced the skills of the machinemen. This has had the effect of increasing the need for electronically based maintenance. There is also an increasing demand for specialist maintenance workers who understand hydraulics. The market for printing presses in the USA is dominated by Goss, who are a subsidiary of Rockwell International – the defence electronics conglomerate – and, as we saw in Britain, their new presses are extremely complex with a wide array of new technologies incorporated within their operating systems. According to BLS projections for the year 1990 (made in 1982) non-printing craft workers (mainly maintenance workers) will increase from about a quarter of all craft workers in printing in 1978 to just under a third by that year. Within the ranks of the craft printing workers themselves, it is clear that typesetters (compositors) and stereotypers, who made the plates in the hot metal system, will decrease in significance whilst machinemen and photographic platemakers will increase.

Clearly, by placing the focus exclusively on typesetting in the contemporary printing industry, there is a strong tendency to ignore the complex profile of changing skills in that industry. The position of typesetters has clearly been broken in the US printing industry. The skills of the remaining compositors would appear to have been significantly reduced so that all they involve are keyboarding on a VDT and paste-up prior to photosetting. However, as was demonstrated in the previous chapter, such a formal description can be highly misleading. Without a clear analysis of the contemporary skills of compositors in the USA, the case for pervasive deskilling remains as yet unproven. Furthermore, the consistent failure to examine changing maintenance work or the changing skills of machinemen and lithographers produces a notably one-sided picture. On balance, the compensatory theory of skill rather than the deskilling thesis of Braverman appears more plausible in this instance. Consequently, falling levels of union density – not peculiar to printing in the USA – cannot be explained simply by the employers using technology to deskill and thereby eradicate unionization, but as the result of a complex interaction of factors. One key factor still to be explained is why the ITU and other unions in America have failed to recruit the new skilled occupations in American printing.

6 Tyres, Textiles, Clothing, Shoes, Meatpacking and Foundries

6.1 Tyres

American companies dominate the world tyre market. Goodyear holds about 22% of the world market and in 1985 it provided 32% of tyres on new vehicles in America.[17] US tyre manufacturers are increasing the capital equipment in their factories – the most significant of which remain centred on Akron, Ohio – for two sets of reasons.[18] Firstly, the advent of the radial tyre in America has meant that the product has become more complex to produce. Secondly, competition from low-wage Asian countries (notably South Korea, where wages are a tenth of US levels) has meant that American tyre manufacturers must compete on quality and flexibility of production runs rather than on low labour costs. Goodyear have invested heavily in new equipment which relies on the skilled knowledge of its operatives. Whilst Goodyear use highly automated equipment for tyre building and calendering (applying rubber to cords), the jobs of the operatives still require extensive knowledge of the tyre building process and allow considerable choice and discretion to the operatives.[19] Furthermore, as the BLS report in 1974 makes clear, 'skills are increasing in the use of advanced instrumentation involving electronics or hydraulics' and 'complex machinery requires more skilled maintenance'. The BLS report presents a picture of reductions in nonskilled work, the transformation of production skills and the enhancement of maintenance skills as the result of technical changes in the American tyre industry.

6.2 Textiles

The American textile industry has a complex structure. It contains three giant conglomerates – J.P. Stevens, Levi Strauss and Burlington – and a very large number of smaller firms not only in New England and the Carolinas but throughout the USA. However, despite a burgeoning interest in the American textile industry,[20] contemporary American sociologists have limited knowledge of changes in the division of labour within textiles. This is largely due to the absence of a systematic plant-based tradition of inquiry which is partly a function of the unwillingness of American employers to permit access to their manufacturing sites.[21] Technical change in the American textile industry (which employed 1 million workers in 1973) is reducing the need for nonskilled labour and changing the nature of skilled work.[22] Unlike tyre production, the US textile giants have not adopted a massive capitalization programme, but have substantially modified existing machinery. This involves the addition of electronic instrumentation to conventional machines. According to the BLS report on textiles in 1974, 'many traditional manual functions requiring dexterity and skill are being replaced by automatic detection and repair devices. Consequently, considerably more of the operator's time is now spent patrolling more machines, primarily to detect malfunctions, than was the case a decade earlier' (p. 7). American textile mills are witnessing the demise of much semi-skilled and labouring work, but an increase in the need for mechanics and fixers (BLS, 1974). Overall, the picture is one of changing production skills, increasingly sophisticated maintenance skills and a reduction in the need for nonskilled labour.

6.3 The Clothing Industry

The US clothing industry employs approximately 1.5 million workers of whom around 80% are female. It is a low-wage, low-technology, low-skill industry with little in the way of mechanization other than some sewing and cutting machinery. Most firms are small with low levels of capitalization and short, non-standard production runs for a fluid market. In 1970, three-quarters of the workforce comprised nonskilled machine operatives and only 7% were craft workers, many of whom were mechanics. At present there are a range of automatic devices that can be added to traditional sewing machines – such as automatic contour seamers, profile stitching machines and numerical control units – but these are few and far between. The 1977 Bureau of Labor Statistics report suggested that the use of these advanced technologies will decrease the levels of skill and training marginally for operatives and engender new training for the more complex mechanical and electronic maintenance skills involved. However, the overall picture for this industry is static with a continuing mass of nonskilled operatives and a small section of skilled maintenance workers.

6.4 Shoe Manufacture

Shoe manufacture represents a similar static picture technologically to the clothing industry. Small firms with simple forms of technology are the norm within the US shoe industry (BLS, 1977). Frequent style changes inhibit the introduction of more automated equipment, particularly given their high cost of installation. However, a number of the machine operations require high levels of skill for their successful completion. Cutting of the shoe uppers and linings remains a highly skilled job and although there are now laser cutting machines available, only a handful of the largest firms have installed such expensive machinery. Stitching of the uppers by sewing machine is the area of most employment and is being continually simplified by modifications to the machines. Overall, both the clothing and shoe industries in the USA have been deskilled since the late nineteenth century by the introduction of new machinery and the evidence suggests that they continue to be so. Such results provide support, therefore, for Braverman's image of modern working conditions.

6.5 Meatpacking

Meatpacking has traditionally been a labour intensive operation in the USA (see Brody, 1964; Sinclair, 1965). Meatpacking plants correspond to the traditional 'pin-factory', simple type of division of labour described so graphically by Adam Smith in *The Wealth of Nations*. In such plants meat carcasses are moved along conveyor belts and successive butchers use hooks, knives and cleavers to make specific cuts to the moving carcass. The variety of carcasses and the need for precise cuts has meant that there has been little mechanization of the process of cutting itself. There are power knives and saws in use and mechanical hide pullers have reduced the skill required for hide removal, but meatpacking remains a lowly mechanized industry in the USA. Since the carcass is processed on an assembly line, a low level of skill is all that is required of individual workers. Each operative on the assembly line only has to master a single cut. Given the low level of mechanization there are few maintenance craftsmen and nonskilled workers accounted for at least 71% of the workforce in 1978, which totalled 361,800 in 1980. A 1982 BLS projection of future employment trends indicated that the nature of the product and the relatively low wages paid to employees (of whom about one-third are female) suggests that there will be little additional technological change within the industry in the next decade. The overall picture is of a fragmented, subdivided, routinized workforce very much as Braverman described the general tendency of all work in American industry. Nevertheless, it is worth pointing out that there are a small number of highly skilled heavy-equipment mechanics in all meatpacking plants who are required for maintenance work, and who are also unlikely to disappear given the technical stasis in the industry.

6.6 Foundries

The foundry industry in the USA has traditionally been a high input operation. At present around 300,000 people are employed in this sector. Energy and raw material consumption have been high and considerable amounts of nonskilled manual labour (see Kornblum, 1974) have been necessary for their transformation into castings. Recently there has been considerable technological change in the foundry sector. These have included new material handling processes, new methods of moulding, coremaking and diecasting, greater use of electric furnaces and extensive use of instrumentation and computerization.

The widespread introduction of conveyor belts, forklift trucks, hoists and cranes have improved materials handling and led to a widespread elimination of routine labouring jobs. Average conveyor footage in use in foundries increased from around 700 per foundry in 1963 to about 1,100 in 1977 (BLS, 1982). New methods of moulding and coremaking have also eliminated much manual labour, particularly the hot and dirty process of shakeout associated with traditional green sand moulding, which has been replaced by a no-bake chemical resin process. The expansion in the use of instruments for testing and inspection has improved the quality of castings and also significantly reduced the numbers of workers required to repair castings, itself traditionally a nonskilled operation for the most part.

These changes have led to a massive elimination of nonskilled tasks within American foundries. Some skilled hand operations performed by moulders and coremakers have also been reduced, but these have been offset by the increased number of skilled maintenance mechanics and repairers required to service the new machinery. This extensive mechanization has produced an interesting structure of occupations between plants. The larger foundries – which tend to be the most mechanized – use less nonskilled labour proportionately than the smaller foundries (almost 80% of US foundries employed less than 100 workers in 1980). However, the smaller foundries use proportionately far more traditionally skilled foundry workers than the larger foundries, whereas the larger foundries employ far more skilled maintenance workers.

7 Conclusions

This chapter has revealed major similarities between the relationship of technical change and skilled work in contemporary Britain and America. The evidence from the coal, paper, metalworking and printing industries are remarkably similar, as is the general picture for maintenance work. It is clear that technological change, particularly the pervasive introduction of micro-electronics, is generating more skilled maintenance work. This is stronger in the areas of electrical and electronic maintenance, but pertains to hydraulic and mechanical maintenance as well. Production skills are also changing but in a wide variety of ways: this can be seen in table 5.2. Production skills in paper manufacturing are increasing, those in mining are changing and the effects of CNC machines upon the skills of machinists is generally to enhance them, albeit with significant counter-tendencies. It was also clear that there was a wide diversity of effects in the printing industry, both within and between the two countries. The evidence from the American tyre, textiles, clothing, shoe, meatpacking and foundry industries should suggest a note of caution. In the tyre and textile industries technical changes are increasing the skills of operatives, whereas in the clothing and shoe industries some traditional hand-based craft skills are being eliminated as the result of mechanization and automation. There is a wide range of industries in Britain and America and this variety is ever increasing. As industrial researchers we are far from having a full picture about the relationship of technical change and skilled work in the contemporary era, and there is a constant tendency within the literature on these issues to inflate one or two examples and hail them as *the* trend of occupational change in modern societies.

Nevertheless, the evidence produced in the last two chapters is not consistent overall with the deskilling thesis. Braverman's insistence that there is a unilinear trend towards the deskilling of modern manual work in the contemporary era has been shown to be implausible. There are some examples of deskilling but there are far more examples of enskilling and continuities in skills conjoined with significant technical changes. The skilling thesis is likewise too simple. It cannot capture the wide diversities and asymmetries within the patterns of occupational change. It is interesting to discover that the same industries in Britain and America are experiencing similar patterns of change. The commonality of the USA and Britain is more apparent than any version of American 'exceptionalism'. The compensatory theory of skill has been shown to have had a valuable heuristic role but it clearly requires modification. Whilst there is evidence of those asymmetries in the developments both of maintenance work in general and of electronic maintenance in particular outlined in chapter 2 (see table 2.1), the picture for skilled production activities is more varied than was allowed for in the original formulation. Skilled production activities are being transformed by technical change in a multiplicity of directions. Some, like those in paper manufacturing, are undoubtedly becoming more skilled, whilst others like composing in the USA and some plumbing and machining occupations are becoming less skilled. In other situations, notably coal mining, the skills of production workers are being changed rather than reduced or enhanced. These varieties of developments in skilled work are fundamental to any adequate understanding of the relationship between technical change and the division of labour in contemporary societies.

This first section of the book has demonstrated that skilled workers continue to be a significant element within the productive systems of modern industrial societies. They are neither disappearing nor expanding dramatically. This suggests that skilled workers are not becoming proletarianized as suggested by Marxist theories. Nor is there, as yet, much evidence to suggest that they are becoming 'embourgeoisified'. They remain skilled manual workers and there is no evidence from either the British or the American case studies to suggest any significant change in their overall status. This evidence on the continuity of skilled workers in modern productive systems is consistent with the imagery of

Table 5.2 Changes in the levels of skill of manual occupations within selected American industries since 1965

	Skilled production occupations	Nonskilled production occupations	Mechanical maintenance	Electrical/ electronic maintenance
Surface mining	?	?	Increasing	Increasing
Deep mining	Changing	Constant	Increasing	Increasing
Paper	Increasing	? (Reduction in numbers)	Increasing	Increasing
Metalworking	Mainly increasing	?	Increasing	Increasing
Printing	Some decreasing, some increasing	?	Increasing	Increasing
Tyres	Increasing	? (Reduction in numbers)	Increasing	Increasing
Textiles	Increasing	? (Reduction in numbers)	Increasing	Increasing
Clothing	Constant	Decreasing slightly	Increasing slightly	Increasing slightly
Shoes	Constant	Decreasing	Constant	Constant
Meatpacking	Constant	Constant	Constant	Constant
Foundries	Decreasing	? (Reduction in numbers)	Increasing	Increasing

Source: case studies reported in this chapter

Dahrendorf, Mackenzie and Form. It also suggests that managements in capitalist societies are required not simply to maximize their control over ever-deskilled labour but rather to coordinate the activities of various skilled groupings. This limits the drive towards deskilling and, most crucially, allows considerable scope for shop-floor leverage by skilled workers. Indeed, as Sabel (1984) has argued, the need for skilled workers in modern production provides a terrain where benefits can be obtained by *both* employers and, at least, skilled workers. Nevertheless, these issues will be re-examined after the next section of the book.

PART II

The Social Organization of Skilled Work in Britain and America

6

Socialization into Skilled Identities

The first section of this book dealt with the structure of skilled work in Britain and America. It involved an examination of various theories about the development of skilled work in relation to comparable data from the two countries. This second section is an attempt to develop the analysis in the direction of the social organization of skilled work. It will examine the processes of socialization into skilled identities, the relationship between skilled workers and trade unions and the issues of gender and ethnic segregation around the axis of skill within the manual working class in both countries. These issues are necessary for analysis in order to address the wider question of the position of skilled workers in the class structure outlined in the first chapter of this book.

This chapter concerns the processes of socialization whereby skilled workers acquire their identities in the sphere of work. It concerns a neglected aspect of skill as currently theorized: namely the norms, values, beliefs and cognitive orientations that skilled workers share and which are created and re-created through broad processes of socialization. Recently it has become commonplace to criticize the debate about skill and work in contemporary economic sociology for its failure to theorize or explain 'subjective' aspects of the labour process. This chapter will attempt to place such phenomena at the centre of the analytical stage.

1 The Social Determination of Skill Model

This model was developed by the author (Penn, 1985a) and is based upon extensive research into the historical situation of skilled manual workers in the British class structure. As a model it has strong links with other work in the field of industrial sociology – notably Turner (1962), Duhm and Muckenberger (1983) and various publications by Jones and his associates (1982, 1985, 1986). These writers strongly criticize the conventional debate about skill and work in modern capitalist societies for its tendency to conduct arguments from an *a priori*, deductivist stance. In particular, two of the leaders of the 'new' economic sociology – Braverman (1974) and Edwards (1979) – have been challenged for their overly deductive approach and their meagre and often arbitrary use of empirical examples. The social determination of skill model has moved the analysis of work on to a more empirical plane and involves the frequent use of systematic historical data with which to assess theoretical arguments and derived hypotheses.

The main elements of the 'social determination' model are three-fold. Firstly, it is argued that *skilled manual work has been a general feature of British industry historically*. Occupations have been organized around the identity of skill and a wide range of social practices focus on the generation and preservation of such identities. Rules and regulations about such issues as vertical and horizontal demarcation, dilution, manning agreements and norms about differentials have been but a graphic representation of a range of complex social processes that sustain skill in the workplace. The second element in this model involves the recognition that *occupations have been actively structured around skilled identities and this has been translated into the formal (trade union) and informal (work group) organization of such occupations within the sphere of work*. The final element of this approach involves the recognition that *machinery historically has required skilled workers* – generally for maintenance but often for their operation. To summarize, the social determination of skill approach emphasizes the importance of maintenance and productive skills historically, the role of organized labour in their preservation and the need for analysing the nature of skilled manual work today through systematic empirical inquiry rather than via deductive reasoning based upon an imputed 'logic' to capitalist development.

The social determination model is, therefore, closely linked with the compensatory theory of skill that was outlined in chapter 2. However, the social determination model involves an examination of skilled occupational identities and can be seen both as an extension of the compensatory theory and as a different perspective on skilled workers in the modern period. If occupational identities are central to this model and to the actions of skilled workers in the world, it becomes of major interest to discover how these identities are generated, what forms they take and how these processes differ between Britain and America.

2 Trajectories into Skilled Work

There are a variety of routes into skilled work in the modern era. The classic form of entry involves an apprenticeship. This institution predates modern industrial capitalism and has roots in medieval craft traditions. However, modern apprenticeships differ from pre-industrial apprenticeships in two ways. Firstly, they do not normally involve close physical or social proximity between apprentice and employer, and secondly, few apprentices expect to become 'Masters' after an interim period as a journeyman. An apprenticeship involves a lengthy period of training, with a combination of formal instruction, informal learning with time-served craftsmen and on-the-job practical experience. At the end of an apprenticeship, the apprentice becomes a qualified craftsman and is eligible for appropriate forms of craft work.

However, it is possible to enter such craft work without the possession of a completed apprenticeship. This can occur in various ways. A nonskilled worker may acquire craft skills by observation, by learning at home, by partial completion of an apprenticeship, by working on a small site in close proximity to skilled workers or by learning as he or she goes along. One obvious example where such entry into skilled work can occur is in the area of carpentry where a nonskilled worker can pass himself off as skilled as a result of knowledge and experience acquired in a variety of nonskilled employments. Another area is welding, where skills can be acquired in a small workshop involved in car repairing and subsequently transferred to, say, the metal construction industry.

The other major route into skilled work involves an extensive internal career ladder, whereby workers begin employment in nonskilled jobs and ascend towards skilled work by a lengthy period of learning in a variety of nonskilled jobs. Eventually, they will be promoted into the skilled occupations that lie at the summit of the occupational hierarchy. Such skilled work does not produce the same kind of credentials as an apprenticeship. A craftsman *can* normally produce evidence of his status if required, although this is rarely done in practice. A skilled worker who has ascended a lengthy internal career ladder does not have such a credential at his or her disposal and often will find that his skills are not transferable to another employer.

There are thus two kinds of skilled worker in modern Britain and America. One set have undergone apprenticeships and are generally referred to as craft workers, whereas the others constitute the rest of the skilled manual workforce. In most of the literature on social stratification and the labour process, skilled workers are normally seen through the narrower frame of craft work. One purpose of this chapter is to examine whether both sets of skilled workers – craft and non-craft – are socialized into similar kinds of occupational identities.

3 Occupational Socialization of Craft Workers in Britain

Craft workers can be defined as those who have completed apprenticeships. An apprentice will normally commence his/her apprenticeship at sixteen in modern Britain. Historically, apprentices began work earlier when the school-leaving age was lower, but in almost all situations, British apprentices are young and inexperienced when they enter paid employment. During their apprenticeships, these young workers will typically spend a great deal of time with older members of their occupation. These older workers are crucial to the transmission of skilled identities at work. This is because an apprenticeship typically involves close interaction between an older craftsman and a younger apprenticed learner. During this close relationship the craftsman, or a series of craftsmen, imparts knowledge about the technical requirements of the skilled occupation, such as tips on how to use oxy-acetylene torches for cutting metals or how to find a fault on a telephone wire. Many of these tips prove invaluable to the learner as they are based upon extensive experience and are not codified in training manuals. Often the craftsman will say with some relish, 'they don't teach you that in class, do they?'. The technical aspect of apprenticeships has received some earlier analyses by sociologists (see Lee, 1972, for Britain; and Riemer, 1977, for the USA) which have shown that apprentices acquire the behavioural aspects of craft work during their apprenticeship period. Electricians' apprentices, for instance, gradually come to know which is the best make of tools, what is an appropriate form of dress, and ultimately the semi-secret language of the craft (Riemer, 1977). However, it is worth adding that the acquisition of appropriate tools and dress predisposes older craft workers to take the apprentice 'seriously' and to be more willing to provide access to the 'tricks of the trade'. Conversely, failure to conform to the role expectations of the older craftsmen can seriously handicap an apprentice. Not only will he become an object of fun and perhaps ostracism, but vital knowledge will be withheld or, at best, only grudgingly provided. As will be shown later in this chapter, these facets of the craftsman/apprentice relationship have significant effects on the processes of recruitment into skilled jobs and upon patterns of anticipatory socialization prior to entry into the labour market. Nevertheless, it is important to realize that the vast bulk of the socialization into skilled trades during apprenticeships is not purely or even predominantly technical in its nature. Most socialization takes the form of instruction into the appropriate norms, values *and* ensuing appropriate actions of the trade. These identities can be analysed in terms of sets of norms and procedures held to be appropriate for dealing with three groupings found in the workplace: 'fellow workers', 'other workers' and management. This triangular orientation to craftsmanship is central to an understanding of the social significance of skilled work in modern societies.

3.1 'Fellow Workers'

The notion of 'fellow workers' is a moral construct, since in any extensive division of labour there is a wide range of potential fellow workers. In practice, the strongest identity transmitted through socialization in apprenticeships is an occupational one. Young adults are taught to conceive of themselves as pipefitters, electricians, welders and the like. As Hughes (1971) and Becker (1963, 1982) have shown, every occupation involves a 'bundle of tasks' and the acquisition of proficiency in these tasks is a central mechanism in the establishment of an occupational identity. Much time is also spent during apprenticeship training in the acquisition of norms of fellowship, solidarity and fraternity which surround the occupational group. Furthermore, a great deal of the training of apprentices by adult craft workers involves the transmission of knowledge of where the occupation begins and ends. For instance, pipefitters in Britain have traditionally never considered welding as part of their role, nor would maintenance fitters traditionally see the dismantling of an electric motor as part of theirs. These orientations are never self-evident but must be transmitted by older workers. The boundaries of specific skills are jealously guarded and fellow workers are seen almost always through the prism of occupational exclusions. *Fellow workers in Britain are essentially people in the same occupation* and such workers form the basis not only for informal groupings within plants but also within the trade union movement. Brotherhood and fellowship follow occupational lines and are often institutionalized in out-of-work activities like Friday-night drinking or shared lifts to work. This strong sense of fellowship or brotherhood has definite effects upon considerations of appropriate actions. Solidarity and support of fellow workers are the essence of skilled occupational actions. Commitment to the informal work group and the formal trade union structure is strong – indeed, according to Goldthorpe et al. (1968a), craftsmen in the three Luton plants investigated revealed a far greater predisposition to engage in such activities as attending union meetings than nonskilled workers. The fellowship of skilled workers is strongly ingrained during the formative apprenticeship period and provides the basis for the strong levels of industrial militancy which have been a traditional feature of skilled workers in Britain (see Penn, 1982 and 1985a).

3.2 'Other Workers'

'Other workers' can be distinguished into two analytically separable categories which correspond to the processes of horizontal and vertical demarcation.

3.2a Other craft workers Here we encounter a paradoxical relationship. Other craft workers are perceived by the skilled as more or less equivalent in skilled status but also as potential competitors for their own skilled jobs. All occupations have arbitrary limits and consequently there are considerable tensions between skilled occupations at the boundaries. For instance, electricians could potentially repair mechanical mechanisms that have broken in the control system on a machine. Perhaps the mechanical failure has caused an electrical short-circuit which initially required the attention of an electrician. However, electrician apprentices are taught by older workers never to attempt such repairs and to call a fitter instead. The reasons are straightforward. As all occupational boundaries are arbitrary, any attempt to encroach on the work of another skilled trade could lead to reciprocal reactions. Such a situation would lead to a war of all against all within the skilled trades. Just as the major oil companies have restricted competition historically (Sampson, 1975) to avoid a damaging internal war, so have the skilled trades. This is because such inter-craft competitiveness would most likely lead to a situation where all crafts had been weakened within the division of labour since both management and nonskilled workers might seek to expand their occupational roles into the areas of work conventionally regarded as skilled. Consequently, we encounter a dual relationship within the skilled trades – intense competitiveness over precise occupational boundaries mixed with broad comradeship around their shared craft identities. This dual relationship can be characterized as 'separate but equal'. Two expressions of this broad equality are, firstly, the general similarity in pay rates[1] for craft workers and, secondly, their strong tendency to act as distinct units within pay bargaining structures. In Britain this solidarity is cemented by their shared experience as apprentices. None the less, socialization into a skilled identity is weaker than socialization into an occupational identity since the former always contains the seeds of potential fragmentation.

3.2b Other workers who are not skilled   To understand the complexity of relations between skilled workers and those who do not fall into this category, it is necessary to understand the position of skilled workers within the broader hierarchy of the division of labour in advanced capitalist societies. Skilled workers stand above the nonskilled in terms of their typical market and work situations. This has been a longstanding feature of intra-class relations in Britain (see Penn, 1985a). The pay of skilled workers has traditionally been higher than that of the nonskilled by a relatively fixed proportion – a situation embodied in the notion of a skilled 'differential'. Skilled workers have a very strong commitment to the belief that they should receive higher pay than the nonskilled: a value system which is a compound of beliefs about their higher intrinsic skills and their period of deferred gratification whilst receiving low pay as apprentices. Skilled workers learn in their apprenticeships to beware of the nonskilled. The nonskilled are seen as beyond the pale of skilled work and a danger to the boundaries of skilled occupations themselves. This is particularly true on the interface of skilled and nonskilled work. If we again accept the assumption of Hughes (1971) and Becker (1982) that occupations are 'bundles of tasks' and that they are largely contingent as to their precise content, then the threat of the nonskilled becomes clear. For the nonskilled could acquire certain parts of the occupation by a process of accretion or 'chipping away' and that could well lead to the skilled core becoming vulnerable to other craft groups within the division of labour. In addition, this model reveals the greatest threat to any craft occupation: an alliance of the nonskilled and management to redistribute tasks and re-characterize the nature of conventional occupational boundaries. As we saw in chapter 4, this has been a longstanding fear of skilled print workers in the contemporary era. In consequence, a great deal of time is spent during apprenticeships on how to relate to nonskilled workers. They are considered inferior but potentially dangerous. Skilled unions have worked out a *modus vivendi* which involves the recognition of nonskilled unions and the utilization of the shared status as 'worker' to resist the alliance of the nonskilled and management. Indeed, it seems likely that the assistance provided by skilled unions to nonskilled unionization in Britain between 1890 and 1910 was partly inspired by such a strategy (see Penn, 1985a, chapter 6).

Here we encounter a third element of the socialization of skilled workers in Britain – their identity as manual workers or as members of the working class. However, just like the skilled identity, the working class identity has a dual aspect. It involves the recognition of a shared antagonism with management but a suppression of the divergent con-flictual occupational divisions within the manual workforce as a whole – many of which centre around skilled exclusions. This leads towards an important insight – apprentices are socialized into a multi-plicity of identities within the workplace by older craft workers in Britain. These identities – occupational, skilled and working class – create multiple resources for the interpretation of situations. It is the contention of this chapter that these identities can be ranked hier-archically, which means that occupational definitions of the situation are more powerful than skilled and, *pari passu*, skilled definitions of the situation are more powerful than working-class ones. One problem of the traditional sociology of economic life has been the conflation of these three forms of identity and awareness and a consequent failure to under-stand the tensions and ambiguities inherent within skilled occupational roles.

Similar orientations are seen in skilled workers' relations with techni-cians – the group who traditionally stand slightly above craftsmen in the division of labour in terms of relative pay and status. Technicians are seen as having greater formal knowledge, usually the result of higher levels of education. They are also seen as inhabiting the 'other side' of the manual/non-manual divide and in consequence they are seen as part of the 'staff': a notion which signifies close cooperation with manage-ment. Technicians are seen as even more dangerous than nonskilled workers; for if the nonskilled represent a threat to the peripheral boundaries of the craft, then technicians pose a danger to the core of the occupation. There is considerable emphasis placed in the socialization processes of craft apprentices on the external threat of technicians to skill. The processes whereby technicians are defined as white-collar, non-manual workers involves the simultaneous emphasis of the manualness of skilled craft work.

It would appear as if the tensions between technicians and craftsmen are increasing in contemporary British industry. Not only is there evident hostility between the two major technicians' trade unions – ASTMS and TASS[2] – and the two dominant craft-based skilled unions – the EETPU and the AEU – but there is also evidence of significant demarcation difficulties. For instance, at British Shipbuilders at Barrow-in-Furness, the EETPU and ASTMS came into headlong conflict over who should install and maintain new machinery which contained micro-electronic control systems at the yard. The technicians (ASTMS) claimed the work as theirs as a result of their formal knowledge in electronics, and the electricians (EETPU) asserted their claim based upon tradition and precedence. Indeed, the rationale for the EETPU's own extensive retraining programme[3] involves a recognition that without access to new forms of knowledge, the core of their skilled tasks will be acquired by groupings of technicians. At Barrow the skilled craftsmen successfully retained their maintenance functions in the new phase of micro-electronic controls, as did skilled maintenance workers in the paper industry at Cropper's and Thames Board (as we saw in chapter 4). However, as was shown in that same section, at Henry Cooke's maintenance was sub-contracted on to the vendor of the machinery (the Measurex Corporation) and they employed technicians not craftsmen for the purpose of maintenance. The outcome at Cooke's reveals the potential threat to skilled manual work by technicians in the present phase of automation.

The present conflicts in the newspaper industry also demonstrate the importance of these points. In the USA the function of skilled compositors has been largely eliminated as a result of automation of typesetting. Journalists and tele-ad girls now generally have direct entry to the computer keyboards that set the type. This is a classic example of a squeeze on a skilled craft from two directions: from above (by journalists) and from below (by nonskilled secretarial labour). In Britain, the compositors continue to resist this squeeze by a strategy of 'following the work'. This is embodied in the National Graphical Association's (1984) 'Strategy for the Printing Industry'. Essentially, the compositors' union is arguing that its work is moving into the area conventionally called sub-editing. 'Following the work' entails asserting the right for NGA members (i.e. compositors) to do these new computerized tasks.

However, this had led to a conflict with the National Union of Journalists, who claim sole organizing rights within the sub-editing sphere. In 1985 open warfare broke out between the two respective unions and newspapers in Wolverhampton and Portsmouth settled the precise form of the division of tasks on the new machinery in radically different ways.

3.3 Management

The general orientation of skilled craft workers to management can be characterized as wary but independent. Wariness can easily become hostility, and one of the central themes of occupational socialization for skilled workers entails learning the principle of never allowing management to tell you what to do. Here there is evident conflict within the relationship of craft workers and management. Management claim, as their prerogative, the right to dispose of labour as it sees fit. However, this is never recognized by skilled workers as legitimate, although routinely they will accept instructions provided they are presented in a satisfactory manner. The historic battles over the managerial prerogative are relived by skilled workers whilst working, during tea-breaks and in the pub, and constitute an essential element of their collective occupational identity and memory.

The latent hostility between skilled workers and management is typified by the former's attitudes towards management's 'uniform' – white collar and tie. This is seen as signifying an unproductive, 'parasitic' role. Skilled workers see the dirtiness and toughness of their own work as the central focus of 'real' work. Management is seen as unproductive and predatory. Particularly disliked are managers without any shop-floor experience as skilled workers: these are characterized as essentially ignorant of the realities of skilled work. In contemporary industry, many such managers are university or polytechnic graduates and this acts as an additional element in the mix of distrust.

As with all stereotyping processes, individual or collective exceptions can be made. However, the stereotype merely remains suspended and becomes a renewed collective resource whenever and wherever management breaks the normative expectations of skilled workers in a plant. A great deal of time is spent by older skilled workers with their apprentices socializing them into appropriate attitudes and behaviour towards management. For example, if a craftsman and apprentice are working together on a job and a manager, or quite often a set of managers and a foreman appear, the craftsman talks for both workers. The apprentice will learn from observation how to relate appropriately in these situations. One central strategy is to ignore managers initially. This is based upon the belief that they must be shown to be interrupting an important activity and that they must await their moment for attention. Doctors, bank managers, Heads of Department at Berkeley and many other occupations use this tactic as a part of their everyday routines. After the manager has gone, then the craftsman will comment about him to the apprentice and often relive and redescribe the encounter. When I was a pipefitter's mate on a Government construction site in the late 1960s, the appearance of the clerk-of-works set off this repertoire of behaviour. The craftsmen would not stop work immediately appeared not to notice his presence. After some time this was acknowledged, and after some more time, activities would stop to see what he wanted.

Control over time is a vital part of skilled activities. For instance, toolmakers – the elite of the skilled engineering occupations – have fought tooth and nail to prevent payment-by-results systems. Central to their beliefs is the view that a job should be well done and not be rushed. A job should take the time necessary for its completion and this timing should remain under the control of the craftsman and not a methods engineer from management. Indeed, at the moment of writing there is a major conflict at a nearby machine making firm between the management, who want to increase the speed of machine construction as a result of a full order book, and the craftsmen making the machine, who wish to maintain their traditional high standards of craftsmanship.

As an apprentice, one is continually told to 'take your time', 'take it easy', 'slow up', 'calm down'. This is not said in relation to any actual speed of working but rather as an aspect of a generalized orientation to skilled workers' control over time and timing in the workplace. One key part of socialization into skilled occupations is learning how to take informal breaks. Whenever an apprentice is sent for more supplies he is told to take his time – 'we'll see you at tea-break' is a common refrain. Whilst the apprentice is away getting bolts, welding rods or stilsons, for instance, the craftsman or craftsmen can legitimately down tools, have a smoke and read the paper. Similarly, skilled tradesmen rarely bother overly about having all their tools with them. Going to get a wrench or a drill presents another opportunity for a break. These phenomena have occurred in my experience even where skilled workers were being paid on a collective bonus whereby the sooner the job was finished, the greater was their final pay.

As can be seen, craft workers are socialized into occupational identities at work through the mechanism of apprenticeships. In Britain apprenticeships occur early in an individual's work experience, normally between the ages of 16 and 20. This socialization takes a strongly normative form and is cemented by the close interpersonal relations of craftsmen and apprentices. However, it is also the contention of this chapter that socialization occurs prior to entry into the apprenticeship system at around the age of 16. This is because skilled craft work is highly prized within the British manual working class, both for its relative pay and for its superior working conditions to either routine manual or non-manual work. Apprenticeships are often filled by word of mouth and routinely involve sponsorship of a 15-year-old boy by an existing skilled worker. These informal structures lead to the selection into apprenticeships of a certain kind of boy – one who has a close relative in skilled work: often a father or an uncle. This familial process of recruitment means that the apprentice will already know a considerable amount about the normative aspects of craft work. He will have heard discussions of 'fellow workers', various types of 'other workers', and, of course, the nature of industrial management at home and in the wider community. This means that he will slip into the belief patterns of existing skilled craftsmen at work with relative ease.

However, not all boys are considered suitable for sponsorship. 'Tearaways' or the kinds of boys described by Willis in *Learning to Labour* (1977) are not thought desirable recruits. A certain degree of seriousness and moral uprightness from a boy is required by a sponsor who already works in a firm. Willis's kinds of boys are unlikely even to seek apprenticeships since they want to maximize their immediate economic rewards upon entry into paid work. They are destined for the nonskilled labour markets described by Blackburn and Mann (1979). Apprentices require a commitment to deferred gratification and continued learning after the end of formal schooling. Such values are far more likely to be prevalent in the homes of skilled workers and help to explain the likelihood of the sons of craftsmen entering apprenticeships themselves. Thus there is an interaction between family, educational and work structures that serves to reproduce a significant differentiation within the British manual working class.

4 Occupational Socialization of Craft Workers in the USA

In many respects occupational socialization of craft workers takes a similar form in the USA. However, there are some important differences.

Firstly, apprenticeships may be entered into at a later age in the USA. In many factories, if an apprenticeship becomes vacant, it is possible for nonskilled workers to take on that apprenticeship as a result of their seniority. This was the pattern that I encountered in several plants in the USA in 1985. This is almost never the case in Britain since adult workers must be paid the full adult craft rate for such work, thereby making it uneconomic for employers to take them on as apprentices. Secondly, it is much more likely that workers in craft industries in Britain will have served apprenticeships than is the case in the USA. This is partly a function of the greater density of craft industries in Britain. It is not often possible in Britain to pick up elements of skilled craft work in a small plant, in a small town and then transfer to craft work in a large city. However, as Strauss (1965) has shown, this is a common pattern in the USA and reflects partly the much greater levels of geographical mobility there and partly the wide dispersion of industrial employment in America. The fact that craft workers may have had extensive prior experience of nonskilled work or have entered the trade without a formal apprenticeship could be thought to dilute the strong occupational identities of craft workers. Certainly this was my working hypothesis prior to investigating these phenomena empirically in the USA in 1985 and 1987. However, the interviews that I conducted in the San Francisco, Oregon, St Louis and Michigan areas all suggested a rather different conclusion.

'Joe', for example, had learned to be a compositor in a small town in California and joined the printers' union after 12 months. Upon moving to San Francisco, he worked as a compositor in a large newspaper plant with apprenticed craftsmen. He had little difficulty in becoming an accepted member of the occupational group. He had learned the 'moves' of the trade and he was assumed to have completed his apprenticeship. Similarly, 'Nancy' had entered into an electricians' apprenticeship in her mid-20s after having worked earlier in the same plant as an assembler. She complained bitterly about the attitudes of fellow craftsmen to her. She had acquired all the attributes of a craft worker detailed above: she disliked management and was scathing about the attitudes of most nonskilled workers. Her complaint was that she was not accepted as a craft worker by her fellow male workers. Such examples suggest that despite the greater permeability of skilled craft work in the USA, the sense of occupational identity seems as strong as it is in Britain with its more traditional system of craft entry. Such conclusions are consistent with the findings of Halle in his recent study of the American worker (1984).

However, the multiple identities of craft workers in the USA take a different form from those in Britain. Whilst American craft workers see themselves firstly as electricians or as compositors and secondly as skilled craft workers, they do not see themselves as straightforwardly part of a 'working class'. As 'Cindy' put it to me: 'Yeah. Sure I'm a skilled worker, but I'm also part of the middle class'. For 'Cindy' and many other craft workers whom I encountered in the USA, their image of their stratification system was one where they were above the nonskilled *and* part of a much wider collectivity – the middle class. In Britain, there is the same sense of superiority in relation to the nonskilled but a feeling that craft workers form part of the working class collectivity. Put in a nutshell, American craft workers see themselves near the bottom of the middle class, whereas those in Britain see themselves as the highest element of the working class. The reasons for this are complex and relate to the differing developments of the respective stratification systems (see Mackenzie, 1970, 1973; Form, 1976, 1985). This is an area where further research is merited to assess the processes at work. In particular, there is a need for a research strategy that integrates the analysis of the workplace with that of the wider social stratification system in contemporary America.

5 Occupational Socialization of Other Skilled Workers in Britain and the USA

The occupational socialization of non-craft skilled workers takes very similar forms in both Britain and America. The paper manufacturing and deep coal mining industries in the two countries are both good examples of these processes. In paper manufacturing, an individual enters production initially as a nonskilled worker. He or she will be directed and supervised to some degree by the machineman or equivalent skilled worker who will be the leader of the work crews, who will be receiving much higher pay, who will also dominate the trade union and will in all likelihood be treated with a degree of caution by the management. Entry into such skilled work is by a process of seniority and selection. The seniority aspect involves extensive acquisition of knowledge and experience which is rarely in any fully codified form. Movement up the career ladder is contingent upon proficiency in the previous job on that ladder and given the nature of the knowledge required for such competence, it is also based upon cooperation with more experienced skilled workers who control the transmission of occupational 'nous'. Failure to comply with the norms and values of these workers will mean that the worker will be deemed insufficiently proficient by these other workers and, in all probability, by the management as well. Seniority provisions in British and American paper plants are the norm but they are not universal and the exceptions are very much connected with forms of occupational deviance. Failure to comply with the norms of the skilled workers in these environments will normally lead to ostracism, an inability to acquire the necessary knowledge for entry into the skilled jobs at the apex of the job trajectory and, ultimately, to a dead-end, nonskilled job elsewhere in the plant. For instance, one machineman whom we interviewed in Britain entered his firm as a cutter boy at the age of 15 and then became a top wire assistant. Then he became a machine assistant, a dryerman and finally a machineman. He spent 14 years as a dryerman before he became a machineman. He was quite philosophical about inducting junior members of his crew into the 'mysteries' of the trade: 'I tend to try and teach my crew as much as I possibly can . . . If I can teach a bloke to do a certain thing I haven't to do it myself. I watch him do it. You know, wander behind him and watch him do it myself '. However, he openly admitted that he could withhold his knowledge from members of the crew. Indeed, within the plant this had happened when a machine assistant had been promoted at a young age contrary to the norms governing seniority provision. The other machinemen would not help him in his initial difficulties with the machinery and, interestingly, the foremen also regarded the promotion as illegitimate and refused to assist the man. Within a couple of months he was demoted since he lacked the experience to run the machine successfully.

The same structures pertain in the respective deep coal mining industries. Skilled work in British and American deep coal mines is, apart from the apprenticed machine maintenance crafts, concentrated at the coalface. Entry into face teams is a product of a lengthy period of training and experience away from the face in such jobs as haulage and transportation. In these jobs, younger coal miners seeking skilled work on the face with its concomitant high pay and status will be monitored by ex-faceworkers who have left the arduous conditions of coal cutting and development work. Ex-faceworkers remain skilled wherever they are working and they supervise and evaluate younger nonskilled men as to their suitability for facework. The central criterion for eligibility both in Britain and the USA is an unwillingness to take risks. In a hazardous environment this entails precise work, attention to detail and a care for the safety of others. It is one of the strange and interesting paradoxes of coal mining in both countries that such a tough and dangerous environment should produce men who have great concern about the welfare of their 'mates'.

Nevertheless, despite the fact that non-craft skilled workers like papermakers or coal miners have entered skilled work via a lengthy period of nonskilled work, there is little evidence that this radically modifies the skilled divide. There is perhaps less overt hostility between skilled and nonskilled in such industries since, as Chapman (1900) pointed out in his classic analysis of the skilled divide within the British cotton industry, the nonskilled are accommodated to their inferior position by the prospect of becoming skilled themselves (see Penn, 1985a, chapter 6). The power of these processes can be seen in the dominance of the coal and paper industries' trade unions in both countries by the skilled workers within these industries.

How, then, do craft workers relate to other non-apprenticed skilled workers? Here we encounter a fundamental division within the ranks of the skilled workforce. Skilled craftsmen regard themselves as more skilled than other skilled workers. This is partly because entry into craft work is restricted to apprentices (at least in theory), whilst many non-craft skilled production jobs are open to the nonskilled. Secondly, it is due to a belief by skilled craftsmen that their training renders them eligible for any pertinent job in whatever industry and with whatever firm. Such transferable skills are the basis for the feelings of superiority of craft workers over other skilled workers. However, such a belief, common to craft workers in Britain and America, is challenged by many skilled non-craft workers. This is particularly noticeable where the craft workers are concentrated in machine maintenance and the non-craft skilled workers engaged in direct production work. In such situations, the non-craft skilled workers have a strong belief that they are the more skilled and that maintenance workers are merely machine menders, whereas they themselves are the core skilled productive group. As will become apparent in the next chapter, these intra-skilled relationships have a significant impact on trade union activities in both America and Britain in the current era.

It is evident that both craft and non-craft skilled workers are socialized into their occupational identities by other skilled workers. Compliance with these norms and beliefs is a condition for successful acquisition of the knowledge and experience upon which skill is based. There are many similarities within these processes in Britain and in America – both for craft workers and for non-apprenticed skilled workers. In Britain there is evidence that these work-based processes are strongly linked to the wider stratification system and that there are processes of anticipatory socialization in this articulation. Parallel evidence for the USA is not available and it would be interesting to know the degree of commonality between the two countries in relation to these issues. These processes whereby skilled identities are produced are central to an understanding of the actions of skilled workers within the wider social structure. As has been shown, there are many similarities in the ways that specific occupational *and* more general skilled identities are produced. However, the salience of the skilled divide differs significantly in relation to the broader class structure. The skilled divide in Britain is one within the working class, whereas in the USA it is the divide between what many Americans refer to as the 'middle class' and the 'lower class.' This conclusion also warrants further research. It is clear from this chapter that the re-creation of skilled identities within the workplace is still central to the social organization of production in both Britain and America. Such identities are not an historic residue but are central to the stratification systems of both societies.

7

Skilled Workers in British and American Trade Unions

Skilled workers have long formed the core of the American and British trade union movements. The purpose of this chapter is to examine the contemporary articulation of skilled workers and trade unions in the two countries. It was shown in the previous chapter that there are, broadly, two kinds of skilled worker in both countries: craft workers and non-craft skilled workers. This chapter will examine the significance of this dichotomy for the current forms of trade union organization in America and Britain.

1 The Development of Trade Unionism in Britain and America

Skilled workers formed the core of organized labour in both the USA and Britain in 1900. In Britain, the earliest trade unions were concentrated amongst apprenticed workers like carpenters and engineers (see Webb and Webb, 1920; Pelling, 1963; Burgess, 1975). A similar pattern held for the USA where, as Commons et al. (1918), Perlman and Taft (1935) and Foner (1947) have shown, skilled workers dominated the early development of American organized labour. There were powerful reasons for such similarities. The development of American unionism was strongly affected by British patterns as the result of immigration from Britain. Furthermore, apprenticed skilled workers were in strong demand in both countries during the period of industrialization after 1850. The scarcity and transferability of their skills permitted the development of a similar structure of unionization. However, in the twentieth century there has been a significant divergence in the development of the unionization of skilled workers in the two countries, which has produced significantly different kinds of labour movements. In the USA there has been a bifurcation of the union movement between industrial unions and craft unions since the 1930s which is not paralleled in Britain.

Craft unionism refers to the organization of all members of a craft across all industrial sectors. A classic example is the Carpenters' Union in the USA which organizes all carpenters wherever they are employed. Industrial unionism involves the organization of all workers in an industry irrespective of their skill level. Industrial unionism is a method of organizing mass production industries like automobile production and tyre manufacture where there is a high proportion of routine nonskilled manual workers. In the USA, the American Federation of Labour (AFL) embodied the principle of craft unionism whereas the Congress of Industrial Organizations (CIO) has stood for industrial unionism. Despite the amalgamation of the two organizations in 1955 as the AFL-CIO, the two forms of union organization still exist and have quite different impacts on the skilled workers within their differing jurisdictions.

2 Skilled Workers and Industrial Unions

The central problem for skilled workers in industrial unions is that they generally constitute a minority of the membership. As Turner (1964) has shown, union leaders are constrained by the internal political structure of their organizations and they are required to pursue policies that gain the support of the majority of their rank-and-file. There are two areas of craft activities that have created longstanding conflicts within industrial unions in the USA. The first issue centres on wages. Skilled craftsmen expect substantial differentials in pay over the nonskilled. These are rewards for skill, status and the deferred gratification incurred during apprenticeship training at low wage rates. Secondly, skilled craftsmen wish to prevent access to the trade by nonskilled workers and to restrict the supply of recruits into their work. As is clear from the previous chapter, this is not simply a matter of monopoly wages. The entire position of skilled workers within the labour process is a function of restricting the numbers of skilled workers. An unrestricted supply of skilled workers would enhance the power of management and increase the possibilities of fundamental changes in the division of labour to the detriment of skilled workers (see Penn, 1985a). However, nonskilled workers resent differentials and also seek to move into the better jobs performed by skilled workers. Clearly, there is a strong potential for conflict between skilled and nonskilled workers within industrial unions.

This has been a persistent source of conflict within the largest industrial union in the USA – the United Auto Workers (UAW). This first surfaced significantly in the period after the Second World War. Skilled earnings differentials over the nonskilled fell from 1.72 to 1.44 between 1947 and 1950 (Weber, 1963) and the Society of Skilled Trades was formed to organize craft workers within the UAW in 1955. By 1967 this body had transmuted into the International Society of Skilled Trades (ISST) and it attempted to oust the UAW from organizing craft workers within automobile plants.[1] This failed when the NLRB (National Labor Review Board) ruled that it was not appropriate to form separate bargaining units for skilled and nonskilled workers in either the automobile or tyre industries. Nevertheless, the threat from the ISST and the conflict within the UAW over ratification of the 1973 Ford contract led to the emergence of a more autonomous skilled trades section. Nevertheless, it is still clear that there are tensions between craftsmen and the UAW leadership over issues of differentials and the apprenticeship system. In 1983, the UAW International Skilled Trades Conference on Collective Bargaining and New Technology reaffirmed its demand that 'historical wage relationships and differentials must be restored', that skilled work should not be contracted out and that skilled work should only be undertaken by time-served craft workers.[2] In the spring of 1987 the Skilled Trades Conference of the UAW reaffirmed these demands and there was considerable criticism of the advent of profit sharing and lump-sum payments which had combined (in the Conference's view) to reduce further the historic differential between skilled tradesmen and production workers. The Conference demanded the restoration of the fixed percentage annual improvement factor (AIF).[3]

Nevertheless, whilst there are many skilled workers in industrial unions in the USA, there are also many others in craft unions such as the Carpenters, Machinists, Plumbers, Sheetmetal Workers, Boilermakers and Bricklayers unions. These labour organizations have received little recent research in the USA,[4] yet they represent the continuation of traditional craft unionism into the modern era. Such craft unions concentrate on the interests of their skilled membership. These involve the preservation of skilled differentials, the exclusion of the nonskilled from skilled work and the strict control over the apprenticeship system. Craft unions in the USA generally operate the apprenticeship system in conjunction with management. A joint apprenticeship committee, usually comprising an equal proportion of union and employer representatives, sets rules concerning eligibility for entry, the ratio of apprentices to craftsmen and the overall duration of an apprenticeship. This contrasts with the practice of industrial unions like the UAW who do not get involved in the selection of apprentices and deal with the issues of the apprenticeship programme through collective bargaining with management. American craft unions are still strongly committed to the preservation of skilled earnings differentials and it would be very valuable if analyses of such unions in the contemporary period were forthcoming.

The pattern of craft unionism parallels the situation in the American International Association of Machinists. The IAM was the exception to the rule in the old AFL with its commitment to craft unionism in that it had pretensions to industrial unionism (see Haydu, 1983, 1984). However, as Perlman (1969) has shown, 'the IAM remains in outlook craftsman-oriented'. This is attributed by Perlman to two key factors. Firstly, all the international officers had served formal apprenticeships and thus embodied the craft ethos; and secondly, as late as 1952, over half (53.4%) of the union's membership were either skilled journeymen or craft apprentices. This still seems to be the case in the metalworking shops that I visited in Michigan in the spring of 1987. In a real sense the IAM can be seen as a craft–industrial hybrid. We shall return to this possibility later in this chapter.

There is a third type of union in America, which is the industrial union where skilled workers are very strongly placed within the internal union structure. The Paperworkers (UPIU), the Steelworkers, the Mineworkers and the Clothing and Textile Workers (ACTWU) are all examples of such unions. The reasons for the different position of skilled workers within these unions lies in the internal career ladders central to the acquisition of skill within these industries. These unions are dominated by skilled production workers who, as was shown in the previous chapters, have risen from the ranks of the nonskilled as the result of an internal promotional system. Skilled maintenance workers in these industries are often dissatisfied with their situation, but they constitute a very small proportion of the overall workforce. In the automobile industry, on the other hand, there are virtually no skilled production workers on the assembly line, and the bulk of the skilled workforce are engaged in machine construction, installation, repair and maintenance.

The classic example of this third type of American unionism is the United Steel Workers. There has been far less evidence of discontent by skilled workers in this union than in the UAW. This has been attributed by Stieber (1959a, 1959b) to the maintenance of skilled earnings differentials in the steel industry. As Weber (1963) has shown, declining skill differentials have been a prime factor in craft discontent in a wide range of American industries since 1940. The different pattern in steel is largely the result of the internal career ladders in that industry whereby there are 'opportunities for relatively rapid promotion to workers at the lower end of the wage structure' (Stieber, 1959a: 179). This has, according to Stieber, produced a different attitude to skilled differentials from that in the automobile industry since 'Employees in low classifications are less likely to object to percentage wage adjustments when they, themselves, can look forward to sharing in the larger increases given to higher skilled workers in the not-too-distant future' (p. 179). It is also significant that skilled workers comprise almost one-third of the production workforce in steel (*Monthly Labor Review*, March 1963), a proportion far higher than in the UAW, and it still appears that these skilled production workers dominate the Steelworkers' Union hierarchy. Nevertheless, there have been a series of attempts by smaller craft groupings to extract themselves from the United Steel Workers. In the period between 1950 and 1959, the Steelworkers' Union led the list of American unions affected by craft severance petitions. However, just as the UAW was saved from internal fissure by the NLRB, the Steelworkers' Union also benefited from the 'National Tube' decision of the NLRB in 1948, which ruled that craftsmen could not gain separate representation in an 'integrated industry'. Similar conflicts have been found elsewhere in the rubber (tyre) and the electrical industries. Indeed, as will be shown in the next chapter, the subordination of skilled workers within industrial unions has had a significant effect on the changing social composition of skilled workers since 1970.

Another example of the effect of skilled production workers dominating a union can be seen in the case of the Paperworkers Union at the James River Paper Mill at Halsey in Oregon in 1985. Here, as was shown in chapter 5, machinemen received considerably more pay than maintenance electricians or fitters. Machinemen received $21 per hour, whereas maintenance workers received $17.50 hourly. The latter objected to this differential but could do little about it since they were all members of the same Paperworkers' Union which was dominated by the skilled machinemen. These machinemen could rely on the support of nonskilled paperworkers for the preservation of this differential since the latter hoped to achieve it one day themselves. This is in stark contrast to the structure of skilled pay relativities in British paper mills, where all skilled workers are paid the same rate of pay. This is because all the skilled groups in British paper plants have effective separate representation by a union pertaining to their specific form of skill, as was shown in chapter 4.

In Britain, on the other hand, there are few examples of the pure type of industrial unionism. The National Union of Mineworkers (NUM) is perhaps the nearest and was unique in its exclusive organization of all underground coal mining manual workers in the period between 1945 and 1984. However, there were still separate unions for pit deputies (NACODS) and colliery managers (BACM). The normal state of affairs in most British factories is for nonskilled production workers to be in a large 'general' union and for maintenance workers to be in an array of craft unions, as was demonstrated in chapter 4. However, many mainte-nance craft workers would be members of the Engineering (AEU) or Electricians' (EETPU) Unions. Both of these unions are ostensibly industrial unions but they are in practice craft–industrial hybrids. The Engineering and Electricians' Unions, whilst both representing skilled and nonskilled workers, and latterly supervisory, managerial, technical and clerical grades, are effectively dominated by their large craft mem-berships. Indeed, it is interesting that the leaders of both these unions continue to emphasize the centrality of craftsmen within their respective unions in their attacks on their opponents within the wider trade union movement.[5] A main factor in this pattern is that it is craft workers who generally take on the role of shop steward and become officials within the union. It is often argued that this is because such workers are gener-ally more free to move around the plant in their jobs and thereby gener-ate a wide constituency of contacts. However, whilst this is to some degree correct, the major reason lies in the strong commitment of skilled workers in such industries to trade unionism, which is implanted during their apprenticeships. Such motivations interact with the historic origins of both the Electricians' and Engineering Unions in classic late nineteenth-century craft unionism to produce what amounts to craft–industrial hybrids within British industry.

In the USA only the International Association of Machinists can be similarly categorized. The IAM is in contrast to the general pattern of US industrial unions, where the skilled membership usually comprises little more than 10% of the overall membership. Both American and British craft–industrial hybrids still behave very much like the tradi-tional craft unions, emphasizing the sectional interests of their skilled members. This is most obvious in the area of pay determination. The AEU has supported the widening of pay differentials within the British engineering industry since 1976. Penn, Martin and Davies (1987) and Penn and Dawkins (1988) have shown that skilled differentials in engineering have now reverted to the traditional pattern that has dominated the industry since 1922 (see Penn, 1983c and 1985a). This is the result of a combination of national union pressure and local shop steward bargaining strategies which have sought to widen skilled relativities in pay. Aronowitz (1973) claimed that similar processes are at work in contemporary US trade unions, although his supporting empirical evidence is scanty.

Recently many of the traditional unions of craft workers in Britain have amalgamated with other unions to form new conglomerates. A conglomerate differs from a general union in that, whilst a general union covers workers from a range of industries, it is concentrated amongst nonskilled workers, whereas a conglomerate covers a wide range of positions in the division of labour. One example is the General, Municipal and Boilermakers' Union (GMBU) – traditionally a nonskilled union – which has recently merged with the craft Boilermakers' Union. The latter have their own section within the union and the officers of their own section must be time-served boilermakers. Likewise, the Technicians' Union (TASS) amalgamated in 1985 with the Sheetmetal Workers' and the Patternmakers, which were both craft unions. These became the craft section of the union and thereby increased tension with the AEU who regarded themselves as the appropriate union for craftsmen in the metal industries. Nevertheless, some separate craft unions remain in Britain, notably the compositors' union (NGA) and train drivers (ASLEF), although both have had discussions with other noncraft unions recently about mergers.

What this complex pattern suggests is that skilled workers still dominate many British trade unions, and where they do not, their interests are often met by apparently autonomous craft sections within wider conglomerate unions. Nevertheless, there are examples of conflicts within British trade unions between different kinds of skilled workers. The NUM (National Union of Mineworkers) presents a good illustration of such tensions. The NUM has traditionally been an industrial union which organized all manual workers underground – both skilled and nonskilled. The research conducted in 1986 in the Lancashire coalfield by Penn and Simpson (reported in chapter 4) revealed that there were three groups of skilled workers underground. These were coalface miners, development miners and mechanical and electrical maintenance craftsmen. The coalface team were engaged in coal cutting, whilst the development teams, which also comprised face-trained miners, were involved in the cutting of tunnels which are used to open new coalfaces in the retreat mining system now used in the Lancashire coalfield. These men have achieved their skilled position as a result of considerable experience elsewhere underground and various periods of formal training. These workers have traditionally dominated the NUM, the bulk of whose members are other coal miners. However, as was shown in chapter 4, the electrical and mechanical maintenance men in the coal mining industry have become increasingly critical of the NUM, both for its failure to secure extra payments for the new skills they had acquired to maintain new equipment, and for their overall levels of pay relative to skilled miners. It is interesting to note that many maintenance workers at the pits visited were members of the Union of Democratic Mineworkers, which had been formed as a breakaway from the NUM after the Great Coal Strike of 1984 and 1985. This new union has close links with one of the large traditional craft–industrial hybrids – the EETPU (Electricians' Union). Such developments clearly warrant further research.

3 Conclusions

It became evident in Part I of this book that skilled workers still remain an important section of the workforces in Britain and America. This chapter has shown that the articulation of skilled workers into contemporary trade unions in the two countries is complex. Both *within* and *between* the two societies, the patterns are heterogeneous. Nevertheless, it is possible to present certain general conclusions.

Firstly, the rate of unionization is greater in Britain than in the USA. In Britain, around half of the workforce has been unionized since 1970, whereas in the USA, unionization has fallen to less than 20%. The US figures mask the wide differences between regions of the USA, where unionization is greater in the traditional North-Eastern and mid-Western centres of manufacturing, but far lower in the Southern and South-Western 'right to work' states. Nevertheless, despite these relative differences, it is also clear that the split between craft and industrial unionism takes a stronger form in the USA. There is a range of effective industrial unions like the Automobile Workers, the Steelworkers and the Rubber Workers, and another set of craft-based unions such as the

Carpenters, the Plumbers and the Sheetmetal Workers. It would seem that despite the decreasing overall rate of unionization of the American labour force, craft unions are more viable in contemporary America than in present-day Britain. This is very much connected to the differential rates of expansion of skilled workers revealed in chapter 3. The rapid expansion of the skilled workforce since the Second World War in the USA has facilitated the continuation of craft unionism. The decline in many areas of skilled work in Britain since 1970 has forced many British craft unions to seek wider forms of organization through amalgamation in order to survive as effective representatives of skilled labour.

The development of craft–industrial hybrids has not emerged as powerfully in the USA as in Britain, nor has there been a similar growth of conglomerate unionism, where craft sections are but a part of a wider range of industrial and social groupings within the union. These are apparent exceptions. Nevertheless, the Teamsters Union and the Service Employees Union (SEIU), which nowadays take on some of the characteristics of a conglomerate union but lack sufficient coverage amongst higher social strata like managers, technicians or clerks to merit the title, must be regarded as more akin to general unions.

The position of skilled workers in US industrial unions depends upon the form of employment within the industries covered. In automobiles and tyres, where the vast bulk of the membership is nonskilled, skilled workers remain subordinated in their own minority sections. In paper, steel, textiles and mining, skilled production workers dominate the union and it is craft maintenance workers who are subordinated. In the craft-based unions like the Carpenters, Plumbers and Sheetmetal Workers, it is evident that skilled craftsmen still dominate the union. These varying patterns of domination have definite effects on the conditions of skilled workers and their position within the wider stratification system. Craft unions are much more committed to traditional skilled earnings differentials than industrial unions and far more concerned about the traditional supports of craft work – the apprenticeship system and the exclusive claim of apprenticed workers to certain kinds of work. These issues can be raised by skilled workers within industrial unions, but they must compete with the demands of nonskilled workers, many of whom challenge such economic bases of skilled superiority.

In Britain, the division between craft and industrial unions is less evident and is complicated by the existence of craft–industrial hybrids and conglomerate unions. In the former case, craft workers dominate larger unions which include a majority of nonskilled workers. This is the result of the domination of union office by apprenticed workers in such unions as the AEU and the EETPU. In addition, in most British plants, skilled workers are represented separately by these two unions. In the case of conglomerate unions, the position is unclear, since they have emerged in Britain significantly only since the late 1970s. However, one can hypothesize that the loose structure of such unions will facilitate the expression of skilled interests by the relevant skilled sections. Nevertheless, only further research into these and related issues will permit a clearer understanding of the processes and structures outlined in this chapter. It is clear, none the less, that the articulation of skilled workers into trade unions, whilst undoubtedly complex, is an important variable within both societies. We lack sufficient secondary literature from which to produce *definitive* statements but it is evident from this chapter that such patterns continue to exist and are central to the internal structuring of a wide range of trade unions in both Britain and America.

Nevertheless, there is little evidence to suggest the demise of skilled workers within the trade union movements in either America or Britain. The mode of their unionization is becoming ever more complex, but beneath the surface, they remain well organized and well positioned to defend their specific interests within the broader system of stratification.

8

The Social Composition of Skilled Workers

1 The Traditional Pattern of Skilled Work in the USA

Skilled workers in the USA have traditionally been white and male. In the nineteenth and early twentieth centuries the skilled trades were overwhelmingly male (see table 8.1). As Walkowitz (1981) has shown in his study of ironworkers in New York between 1855 and 1884, the skilled trades in iron manufacture were heavily occupied by Irish immigrants whilst the specialist crafts like patternmaking were filled mainly by native Americans. Rapid American industrialization in the last quarter of the nineteenth century coincided with massive immigration into the USA, and there was a powerful tendency to restrict skilled work to either native white Americans or to North and Western European immigrants (see table 8.2). There are various reasons for this discriminatory pattern. Skilled work was highly prized within the American working class, particularly that involving apprenticeships. Such jobs involved relatively high pay (see Gustman and Segal, 1974; Orton, 1976) and status (see NORC, 1947; Penn, 1975) and significant degrees of job autonomy (see Montgomery, 1976; Dawson, 1979). As Taft (1964) has shown, few white working-class families could afford the expense of higher education for their children and this led to a strong desire by skilled workers to restrict entry into the skilled trades to their sons or close male relatives. Such strategies of exclusion were reinforced by negative gender and ethnic cultural stereotyping. Non-whites and women in particular were seen as unsuitable for skilled work. The cultural mix surrounding apprenticeships outlined in chapter 6 tended to rule women and non-whites out of serious consideration. The close social and physical proximity of craft worker and apprentice predisposed craftsmen to seek boys for such learning periods. This was reinforced by stereotypes of non-whites as 'idle, shiftless and unreliable' and of women as only marginally committed to full-time paid employment and of being incapable of understanding the complexities of skilled work. This could all be labelled racism and sexism. However, such blanket terms disguise the form and content of discriminatory practices in the sphere of employment and thereby fail to suggest the most sensible *point d'appui* for its elimination. This can be seen when we examine in further detail the traditional practices of exclusion as they evolved in the USA in the first 60 years of the twentieth century.

Table 8.1 *Gender composition of five selected crafts (including apprentices) in the USA in 1890 and in 1930*

Occupation	1890		1930	
	Male	*Female*	*Male*	*Female*
Blacksmiths } Apprentices }	209,521	60	124,365 682	8 0
Boilermakers} Apprentices }	21,333	6	49,923 631	0 0
Electricians } Apprentices }	14,897	103	280,279 4,604	38 7
Machinists } Apprentices }	186,677	151	640,285 13,600	4 6
Compositors, linotypers and typesetters	N/A	N/A	173,363	10,269

Source: A.E. Edwards, *Population: Comparative Occupation Statistics for the United States, 1870–1940* (Washington DC, United States Department of Commerce, 1943), Tables 9 and 10

As we saw in chapter 6, there are essentially two forms of skilled manual work in modern America: apprenticed crafts and skilled work that stands at the apex of an internal career trajectory. It is important to grasp that different discriminatory practices have been associated with each of these broad types of skilled work. There are two kinds of apprenticeship programmes in American industry – those run by craft unions

Table 8.2 *Ethnic origins and gender in five selected crafts in the USA in 1910*

Occupation		Native white		Foreign-born white	Negro
		Native parents	Foreign/ mixed parents		
Blacksmiths, forgemen and hammermen	Male	117,629	45,766	66,676	9,834
	Female	8	9	11	3
Boilermakers	Male	19,189	13,638	11,443	475
	Female	–	–	–	–
Electricians and electrical engineers	Male	76,719	39,282	16,695	703
	Female	42	40	10	0
Machinists, millwrights and toolmakers	Male	212,361	137,946	134,232	3,322
	Female	41	38	13	1
Compositors, linotypers and lithographers	Male	57,574	37,579	17,249	2,304
	Female	8,688	4,465	740	151

Source: A.E. Edwards, *Population: Comparative Occupation Statistics for the United States, 1870–1940* (Washington DC, United States Department of Commerce, 1943), Tables 14 and 15

and those run by industrial unions. Almost half of all labour contracts (see Holley and Jennings, 1984) have detailed provisions concerning the regulation of apprenticeships, although in certain industries the proportions are far higher. For instance, in printing 85% of labour contracts have such provisions, whilst in primary metals (like steel) the proportion is 88%. Craft unions generally operate the apprenticeship system jointly with management. A joint apprenticeship committee usually comprises an equal proportion of union and employer representatives and sets rules concerning entry criteria, the ratio of apprentices to craftsmen and the overall length of the apprenticeship. This strong involvement of craft workers in the day-to-day operation of the apprenticeship system has facilitated considerable pressure from the skilled workforce as to the characteristics of apprentice intakes. Often boys have been 'spoken for' by their fathers and uncles. It is the policy of restricting apprenticeships to the sons or male relatives of existing workers that has maintained the maleness of such jobs and, given their ethnic homogeneity, prevented the entry of recruits from a wider range of ethnic backgrounds. These traditions have produced expectations amongst craftsmen as to what an apprentice would look like – young, male and white – and also influenced managerial images about the boundaries between 'male' and 'female' and 'white' and 'black' work. Such discriminatory expectations have been powerful traditionally in American industry. Even in those industries like automobiles and steel where the unions did not get involved in the selection of apprentices, there were strong factors disposing management to select young white males. A major factor was the willingness or otherwise of skilled workers to countenance women or non-whites as apprentices. As Taft notes, 'the members rather than the leaders, as was shown at the 1963 Convention of the Brotherhood of Firemen and Enginemen and in many others in the past, are the most guilty of discrimination and anxious to continue such a policy' (1964: 681).

However, as was shown in chapter 6, not all skilled manual occupations are entered via apprenticeships. In a range of industries – such as steel, paper, textiles and coal – entry into many forms of skilled work forms part of an internal career trajectory. Not all entrants to the bottom of the ladder will make it to the skilled apex; nevertheless, all skilled workers will have moved up the ladder from the bottom. It is here that we encounter the interaction of internal career trajectories with the seniority system. Seniority is a fundamental feature of American labour relations (see Holley and Jennings, 1984) and refers to the length of an employee's continuous service. It characterizes two sets of rights for employees – job rights and benefit rights. Job rights relate to constraints on management in relation to such areas as promotion, shift preference, overtime and job transfers. The most senior employee will be given preferential treatment – he or she will be laid off last, recalled first and get the first bite of the cherry in relation to transfers, shift choice and overtime. Benefit rights relate to the eligibility of employees to benefits such as holidays, sick leave and health insurance. Seniority provisions are endemic within American industry, with almost 90% of all labour contracts in manufacturing containing seniority rules. However, seniority, in practice, may be measured in a variety of ways. The broad distinctions concern length of service with an employer (usually called 'plant seniority'), length of time in a job classification and length of time on a job progression.

However, when we examine entry into skilled work, the use of seniority along a specified progression line (or internal career trajectory) will discriminate against workers who occupy lower status jobs that are not deemed part of the progression or trajectory. Such segmentation of the practices of seniority have traditionally preserved entry into skilled work in industries like steel (see Kornblum, 1974) or paper manufacturing to white males. Despite the accruing of significant seniority by non- whites and women in such plants in the areas of general nonskilled work, they were not able to use their seniority to enter the higher levels of skilled work since this presupposed seniority *within* the internal career trajectory. The absence of recruits into the jobs that constituted the beginning of the career ladder was affected by the interlocking matrix of managerial and skilled workforce expectations and demands described earlier. As has been shown, the acquisition of skill within these internal career trajectories is contingent, critically, upon the willingness of the skilled workers to teach junior, lesser skilled workers the 'tricks of the trade'. Traditionally, such skilled workers have strongly resisted the introduction of women and non-whites to this sphere of intimacy at work. Such attitudes and beliefs have been powerful discriminatory forces in traditional American industry.

2 The Changing Pattern of Skilled Work in the USA

There has been a long history of ethnic discrimination amongst US trade unions. In the 1870s and 1880s the Knights of Labor attempted to recruit black members and to overcome the previous traditions of ethnic exclusion. However, with the demise of the Knights of Labor, it was left to the American Federation of Labor to attempt to remove ethnic discrimination amongst its constituent unions. Samuel Gompers, leader of the AFL, found this easier said than done, particularly in the area of informal union practices and rites. For example, the International Association of Machinists dropped its formal prohibition of black members in 1895 in order to gain its AFL charter. Nevertheless, it continued to exclude blacks from its initiation ceremonies until 1948. The racial animosity of white union members was exacerbated by the occasional use of black strike-breakers. This reinforced the negative stereotypes that white trade unionists held of non-whites in American society.

Skilled craft jobs in America have thus traditionally been the preserve of white male workers. The data reported in table 8.1 showed that women represented a minuscule proportion of craft workers in 1890 and 1930. Only in the printing trades was there any significant number of females in 1930. The picture was similar for blacks. From table 8.2 it is evident that there were very few black craft workers in 1910, and table 8.3 shows that the picture had changed little by 1940. However, since 1940 there has been increasing awareness of these forms of economic discrimination, both for women and for blacks. Since the 1950s there has been a growing social movement to eliminate such discriminatory practices. The 1964 Civil Rights Act forbade racial or ethnic (and sexual) discrimination in employment; and in 1972 the Coalition of Black Trade Unionists was formed as an explicit effort to remove ethnic discrimination within the trade union movement itself. The Civil Rights Act was swiftly followed by President Johnson's Executive Order 11246 which required all contractors, servicers and producers engaged in work on federal contracts worth $10,000 or more per annum to give proof that they were equal opportunity employers. Failure to do so could lead to the cancellation of their projects and their future debarring from such federal projects.

In relation to the skilled trades – traditional bastions of exclusion – the main Government effort has been to improve the chances of non-whites and women of obtaining entry to such work. In 1969 there was the Philadelphia Plan which set up quotas for minorities in six building unions working on federally funded construction contracts in the Philadelphia area (see Filippelli, 1984). This was followed by a series of voluntary Hometown programmes whereby union trade councils and contractors' associations in over 70 areas in America agreed to affirmative action in the area of recruitment into skilled work. The criticisms of

Table 8.3 Percentages of males in selected occupational aggregates in the USA: 1940

		Whites		Blacks	
	Overall percentage male	Numbers	Percentage male	Numbers	Percentage male
Unskilled	73.9	6.2m	79.6	1.7m	58.5
Semiskilled	66.8	5.8m	67.1	344,228	62.4
Skilled	98.3	5.0m	98.3	128,762	98.6
Clerical	59.6	4.7m	59.3	75,738	77.8
Professional	54.3	1.7m	54.7	49,485	43.1

Source: A.E. Edwards, *Population: Comparative Occupational Statistics for the United States, 1870–1940* (Bureau of the Census, Washington, 1943), Table 28, p. 189

the lack of enforcement of affirmative action by Government agencies such as the Office of Contract Compliance Programs, and the lack of any enforcing authority in the Hometown programmes, have led to an increasing emphasis on efforts to change the patterns of recruitment into apprenticeships. The traditional pattern of nepotism has been severely weakened by the implementation of the 1972 Equal Employment Opportunity Act (Burstein, 1985). In particular, unions and employers are required to advertise vacancies for apprenticeship programmes and to base selection upon standardized tests. By 1975, 18.4% of apprentices in construction trades were non-white, which represents a significant improvement historically. Nevertheless, as Strauss (1973) has shown, blacks have tended to be concentrated in the 'mud trades' such as plastering, cementing and bricklaying, which were the trades in which there was a high proportion of blacks during the slave era. Blacks traditionally have found it far harder to enter the newer, higher status trades like electrician or sheetmetal worker. This asymmetry still remains a force in contemporary America, but there is some evidence that there is a convergence of ethnic proportions in skilled work (see table 8.4).

The central battle in many plants has been over the seniority system. As was shown earlier, this can have two significant effects on entry into skilled work. Firstly, seniority is a prerequisite for movement into skilled positions at the end of an internal career trajectory, and secondly, seniority can be used by nonskilled workers as a means of entering apprenticeship programmes. However, to be effective in the area of ethnic and gender discrimination, both require the existence of, at least, a plant-wide seniority system and the removal of traditional departmental seniority listings. A wide range of changes have been made by the courts in an attempt to improve the chances of blacks and women entering skilled work. Perhaps the most important was the decision of the US Supreme Court in 1977 in the case between Weber and the United Steelworkers of America. The Steelworkers had signed an agreement with Kaiser Aluminum to set up an apprenticeship programme for craft work wherein half of each intake would be reserved for female and/or minority workers. Weber, a white worker employed at Kaiser, who had more seniority and better qualifications than some of those selected for the programme, argued reverse discrimination. The Supreme Court ruled that collective bargaining could be used legitimately to correct prior discriminatory practices, provided that it was a temporary measure designed to achieve proportions of minority and female craft workers equivalent to those in the wider population (see Holley and Jennings, 1984).

Table 8.4 Percentages of blacks and Hispanics in selected skilled occupations in the USA, 1970–1980

Occupation	1970			1980		
	Blacks	Hispanics	Total	Blacks	Hispanics	Total
Carpenters	5.3	3.8	9.1	5.2	5.6	10.8
Electricians	3.0	2.7	5.7	5.0	3.9	8.9
Tool and die makers	1.6	1.9	3.5	3.3	2.9	6.2
Telephone line installers and repairers	3.7	2.2	5.9	6.1	3.9	10.0
Telephone installers and repairers	4.3	2.9	7.2	7.1	4.5	11.6
Typsetters and compositors	5.1	3.7	8.8	3.5	3.2	6.7
Sheetmetal workers	3.2	4.3	7.5	5.2	6.4	11.6
Mining operatives	4.6	6.5	11.1	–	–	–
Mining machine operators	–	–	–	4.5	5.8	10.3

Source: 1980 Census of Population, PC80-1-D1-A, 'Detailed Population Characteristics', *United States Summary*, US Department of Commerce Bureau of the Census, Table 287, March 1984; and 1970 Census of Population, United States Summary, Table 223

These political and legal processes have produced significant changes in the ethnic and gender composition of skilled workers in the USA, as can be seen from tables 8.5 and 8.6. It is interesting to note that the opening up of skilled work has not been the same for all occupations nor isomorphic as to gender and ethnic change. The proportion of women in the skilled occupations listed in table 8.5 has generally increased between 1970 and 1980. However, the rate of change was very slow in the case of carpenters, electricians and tool and die makers, whilst far faster in the areas of telephone engineering and mining. The skilled composing jobs in printing have become heavily feminized during this decade. In 1970 women were approximately one-sixth of this occupation, whereas by 1980 they were more than half. This change relates to the impact of new technology in this area of printing (see Rogers and Friedman, 1980) and the concerted efforts of US newspaper producers to de-unionize their plants (see SOGAT '82, 1985). However, the ethnic character of this work has become more exclusive over this period as white women have increasingly taken over from both white and non-white men. Such a pattern is not, however, general. In most of the skilled work presented in tables 8.5 and 8.6 the proportion of blacks and Hispanics has risen quite fast between 1970 and 1980. The rate of change is more uniform than for women, with traditional crafts like carpentry and electrics becoming less exclusive just as much as modern crafts such as telephone engineering have done. Overall, it is clear that gender segregation in skilled work is *more powerful* than ethnic segregation in modern America. This is probably because craft work is a quintessentially male world and that, as a consequence, there is more pressure from non-white males than women to enter this area of employment. Conversely, it would appear that employers find their workforces more receptive to minority males than women in this area of the division of labour.

3 The Pattern in Britain

Skilled workers in Britain have also traditionally consisted of white males. The craft unions of the later nineteenth century excluded women explicitly from membership (see Walby, 1986). The Amalgamated Society of Engineers did not permit women's membership of the union until 1943 and they strongly opposed the presence of women in craft areas of metalworking during the First World War (see Cole, 1923; Penn,

Table 8.5 *Males and females in selected occupations in the USA, 1970–1980*

Occupation	1970			1980		
	Males	*Females*	*% Female*	*Males*	*Females*	*% Female*
Carpenters	915,393	10,534	1.2	1,284,947	20,921	1.6
Electricians	475,887	10,208	2.1	612,614	13,199	2.2
Tool and die makers	199,485	2,848	1.4	190,386	3,504	1.8
Telephone line installers and repairers	53,670	1,860	3.5	59,363	3,243	5.5
Telephone installers and repairers	233,004	6,682	2.9	226,960	29,619	13.1
Typesetters and compositors	72,040	14,531	20.2	31,205	39,310	126.0
Sheetmetal workers	151,432	2,938	1.9	126,766	5,324	4.2
Mining machine operators	34,812	0	–	90,463	2,751	3.0

Source: 1980 Census of Population, PC80–1–D1–A, 'Detailed Population Characteristics', *United States Summary*, US Department of Commerce, Bureau of the Census, Table 276, March 1984; and 1970 Census of Population, United States Summary, Table 221

1985a). Skilled work was also ethnically homogeneous. In the context of the second half of the nineteenth century this mainly meant the exclusion of Irish and Jewish immigrants. Skilled work in the Glasgow and Belfast shipyards and in the Liverpool docks were reserved for white Protestant workers. These ethnic and religious divisions around the axis of skill were powerful factors in the internal stratification of the British working class at this time (see Penn, 1985a). In many areas of skilled work, the trade unions, or more precisely the trade unionists, had a powerful voice in the selection of apprentices. In the cotton industry, the loom overlookers (maintenance and supervisory workers in the weaving sheds) voted on the desirability of potential recruits for apprenticeships in a manner identical to the 'black-balling' used by exclusive patrician organizations like London clubs. In printing the compositors had the effective right of veto over applicants for apprenticeships, and there has been a longstanding tradition of 'speaking for' young lads by older skilled workers. These processes are by and large the same as those catalogued in the USA and the reasons are likewise very similar.

It is evident from table 8.6 that the skilled trades in Britain were overwhelmingly male in 1951. It is also interesting to note that there has been little change in the proportion of females in such skilled trades since then. Indeed, there has been a decrease in the proportion of female sheetmetal workers and precision instrument-makers and repairers. The decline in apprenticeship programmes since 1970, which accelerated dramatically after 1980, has meant that there are few opportunities

Table 8.6 *Percentage of women in selected crafts in Britain, 1951–1981*

Occupation	1951	1961	1971	1981
Carpenters, joiners	0.3	0.4	0.3	1.0
Painters, decorators	0.2	4.0	2.1	0.6
Sheetmetal workers	4.3	2.0	1.0	1.4
Toolmakers	0.5	0.1	0.6	1.3
Welders	6.1	6.4	5.7	6.7
Electricians	0.1	2.2	4.8	1.6
Compositors	1.3	0.9	2.7	4.6
Motor mechanics	0.2	—	0.3	0.9
Precision instrument-makers and repairers	11.1	10.7	17.5	4.3

Source: Censuses of Population (see chapter 3)

for youngsters to enter any skilled work in contemporary Britain and those who do continue to be overwhelmingly male. In 1980, only 0.3% of engineering craft apprentices in Britain were female (EITB, 1981). As Cockburn (1983b: 16) concludes in her analysis of these data, 'when we look at the trends [in the gender segregation of engineering employment] we find little movement'. This is despite legislation in Britain passed during the 1970s outlawing sexual discrimination at work.

Despite the efforts of the Engineering Industry Training Board, various local councils and employers themselves, there is little change in the pattern of male exclusivity in skilled work. Why should this be so? Recent research in Rochdale undertaken as part of the Economic and Social Research Council's Social Change and Economic Life Initiative has shown that despite efforts by employers to recruit female apprentices, they receive very few applicants. This is perhaps surprising since 7% of engineering and technology undergraduates in Britain by 1981 were female (see Cockburn, 1983b; 17). It appears that young women of 15 or 16 years of age perceive apprenticeships and skilled manual work as 'dirty', 'greasy', 'unglamorous' and generally undesirable. On the other hand, nursing, which is also a dirty job at times, is seen as glamorous and desirable work. The contrast is seen as between the crisp white overalls of nurses and the oil-stained overalls of motor mechanics, fitters and turners. The 1975 Sex Discrimination Act has made discrimination illegal, but it cannot generate female applicants given the lack of any affirmative action programmes in Britain. Furthermore, the restriction of entry into apprenticeships to 16-year-olds as a result of the union-regulated payment system in Britain means that women with industrial experience in nonskilled work cannot enter skilled crafts in their 20s or 30s as they can in the USA, and consequently any affirmative action programme must be relevant to the transition from school to paid employment.

Nevertheless, if the picture concerning women's participation in skilled work is poor, it is undoubtedly worse in the case of ethnic minorities. Britain has experienced a long tradition of ethnic exclusion in the skilled trades. In the nineteenth century this was centred upon the exclusion of Irish and Jewish immigrants. However, since 1945 the central axis of exclusion has been between whites and non-whites. The latter comprise people whose origins are generally either West Indian or from India and Pakistan. Britain does not collect census data on the ethnicity of the population and we lack systematic data on ethnic exclusion. However, the work of Lee and Wrench (1981a, 1981b) on recruitment into skilled work in the city of Birmingham has shown that there are a variety of practices which are discriminatory in their effects. Many firms prefer to recruit locally which has the effect of excluding non-whites, who are concentrated residentially in the decaying inner areas of the city, from obtaining apprenticeships in the predominantly white suburbs. Lee and Wrench also emphasize the significance of family connections:

> Some firms have a clear policy of recruiting disproportionately from the kin of existing employees. More common is the statement 'if two lads apply and they are absolutely equal we will take the employee's son' ... The problem is that craft areas are predominantly white, and thus will remain so as long as the relatives of white craft employees get preference (1981a: 517).

These practices, which have come to be labelled the 'lads of dads syndrome', have been exacerbated by the effects of mass unemployment in Birmingham – long the heartland of the West Midlands metals and engineering industrial complex. Fewer firms nowadays advertise apprenticeship vacancies – rather they rely on informal networks based upon their existing skilled workforces. The craft unions support these practices. One shop steward in Birmingham stated that 'as trade unionists we insist that the employees' families get preferential treatment. We say academic criteria are not the main thing' (Lee and Wrench, 1981b: 8).

Indeed, there is powerful evidence that in many firms, craft work is restricted deliberately to white workers as the result of pressure from the existing craft workforces. An infamous example of this occurred at the Castle Bromwich plant of BL Cars Ltd in Birmingham. It was alleged that in 1977 two shop stewards (both representing members of the Amalgamated Union of Engineering Workers) successfully forced a supervisor to reject a black recruit into the toolroom. Eventually this was admitted, as was the existence of a resolution passed by toolfitters not to accept non-white recruits. The firm argued before an Industrial Tribunal that they were not guilty of discrimination – rather their workforce was! In the words of the Company Solicitor, 'the reason for not appointing him was not because he was black but because others would not work with him because he was black' (CRE, no date). This specious argument was rejected by the Commission for Racial Equality since on such reasoning an employer could decide not to appoint a black foreman because his employees would refuse to obey him; or a housing authority could decide not to allocate an apartment to a non-white family because the neighbours would object. It is extremely likely that these patterns still pertain in Britain in the 1980s given the general reduction of opportunities for entry into skilled work.

4 Conclusions

It is clear that the traditional social composition of skilled work still pertains in both Britain and America. Most skilled workers remain white and male. However, such a pattern has begun to change in the USA, whereas there is little change in contemporary Britain. Why should this be so? The proximate answer is that there has been far more effort made in the USA, by Government, employers and unions, to rectify the longstanding structures of discrimination. This has been particularly so in those industrial unions like the UAW where skilled workers have constituted a relatively small minority of the overall union membership. Affirmative action programmes have effected the social composition of skilled work in the USA. The changes should not be overestimated and are uneven in their extent, but there has been a profound transformation in skilled work in America since the mid-1960s. Legislation on discrimination in Britain has been weak and its enforcement half-hearted at best. This is because there are no equivalent movements in Britain to those of women, blacks and Hispanics in the USA. This is partly due to the hegemony of the labour movement in British society (see Lash and Urry, 1987). In America, the labour movement determines the political agenda for reform far less than in Britain. In its absence, the women's and ethnic movements have had more salience. Such factors interact with the longstanding differing political traditions in America and Britain. American governments were far more likely to intervene in economic relationships in the USA, at least prior to the advent of President Reagan, than British governments who have shown a marked reluctance to act decisively in these areas of discrimination. In Britain, until very recently, it was the tradition to permit employers and employees to forge their own accommodations unfiltered by extensive interventionist legislation. The absence of a strong commitment by the labour movement in Britain to affirmative action on gender and ethnic discrimination, when coupled with a lack of systematic pressure from other types of social movements, has left the social composition of skilled work very much as it was at the beginning of this century. It is also clear that ethnic and gender segregation and exclusion are contingent features of modern capitalist societies. It is of major significance that these features of the traditional occupational structure have been weakened in what is arguably the purist example of contemporary capitalism. This is not to suggest, of course, that they have been eradicated in the USA. Landry (1988), amongst many, has shown that there remain marked ethnic differences in employment in contemporary America, and a recent report on 'Women at Work' (1983) from the US Bureau of Labor Statistics confirms that this is also true for gender relations in the labour market. None the less, it is clear that modern capitalism acts as a corrosive to these patterns of discrimination. This chapter demonstrates that ethnic and gender issues are neither universal, immutable nor inevitable in advanced societies. Their transformation remains a continuing political challenge.

9

Conclusions

1 Skilled Work and Skilled Workers in Modern Industry

The first section of this book demonstrated that skilled workers remain a central grouping within the division of labour in both America and Britain. There is no evidence to support the thesis that there has been any significant numerical decline of skilled workers. Indeed, in the USA the proportion of skilled craft workers rose from 11.1% in 1940 to 13.0% by 1980. Some skilled occupations have declined but this has been compensated for by the rise of new skilled occupations; for example, the decline of composing skills in printing and machining skills in metal-working have been compensated for by the rise of welding, sheetmetal working, car repairing and machine maintenance skills. There is a clear difference in the buoyancy of skills between America and Britain, which is linked to the relative dynamism of the two countries' economic systems. In particular, skilled work associated with machinery manufacture has been more strongly based in the USA than in Britain. However, this relative advantage for the USA may be disappearing.

Both Britain and the USA have fallen behind Japan and West Germany in the shipment of machine tools since the early 1970s. In Britain, imports of machines from Japan, Germany, Switzerland, Scandinavia and elsewhere accounted for almost 60% of domestic consumption by 1985. The Japanese, whose industry is five times as large as Britain's, have now directly entered Britain's home market with the arrival of Yamazaki, one of the world's largest machinery makers, in Worcester. The American machine-tool industry, which as late as 1981 had greater shipments than Japan, was half the size of Japan's by 1985. In the USA, machine-tool imports rose from 16% in 1976 to over 40% by 1985. West German imports quintupled from $51.6 million in 1973 to $248.9 million by 1985, whilst Japanese imports rose from $22 million in 1973 to $854.1 million in 1985. Over half the American companies producing machine tools in 1981 had disappeared by 1986, which prompted President Reagan in May 1986 to attempt to obtain a voluntary restraint agreement covering selected machine-tool imports from Japan, West Germany, Taiwan and Switzerland – the four largest exporters of machine tools to the USA.

The production of machinery remains a skill-intensive operation, as was seen in the analysis of Goss – the printing press manufacturer – in chapter 4, with extensive demands for highly trained craft workers. Consequently, the relative shift of machine construction to Japan and West Germany, which itself parallels their overall relative economic success, is producing a significant transformation in the balance of national skill structures.

These shifts are paralleled by the increasing internationalization of production itself. In 1986, there were over 500 plants in the USA wherein the Japanese held a majority of the shares. The well publicized deals between General Motors and Toyota, Chrysler and Mitsubishi, and Ford and Mazda are but the tip of a massive industrial iceberg. Reich and Mankin (1986) have shown how these Japanese-dominated joint ventures are exacerbating the transformation in the net balance of skills discussed above. They demonstrate that Japanese investment in American factories gives the US workforce jobs in assembly but not in design and research. The core skilled jobs within the international productive system remain in Japan despite legislative efforts to ensure high local content to the commodities being assembled. Reich and Mankin also argue that this is a vicious circle, since the absence of core jobs in America will inevitably mean that the next generation of product changes will be researched, designed and tested in Japan. In some respects this is ironic, since US multinationals have traditionally dominated the processes of internationalization since 1945. However, US investment in Britain – which stood at $32.1 billion by 1984 – has not hitherto generally restricted research and development to the USA. Certainly, firms like IBM, Ford, Heinz and Kellogg have substantial research and development facilities in Britain. Nevertheless, there *is* some tendency for skilled work to remain in the USA rather than come to Britain, but this is not as pronounced as the example of Japanese investment in the USA or, in all likelihood, Japanese investment in Britain. The international balance of skilled work is changing on terms increasingly unfavourable to both Britain and the USA, and the analyses of skilled work within Britain and within the USA earlier in this book must be seen in this light.

Such conclusions demonstrate that the relations between capitalism, technology and skilled work are global. In the main, social science as yet has not really begun to unpack this idea in terms of its implications for empirical research. Nevertheless, it should be clear from the analysis of the numbers of skilled workers and the investigation of the job content of their skilled work that the compensatory theory of skill best approximates the complex social processes involved in these developments. However, whilst there is little support for a general skilling thesis and even less for a Bravermanian vision of endemic deskilling, the compensatory theory does require some modification. There is indeed a difference *on average* between maintenance and production skills, but there is a complex pattern of heterogeneity amongst production skills that requires a modification of the initial theory. The central difference is between technical change that involves machinery which takes over the generality of skills and that which modifies and even enhances the utilization of such skills. Clearly, there can be cases where delineation of the precise balance between these developments can be difficult to assess. Further research is required in this area, but it is clear from the research reported in this book that there is a range of examples where computerization of production has not been associated with the elimination of skills, but rather with their modification. Indeed, in the paper industry, there were clear indications of skill enhancement. On the other hand, there is virtually no empirical evidence to support the view that maintenance work or maintenance skills are being eliminated by modern technological developments.

2 Skilled Workers and Politics

It is clear that skilled workers remain a distinct grouping within the systems of production in America and Britain. In both countries, their unions have been strongly involved in the development of a wider Labour Movement. In Britain there is a powerful organic link between the Labour Party and the trade union movement, and in the USA the AFL-CIO has strongly supported the Democrats for most of the post-war period. However, despite these institutional links in America and Britain between organized labour and one major political party in a predominantly two-party political system, there is powerful evidence to suggest that skilled workers are decreasingly likely in practice to support either the Labour or Democratic Parties.

McNamee (1975), building upon earlier work by Hamilton (1965), examined the relationship between skill and voting behaviour in six American Presidential elections since the Second World War. He demonstrated that skilled workers were consistently less likely to support the Democrats. Indeed, in the 1952, 1956 and 1972 Presidential contests, over half of skilled workers voted for the Republican candidate. Glenn and Alston (1968) revealed that the political values of skilled workers resembled those of clerical and professional employees more than those of the nonskilled manual working class. These findings were confirmed by Mackenzie's (1973) study in Providence in the mid-1960s which showed that many skilled workers had middle-class aspirations and attitudes. Nevertheless, the skilled workers in Providence remained strongly in favour of the Democratic Party at that time. However, this was no longer strongly in evidence in Providence by the time of the 1972 contest between Nixon and McGovern. Skilled workers in Rhode Island strongly disliked McGovern's stance on the Vietnam War and his desire to raise taxes in order to pay for his proposed welfare plans.

Indeed, it is likely that skilled workers are even less strongly committed to the Democratic Party in present-day America. During my fieldwork in the USA in 1985 and 1987, there appeared to be little evidence of strong support for the Democrats amongst the skilled workers with whom I spoke. Such a viewpoint is confirmed by Form's (1985) recent study of the American working class. He concludes that 'The skilled, in turn, are more conservative than are the less skilled workers . . . The skilled are primarily concerned with protecting their economic and status advantages' (p. 191). However, the full contours of the

Table 9.1 *Skilled workers and party allegiance (percentage support), 1970–1987*

Party vote	1970 %	1974 (Oct) %	1979 %	1983 %	1987 %
Labour	55	48	47	35	34
Conservative	35	27	46	39	43
Liberal/Alliance	7	20	11	27	24

Sources: Figures for 1970, 1974 and 1979 taken from D. Thomas, 'Will the man who put Mrs. Thatcher in do so again,' *New Society*, 26 May 1983; figures for 1983 and 1987 taken from I. Crewe, 'Why Mrs. Thatcher was returned with a landslide', *Social Studies Review* 3, 1, September 1987

disaffection of skilled workers from the Democratic coalition remain to be studied. Nevertheless, given that similar processes appear to be under way in Britain, it is possible to throw light upon American trends by means of an examination of the disaffection of skilled workers from the British Labour Party.

Skilled workers were in the vanguard of Labour politics in the period between 1920 and 1970; they provided massive electoral support for the Labour Party and also many activists and candidates throughout this period (see Penn, 1982 and 1985a, for a discussion of this historical pattern). However, since 1970 there has been a sharp decline in support for Labour by skilled workers. As is clear from table 9.1, there has been a massive decline in Labour support amongst skilled workers since 1970. In that year more than half of skilled workers supported the Labour Party whereas by the 1980s only one-third retained the traditional pattern of allegiance. A series of inter-related factors have been shown to be crucial in this process. Firstly, it is clear that in the period between 1962 and 1984, Labour Governments were associated with declining skilled earnings differentials within the manual working class (see Penn and Dawkins, 1988). This was associated with Labour Party economic policies that, through the medium of Government-imposed incomes policies, effected a redistribution of income within the manual working class. This reached its apogee in the Callaghan Labour Government after 1975 and led to considerable industrial unrest. This was manifest both in the BL Toolroom dispute and during the Heathrow airport maintenance dispute in 1978. Part of the reason for these developments was the increasing power of unions representing low-paid, nonskilled workers within the Party and trade union organizations. It was also associated with the serious dislocation caused by the oil price rise by OPEC in 1973.

The reduction of differentials within the British working class during the late 1960s and in the mid-1970s challenged basic norms and beliefs amongst skilled workers. Skilled workers feel that their training and responsibility lead them to deserve considerably more pay than the nonskilled. Indeed, much of the rationale of skilled trade unionism is to defend the economic advantages that skill can and, in the mind of skilled workers, should accrue. As was shown in chapter 6, these beliefs about skill are central to the socialization of skilled workers in both countries. Skill is strongly associated in most people's minds with extensive training periods. Eighty per cent of respondents in Rochdale in 1986, when asked what was the basis of skilled work, replied that it was associated with training. Indeed, over a quarter explicitly mentioned apprenticeships. Skill is further seen both as a basis of prestige and a legitimation for additional economic rewards (see Penn, 1975; Goldthorpe and Hope, 1974).

Skilled workers are strongly committed to the inequality of income inherent in modern economic systems. In 1979 they were three times as likely to own a car as were unskilled workers in Britain and their household incomes averaged twice those of the unskilled (Thomas, 1983). Indeed, many skilled workers work long hours to support the standard of living of their families. In 1979, over a third worked over 46 hours a week (Thomas, 1983). This affluence intersected with a central issue of the 1979 General Election campaign – the sale of municipally owned council houses (Kellner, 1982). The Conservative Party under Mrs Thatcher promised to sell these homes (under certain qualifying conditions) to their existing tenants. Over a third of skilled workers lived in such housing at that time and many were attracted to the possibility of home ownership. The sight and sound of middle-class Labour politicians, few of whom lived in council housing, telling those who did that they must retain the dubious benefits of municipal control was a powerful additional factor in the disaffection of skilled workers. In the 1980s, the situation has not been reversed. The Labour Party has moved further to the left, a tendency closely connected with the departure of the Social Democrats from the Party and the rise of the centrist 'Alliance' between the Liberal Party and the newly formed SDP. The 1987 General Election revealed the depth of the collapse in support for Labour amongst skilled workers and the continued success of the Thatcherite Conservative Party in obtaining electoral support from such workers.

For the Labour Party to regain the support of skilled workers, they would have to adopt policies that articulated such workers' perceived interests. Given that these manifestly no longer include state ownership of industry or of housing nor an eradication of income inequalities within the working class, this will be no easy task for a party that is powerfully constrained by the egalitarian and statist beliefs of its rank-and-file activists and, more critically, many of the largest trade unions.

Indeed, there is growing tension within British trade unions over the future development of the Labour movement. The recent rise of large conglomerate unions has led to serious jurisdictional problems (see Penn, 1986). For instance, the Electricians' Union (EETPU) has claimed the right to organize all the new work tasks generated by microelectronic technologies. This is a classic tactic of skilled unions in the face of technological change and is called 'following the work'. This has led the EETPU to organize 'green-field' plants in the paper industry (UPM at Shotton and Kymmene at Irvine) and in the newspaper industry (*Today*). The EETPU was also involved in the bitterly fought dispute at News International where the traditional print unions were excluded from the new plant at Wapping. At the present moment, the EETPU are engaged in attempts to organize workers in the television industry. These actions led the EETPU to contemplate leaving the TUC and at the Trades Union Congress in September, 1988, they were expelled for their unwillingness to comply with TUC directives to abandon two new single-union agreements. It remains a strong possibility that some alliance of the EETPU and the AEU could form the basis of a rival trade union federation in Britain. What is centrally important about these developments is that they signal both a growing alienation of unions representing large numbers of skilled workers in Britain from the socialist inclinations of other large British unions such as the newly formed MSF (Manufacturing, Science and Finance Union) and the TGWU (Transport and General Workers' Union). More than any other group in Britain, and certainly far more than the mass of industrial sociologists who are locked into a conceptual time-warp, the EETPU and AEU recognize the contradictory effects on the division of labour inherent within contemporary technical change. There are both losers *and* gainers and these unions are strongly committed to the notion that their members, and particularly their core membership of skilled workers, must be amongst the leading gainers. Indeed, both the EETPU and the AEU have developed training systems that are available for their members and which are central to their strategy of 'following the work'. Such strategies emphasize the central commitment of skilled workers to maintaining their position within the occupational system and flows naturally from the matrix of socialization into skilled identities outlined in chapter 6.

3 Skilled Workers in the Class Structure

Skilled workers remain a significant element within the class structures of British and American society. How should they be seen in terms of their class situation? Neither the image of the labour aristocracy nor of the militant craftsman is satisfactory in its entirety. There is clear evidence that skilled workers in Britain and America remain committed to the preservation of an economic hierarchy within the working class. There is also evidence that they are decreasingly enamoured of left-of-centre politics as witnessed by their waning support for either the Democrats or the Labour Party. These political developments are conjunctural in so far as skilled workers formed both the core of the Rooseveltian coalition and were in the vanguard of British socialism in the period between 1910 and 1950. Nevertheless, skilled workers remain powerfully organized at work and this collective strength is often harnessed in challenges to the fullest implementation of the managerial prerogative. Skilled workers, unlike most nonskilled workers, are strongly committed to occupational forms of solidarity that often predate industrial capitalism and which generate a collective awareness of their own importance. The possession of 'skill', based as it is upon lengthy training and extensive experience provides a strong sense of individual and collective worth. These identities generate a powerful collective capacity to challenge management, technicians, the nonskilled and, on occasion, the owners of productive resources. This combination of industrial militancy in support of skilled work with a rigorous defence of sectional advantage is never grasped adequately in the literature on either the militant craftsman or on the labour aristocracy. The latter theorists fail to comprehend that skilled workers are combative in defence of their interests, and not merely stooges of capitalism. The militant craftsman tradition fails to recognize that industrial militancy may not necessarily be combined with radical politics of the left. Indeed, as has been shown, they have been noticeably attracted by the radical policies of the Reaganite and Thatcherite right during recent years.

Such political orientations do not signify a process of 'embourgeoisement'. Skilled workers in Britain and America retain a common condition – as manual workers. They are recipients of commands from management and whilst they retain considerable discretion and autonomy within their job tasks, they must constantly battle with management to preserve such working conditions and to secure adequate compensation for such labour. In both societies, skilled workers maintain a common status as manual workers. Despite a long tradition of research into class consciousness in both Britain (Bulmer, 1975) and America (Jackman and Jackman, 1983; Vanneman and Cannon, 1987), the question of the class identity of skilled workers has rarely been subject to systematic investigation. In the USA, skilled workers are able to sustain the identities of being both a 'worker' and 'middle-class'. As was revealed in chapter 6, multiple identities are the norm for skilled workers and attempts to press them into a single mould in terms of their identity is misconceived. There is less evidence from Britain to support the notion that skilled workers see themselves as manual workers and middle class. Nevertheless, it remains a possibility and further research is needed in these areas.

Neither the political orientations nor the cultural beliefs of skilled workers are a solid basis upon which to determine their contemporary class situation. However this is decided, it is evident from this research that the structural position of skilled workers in the division of labour is similar in both Britain and America. It is also clear that there has been no dramatic structural transformation under way in their work situations since the Second World War. The present class situation of skilled workers seems similar to that throughout the period of industrial capitalism since the mid-nineteenth century. There is consequently no reason to suggest that skilled workers are becoming more 'proletarian' in their condition nor to suppose that they are becoming 'embourgeoisified'. They remain a distinct stratum, and consequently there is little evidence to support notions of progressive differentiation. Skilled workers are certainly a differentiated category within the contemporary British and American workforces but this is a persistent condition and cannot be characterized as new. I am led to the inexorable conclusion that skilled workers remain a significant element within the contemporary class structures of advanced industrial societies. This has been the case since the advent of industrial capitalism and it remains so today. To understand the class structures of modern societies, it is necessary to understand the skilled worker stratum. As I suggested at the inception of this book, skilled workers have been used by sociologists as the embodiment of alleged transformations in the structure of class inequality within advanced societies. Much of this literature is more concerned to develop contemporary myths than to present rigorous, empirical research. I hope that the analysis presented in this book will go some way to dispel these myths and to stimulate a renewal of empirical inquiry into the significance of contemporary developments, both in the workplace and within the wider society.

Notes

Notes to chapter 1

1 For Gorz (1975), the entire Western working class is defined as a labour aristocracy confronting the Third World proletariat, whilst for Gronan (1971) administrative and clerical employees constitute the new aristocracy of labour in Western Europe. Within neo-Marxism any division within their category of labour is a potential recruit to the ranks of the aristocracy of labour.

2 See P. Joyce (1980) and M. Savage (1987) for graphic analyses of factory politics at this time.

3 Information taken from R. Smith, 'History of the Lancashire Cotton Industry Between the Years 1873 and 1896', University of Birmingham PhD thesis, 1954. Also relevant is D. Farnie, 'The English Cotton Industry 1850–1896', University of Manchester MA Thesis, 1953; see also Turner (1962). Haydu (1988) continues this tradition of ignorance. He claims that mule spinners in the latter nineteenth century displayed an 'absence of industrial conflict' (p. 19). Haydu should at least have read Turner's account which details the high levels of industrial conflict in textiles at that time.

4 See Penn (1985a, chapter 3) for a detailed analysis of these confusions.

5 C. Kerr et al., *Industrialism and Industrial Man* (1962) presents the classic statement of the convergence thesis.

6 The relative affluence of skilled workers is well attested in the literature. For Britain, see H. Phelps Brown, *The Inequality of Pay* (1977); G. Routh, *Occupation and Pay in Great Britain, 1906–60* (1965); and K. Knowles and D. Robertson, 'Differences between the Wages of Skilled and Unskilled Workers, 1880–1950' (1951). For the USA, see E.E. Muntz, 'The Decline of Wage Differentials Based on Skill in the United States' (1955); R. Ozanne, 'A Century of Occupational Differentials in Manufacturing' (1962); and P. Skergold, 'Wage Differentials Based on Skill in the United States, 1899–1914' (1977).

7   Such a current reached its nadir recently in R. Bellah et al.'s *Habits of the Heart: Individualism and Commitment in American Life* (1985).

8   This still remains Dahrendorf's view as can be seen in his 'Twenty-Five Years of Socio-Political Analysis: Notes and Reflections' (1980).

9   Form's earlier works include 'The Internal Stratification of the Working Class', *American Sociological Review* (1973), and *Blue-Collar Stratification: Auto Workers in Four Countries* (1976).

10 Mackenzie's and Dahrendorf's views parallel those of Touraine (1969) and Gorz (1967) in France, who suggest that technicians are the new skilled workers within modern production. See D. Gallie (1978) for an extensive discussion of these issues.

11 *The Affluent Worker* series never analyses adequately the skilled maintenance workers who were sampled in the three Luton factories. A detailed reading of these texts reveals significant differences between these skilled workers and the responses of the nonskilled assembly line workers in the plants.

12 This has been severely analysed by Holmwood and Stewart (1983).

13 This can best be seen in K. Marx (1970), *Capital: Volume 1* (Moscow: Progress).

14 In particular, see M. Weber, *General Economic History* (1961).

Notes to chapter 2

1   See D. Lockwood (1981), 'The Weakest Link in the Chain? Some Comments on the Marxist Theory of Action', in R.L. Simpson and I.H. Simpson (eds), *Research in the Sociology of Work: Volume 1* (Greenwich, Conn. JAI Press) for an extensive criticism of Braverman's methodology along with that of a wide range of neo-Marxist accounts of economic change. See also R. Penn (1988).

2   See, for instance, P. Armstrong, 'Management, Labour Process and Agency', and D. Knights and H. Willmott, 'Management as a Capitalist Labour Process', papers presented at the 'Workshop on the Study of Managerial Labour Processes', European Institute for Advanced Studies in Management, Brussels, May 1988.

3   See R.D. Penn, 'Technical Change and Work Organization in Contemporary Britain', *Sociologia del Lavoro*, 1989 (forthcoming).

4   There is an increasing body of international research on technical change and the division of labour. Examples are Duhm and Muckenberger (1983); and A. Sorge et al. (1983).

5   For Britain, see Penn (1985a); and for the USA see, for example, Montgomery (1976) and Haydu (1984).

Notes to chapter 3

1 In 1984, 18.8% of employed Americans were members of trade unions; see Bureau of Labor Statistics, *Employment and Earnings*, January, 1985. In Britain, the proportion in 1984 was around 45% and falling swiftly; see *Employment Gazette*, January, 1986.

2 The concentration of aerospace, electronics and chemicals in the USA makes it probably the strongest economy technologically in the world. Only Japan and West Germany would seem to offer any degree of challenge to such a view.

3 See *1980 Census of Population, Characteristics of the Population, Detailed Population Characteristics, United States Summary, Section A: United States, Appendix B* (PC80-1-D1-A, US Summary, Bureau of the Census, Washington DC, 1981).

4 See Appendix B of PC80-1-D1-A (note 3 above) for full reference.

5 Office of Population Censuses and Surveys, *Classification of Occupations 1970* (London, 1970).

6 The sources for table 3.1 are as follows:
1940: The Sixteenth Census of the United States: 1940. Population - volume III, The Labor Force, Table 58, 'Detailed occupation of employed persons (except on public emergency work) by sex for the US' (US Government Printing Office, Washington, 1943).
1950: Census of Population: 1950, volume II, Characteristics of the Population, Part I: United States Summary, Table 124, 'Detailed occupation of the experienced civilian labor force' (Bureau of the Census, Washington DC, 1953).
1960: The Eighteenth Census of the United States: Census of Population, 1960; volume 1, Characteristics of the Population, Part I, United States Summary, Table 201, 'Detailed occupation of the experienced civilian labor force, by sex, for the United States: 1960 and 1950', pp. 522–527 (Bureau of the Census, Washington DC, 1964).
1970: The Nineteenth Census of the United States: volume 1, Characteristics of the Population, United States Summary Section 2, Table 221, 'Detailed occupation of the experienced civilian labor force and employed persons 16 years and over' (Bureau of the Census, Washington DC, 1973).
1980: Detailed Population Characteristics: United States Summary, PC 80-1-D1-A: US Summary, Table 276, 'Detailed occupation of the epxerienced civilian labor force and employed persons by sex: 1980 and 1970', pp. 1–166–175 (US Department of Commerce, Bureau of the Census, Washington DC, 1984).

7 In 1940, the clerical category includes salesworkers. In 1950, 1960 and 1970 it does not. In 1980 the clerical section refers to 'administrative support occupations, including clerical'. In 1980, the combined category of

farmers and farm labourers also includes occupations from forestry and fishing. In 1980 service workers includes private household occupations and service occupations, including protective occupations like firefighters and the police.

8   This is argued in chapter XIV of A.M. Edwards (1943), *Sixteenth Census of the United States: 1940 – Population: Comparative Occupation Statistics for the United States, 1870–1940* (US Government Printing Office, Washington DC).

9   See R. Penn, 'Technological Change, Skilled Workers and the Division of Labour', *Skilled Worker Project Working Paper* (Department of Sociology, Lancaster University, February 1984).

10 See R. Penn, 'The Skills of the Welder', University of Lancaster, Social Change and Economic Life Project in Rochdale, *Working Paper 8*, February 1986 (Department of Sociology, Lancaster University).

11 School of Business and Public Administration, Washington University, St Louis, Missouri (1957), *A Study of the Supply and Demand for Certain Selected Skills, 1956–1961, in Five Metalworking Industries, St Louis Survey Area* (St Louis).

12 Ibid., p. 27, Table 14, 'Status of training of selected skilled workers in metalworking industries, St Louis survey area'.

13 See International Brotherhood of Electrical, Radio and Machine Workers, AFL-CIO, *The IUE Skilled Trades Program*, Washington DC, December 1959.

14 See R. Penn (1986), 'The Skills of the Welder'. In 1971, there were 140,000 welders in Great Britain (GB Census), and 40,000 welding machines (C. Huggett, 'Welding', in Swords Isherwood and Senker (eds) (1980)), of which at least 10,000 probably require considerable skill from the operative (see Huggett, pp. 33 and 36).

15 See R. Penn (1985a) for a discussion of these changes between 1911 and 1961.

16 For example, Engineering Industry Training Board, *Operator Training Elements: Manual Metal Arc Welding* (Watford, n.d.); Engineering Industry Training Board, *Module Instruction Manuals: Fabrication Engineering Practices* (Watford, n.d.).

17 J. Northcott and P. Rogers (1984) reveal that 40% of British factories use micro-electronics in their production processes whereas only 10% incorporate them in their products.

18 The managing director of Lex Vehicle Leasing, which operates a fleet of 16,000 cars in Britain, said in February 1986 that electronic engine management systems are 'very prone to failure. Often the fault is very minor . . . but it does bring the car to a complete stop and the systems are so complex that expert help is almost always needed. We believe that many of the problems stem from the fact that dealer servicing is lagging behind the rapid development in electronics due to problems involved in training

staff'. Cited in *Financial Times*, 11 February 1986.

19 One paradox of the 'labour process' debate in Britain has been an increasing belief that Braverman's account only fits the USA and is a poor guide to developments in Britain. This is held to be a result of a lacuna in Braverman's analysis which leaves trade union responses to technological change and scientific management out of the explanatory equation. Most British analysts take this to be more or less acceptable under American conditions, where trade unions are held to be very weak when compared with Britain.

20 See R. Penn, 'Continuities and Change in Skilled Work: A Comparison of Five Paper Manufacturing Plants in the UK, Australia and the USA', *British Journal of Sociology*, XXXIX, 1 (March 1988).

Notes to chapter 4

1 An establishment is defined by a separate address and/or a separate payroll. In everyday terms it corresponds closely to most people's idea of their employer.

2 AUEW-E: Amalgamated Union of Engineering Workers – – Engineering Section. EETPU: the Electrical, Electronic, Telecommunication and Plumbing Union.

3 In 1986 the American Parent company (Scott) took over the operation in its entirety.

4 General Municipal, Boilermakers' and Allied Trades' Union. Now General Municipal and Boilermakers' Union (GMBU).

5 Association of Scientific, Technical and Managerial Staffs.

6 Amalgamated Union of Engineering Workers – – Engineering Section: now the Amalgamated Engineering Union (AEU).

7 Society of Graphical and Allied Trades.

8 Electrical and Engineering Staff Association.

9 Transport and General Workers' Union.

10 Union of Construction, Allied Trades and Technicians.

11 Technical, Administrative and Supervisory Section of the AUEW. Subsequently a separate union (TASS). TASS recently merged with ASTMS to form a new union called the Manufacturing, Service and Finance Union (MSF).

12 Association of Professional, Executive, Clerical and Computer Staff.

13 This is despite the fact that the Fleet Street printing branch of the EETPU has long been a focus of left-wing opposition to the contemporary leadership of the union.

Notes to chapter 5

1 For example, Caudill (1983), Corbin (1981), Dix (1977, 1979), Eller (1982), Gaventa (1980), Hammond and Mahoney (1978), Seltzer (1985), Taplin (1986a, 1986b) and Yarrow (1979, 1982).

2 The exceptions are Dix (1979) and Yarrow (1979). Both these papers appear in Zimbalist (1979) and neither have much to say about modern American mining work. None the less, they do contradict each other. Dix argues that the advent of the longwall into the contemporary American mining industry has increased the autonomy of the face teams, whereas Yarrow suggests that the introduction of longwall mining decreases the traditional autonomy of continuous mining.

3 Data from R.L. Marovelli and J.M. Karhnak, 'The Mechanization of Mining', *Scientific American*, September 1982, p. 91.

4 For a description of open-cut, surface mining in Australia, see C. Williams (1981).

5 See *Coal Age*, 'Surface Mining of Coal . . . Growth Through Evolution', June 1986, pp. 69–81.

6 See *Coal Age*, 'Longwall Output Continues to Rise', August 1986, pp. 58–60.

7 See Bureau of Labor Statistics, 1981, p. 16, table 13.

8 Ibid.

9 Ibid.

10 See *Coal Age*, 'Longwall Census', August 1986, pp. 47–57.

11 Cited in Marovelli and Karhnak, 1982: 98.

12 Ibid.

13 Ibid.

14 62% of US output comes from surface mining.

15 See L.J. Mills and K. Jones (1983), *Confidential Report on Visit to USA*, National Coal Board; and see National Coal Board (1985), *Group 2 Report on USA*.

16 ASC are a supplier to the US auto industry. They are involved primarily in the automizing of standard production models by the addition of sun roofs or soft tops (convertibles).

17 *Financial Times*, 4 April 1986, 'Tyre Sales'.

18 *Financial Times*, 16 February 1986, 'Goodyear Steers a Global Course'.

19 Ibid.

20 This is revealed in the Textile Database compiled by Professor J. Leiter of the Department of Sociology and Anthropology, North Carolina State University, Raleigh. Examples of recent sociological analyses of textile workers are: J. Leiter (1982), 'Continuity and Change in the Legitimation of Authority in Southern Mill Towns'; B. Farrell, 'Kinship and Class in Nineteenth Century Boston', PhD thesis, Harvard, 1982; J. Leiter (1985), 'Work Alienation in the Textile Industry: Reassessing Blauner'; J. Leiter (1986),

'Reactions to Subordination: Attitudes of Southern Textile Workers'; M. Schulman, R. Zingraff and L. Reif (1985), 'Race, Gender, Class Consciousness and Union Support: An Analysis of Southern Textile Workers'; L. Frankel (1984), 'Southern Textile Women: Generations of Struggle and Survival'.

21 These comments are based upon discussions held in April 1987 at the Sourthern Sociological Association Meeting in Atlanta, Georgia, and with various scholars in Raleigh, North Carolina.

22 I learned much about the technologies utilized in the modern American textile industry from my visit to the School of Textiles at North Carolina State University and my discussions with the head of the Department of Textile Management and Technology, Professor Gordon Berkstrasser.

Notes to chapter 6

1 The dispute at the Isle of Grain power station in the early 1980s centred upon the attempt by laggers to use their strategic position at the end of the construction process to acquire larger differentials. The unions representing other craftsmen, the AUEW and the EETPU, regarded this as an attack on the traditional structure of relative pay and not only crossed the picket lines set up by the laggers' union (GMBATU) but also undertook the lagging work themselves. This episode marked the beginning of serious hostilities between these and other conglomerate unions in the 1980s.

2 These two unions recently merged to form the Manufacturing, Science and Finance Union (MSF).

3 This is outlined at length in Penn and Wigzell (1987).

Notes to chapter 7

1 See M. Beach, 'The Problems of the Skilled Worker in an Industrial Union: A Case Study', *ILR Research*, Fall – Winter, 1961, pp. 8–15; and the *Daily Labor Report*, 29 December 1975, on 'The Skilled Trades Society'.

2 I should like to thank Mr Thomas Weekley, Assistant Director of the UAW Skilled Trades Department, for his assistance with this and related points on skilled trades in the UAW.

3 See *Detroit News*, 12 April 1987.

4 See, for example, their relative absence from Renfield et al. (eds), *American Working Class History: A Representative Bibliography* (1984).

5 See, for instance, the June 1988 issue of the *AEU Journal* where both Eric Hammond, leader of the EETPU (p. 13) and Bill Jordan, leader of the AEU (p. 7) emphasized the importance of skilled workers in contemporary Britain. Jordan stated that 'In the wake of a third election defeat, Labour should pay more attention to the skilled worker – as articulated by our union'.

Bibliography

Anderson, P. (1965), 'Origins of the Present Crisis', in P. Anderson and R. Blackburn (eds), *Towards Socialism*, London: Collins.

Anderson, P. (1966), 'Socialism and Pseudo-empiricism', *New Left Review*, 35.

Armstrong, P. (1988), 'Management, Labour Process and Agency', Paper Presented to the EIASM Workshop on the Study of the Managerial Labour Process, Brussels, May.

Aronowitz, S. (1973), *False Promises: The Shaping of American Working Class Consciousness*, New York: McGraw.

Aronowitz, S. (1983), *Working Class Hero*, New York: Adama Books.

Beach, M. (1961), 'The Problems of the Skilled Worker in an Industrial Union', *ILR Research*, Fall – Winter, 8–15.

Becker, G. (1964), *Human Capital*, New York: National Bureau of Economic Research.

Becker, H. (1963), *Outsiders: Studies in the Sociology of Deviance*, Glencoe: Free Press.

Becker, H. (1982), *Art Worlds*, Berkeley: University of California Press.

Bell, D. (1962), *The End of Ideology*, New York: Free Press.

Bell, D. (1974), *The Coming of Post Industrial Society*, London: Basic Books.

Bellah, R., Madsen, R., Sullivan, W.W., Swidler, A. and Tipton, S.M. (1985), *Habits of the Heart: Individualism and Commitment in American Life*, Berkeley: University of California Press.

Bernstein, I. (1960), *The Lean Years: A History of the American Worker, 1920–1933*, New York: Houghton Mifflin.

Blackburn, R.M. and Mann, M. (1979), *The Working Class in the Labour Market*, London: Macmillan.

Blauner, R. (1964), *Alienation and Freedom: The Factory Worker and His Industry*, Chicago: Chicago University Press.

Braverman, H. (1974), *Labor and Monopoly Capital*, New York: Monthly Review Press.

Brody, D. (1964), *The Butcher Workmen: A Study of Unionization*, Cambridge,

MA: Harvard University Press.

Brody, D. (1980), *Workers in Industrial America*, Oxford: Oxford University Press.

Bulmer, M. (1975), *Working Class Images of Society*, London: Routledge & Kegan Paul.

Burawoy, M. (1979), *Manufacturing Consent*, Chicago: University of Chicago Press.

Bureau of Labor Statistics (1966), 'Technological Trends in Major American Industries', *Bulletin 1474*.

Bureau of Labor Statistics (1974), 'Technological Change and Manpower Trends in Six Industries', *Bulletin 1817*.

Bureau of Labor Statistics (1975), 'Technological Change and Manpower Trends in Five Industries', *Bulletin 1856*.

Bureau of Labor Statistics (1977), 'Technological Change and its Labor Impact in Five Industries', *Bulletin 1961*.

Bureau of Labor Statistics (1981), ' Technology, Productivity and Labor in the Bituminous Coal Industry, 1950–1979', *Bulletin 2072*, February.

Bureau of Labor Statistics (1982), 'Technology and Labor in Four Industries', *Bulletin 2104*.

Bureau of Labor Statistics (1983), 'Women at Work: A Chartbook', *Bulletin 2168*.

Burgess, K. (1975), *The Origins of British Industrial Relations*, London: Croom Helm.

Burns, A., Feickert, D., Newby, M. and Winterton, J. (1983), 'The Miners and New Technology', *Industrial Relations Journal*, 14, 4.

Burns, A., Newby, M. and Winterton, J. (1985), 'The Restructuring of the British Coal Industry', *Cambridge Journal of Economics*, 9.

Burstein, P. (1985), *Discrimination, Jobs and Politics: The Struggle for Equal Employment Opportunity in the United States since the New Deal*, Chicago: Chicago University Press.

Bythell, D. (1969), *The Handloom Weavers*, Cambridge: Cambridge University Press.

Caudill, H.M. (1983), *Theirs Be the Power*, Urbana, IL: University of Illinois Press.

Chapman, S.J. (1900), 'Some Policies of the Cotton Spinners' Trade Unions', *Economic Journal*, X.

Coal Age (1986), 'Surface Mining of Coal . . . Growth Through Evolution', June.

Coal Age (1986), 'Longwall Census', August.

Coal Age (1986), 'Longwall Output Continues to Rise', August.

Cockburn, C. (1983a), *Brothers*, London: Pluto Press.

Cockburn, C. (1983b), ' Caught in the Wheels', *Marxism Today*, November.

Cole, G.D.H. (1923), *Trade Unionism and Munitions*, Oxford: Clarendon Press.

Commission for Racial Equality (no date), *BL Cars Ltd: A Summary*, London: CRE.

Commons, J.R., Saposs, D.J., Sumner, H.L., Mittelman, E.B., Hoagland, H.E., Andrews, J.B. and Perlman, S. (1918), *History of Labor in the United States* (2 vols), New York: Macmillan.

Corbin, D.A. (1981), *Life, Work and Rebellion in the Coal Fields*, Urbana: University of Illinois Press.

Corrigan, P. (1979), *Schooling The Smash Street Kids*, London: Macmillan.

Cox, C.B. and Boyson, R. (eds) (1977), *Black Paper 1977*, London: Temple Smith.

Crewe, I. (1987a), 'A New Class of Politics', *The Guardian*, 15 June.

Crewe, I. (1987b), 'Why Mrs. Thatcher was returned with a landslide', *Social Studies Review*, 3, 1.

Cross, M. (1985), *Towards the Flexible Craftsman*, London: Technical Change Centre.

Dahrendorf, R. (1959), *Class and Class Conflict in Industrial Society*, Stanford: Stanford University Press.

Dahrendorf, R. (1980), 'Twenty-five Years of Socio-Political Analysis: Notes and Reflections', *Government and Opposition*, 15, 3/4.

Daniel, W.W. (1987), *Workplace Industrial Relations and Technical Change*, London: Frances Pinter.

Davis, R.L. and Cousins, J. (1975), 'The "New Working Class" and the Old', in M. Bulmer (ed), *Working Class Images of Society*, London: Routledge & Kegan Paul.

Dawson, A. (1979), 'The Paradox of Dynamic Technological Change and the Labor Aristocracy in the United States, 1880–1914', *Labor History*, 20, 3.

Dennis, N., Henriques, F. and Slaughter, C. (1956), *Coal is Our Life: An Analysis of a Yorkshire Mining Community*, London: Tavistock.

Dix, K. (1977), *Work Relations in the Coal Industry*, Institute for Labor Studies: University of West Virginia.

Dix, K. (1979) 'Work Relations in the Coal Industry: The Handloading Era, 1880–1930', in A. Zimbalist (ed), *Case Studies on the Labor Process*, New York: Monthly Review Press.

Doeringer, P. and Piore, M. (1971), *Internal Labor Markets and Manpower Analysis*, Lexington, MA: Heath.

Douglass, D. and Krieger, J. (1983), *A Miner's Life*, London: Routledge & Kegan Paul.

Dubois, P. (1981), 'Worker's Control Over the Organisation of Work', *Organization Studies*, 2.

Duhm, R. and Muckenberger, U. (1983), 'Computerization and Control Strategies at Plant Level', *Policy Studies* 3, 4.

Edwards, R.C. (1979), *Contested Terrain: The Transformation of the Twentieth Century*, New York: Basic Books.

Eisen, D.J. (1986), 'Union Response to Changes in Printing Technology: Another View', *Monthly Labor Review*, May.

Eller, R.D. (1982), *Miners, Millhands and Mountaineers*, Knoxville: University of Tennessee Press.

Engels, F. (1971), 'England in 1845 and 1885', in K. Marx and F. Engels, *On Britain*, Moscow: Progress.

Engineering Industry Training Board (1981), *Women in Engineering*, Watford: EITB.

Farrell, B. (1982), 'Kinship and Class in Nineteenth Century Boston', PhD thesis, Harvard University.

Filippelli, R.L. (1984), *Labor in the USA: A History*, New York: Alfred Knopf.

Fincham, R. (1983), 'The Diffusion of New Technology: A Study of some Firms in the Edinburgh Area', in Napier College Social Research Working Paper Number 4, *Essays on the New Technology*, Edinburgh.

Foner, P.S. (1947), *History of the Labor Movement in the United States. Volume 1: From Colonial Times to the Founding of the American Federation of Labor*, New York: International Publishers.

Foner, P.S. (1955), *History of the Labor Movement in the United States, Volume II: From the Founding of the American Federation of Labor to the Emergence of American Imperialism*, New York: International Publishers.

Foner, P.S. (1964), *History of the Labor Movement in the United States. Volume III: The Policies and Practices of the American Federation of Labor, 1900–1909*, New York: International Publishers.

Foner, P.S. (1965), *History of the Labor Movement in the United States. Volume IV: The Industrial Workers of the World, 1905–1917*, New York: International Publishers.

Form, W.H. (1973), 'The Internal Stratification of the Working Class', *American Sociological Review*, 38.

Form, W.H. (1976), *Blue-Collar Stratification: Autoworkers in Four Countries*, Princeton: Princeton University Press.

Form, W.H. (1985), *Divided We Stand: Working Class Stratification in America*, Urbana: University of Illinois Press.

Foster, J. (1976), 'British Imperialism and the Labour Aristocracy', in R. Skelley (ed), *The General Strike*, London: Lawrence and Wishart.

Frankel, L. (1984), 'Southern Textile Women: Generations of Struggle and Survival', in K. Sachs and D. Remy (eds), *My Troubles are Going to Have to Trouble with Me: Everyday Trials and Triumphs of Women Workers*, New Brunswick, NJ: Rutgers University Press.

Frobel, F., Heinrichs, J. and Kreye, O. (1980), *The New International Division of Labour*, Cambridge: Cambridge University Press.

Fuchs, V. (1968), *The Service Economy*, New York: Basic Books.

Gallie, D. (1978), *In Search of the New Working Class*, Cambridge: Cambridge University Press.

Gans, H. (1962), *The Urban Villagers*, New York: Free Press.

Gaventa, J. (1980), *Power and Powerlessness: Quiescence and Rebellion in an Appalachian Valley*, Urbana: University of Illinois Press.

Giebel, G. (1970), 'Corporate Structure, Technology and the Printing Industry', *Labor Studies Journal*, Winter.

Glenn, N.D. and Alston, J.P. (1968), 'Cultural Distances among Occupational Categories', *American Sociological Review*, 33.

Goldthorpe, J.H. (1979), 'Intellectuals and the Working Class in Modern Britain', *Fuller Bequest Lecture*, Essex University (mimeo).

Goldthorpe, J.H. (1980), *Social Mobility and Class Structure in Modern Britain*, Oxford: Clarendon Press.

Goldthorpe, J.H. and Hope, K. (eds) (1974), *The Social Grading of Occupations: A New Approach and Scale*, Oxford: Clarendon Press.

Goldthorpe, J.H., Lockwood, D., Bechhofer, F. and Platt, J. (1968a), *The Affluent Worker: Industrial Attitudes and Behaviour*, Cambridge: Cambridge University Press.

Goldthorpe, J.H., Lockwood, D., Bechhofer, F. and Platt, J. (1968b), *The Affluent Worker: Political Attitudes and Behaviour*, Cambridge: Cambridge University Press.

Goldthorpe, J.H., Lockwood, D., Bechhofer, F. and Platt, J. (1969), *The Affluent Worker in the Class Structure*, Cambridge: Cambridge University Press.

Gorz, A. (1967), *Strategy for Labor*, Boston: Beacon.

Gorz, A. (1975), *Socialism and Revolution*, Harmondsworth: Penguin.

Gray, R.Q. (1976), *The Labour Aristocracy in Victorian Edinburgh*, Oxford: Oxford University Press.

Gronan, M. (1971), 'Die Angestellte technische Intelligenz – eine Lohnarbeiterschichte', *Marxismus Digest*, 1.

Gustman, A.L. and Segal, M. (1974), 'The Skilled – Unskilled Wage Differential in Construction', *Industrial and Labor Relations Review*, 27, 2.

Habermas, J. (1976), *Legitimation Crisis*, London: Heinemann.

Hacker, S.L. (1979), 'Sex Stratification, Technology and Organizational Change: A Longitudinal Case Study of AT & T', *Social Problems*, 26, 5, June.

Hacker, S.L. (1981), 'The Culture of Engineering: Women, Workplace and Machine', *Women's Studies International Quarterly*, 4, 3.

Halle, D. (1984), *America's Working Man*, Chicago: University of Chicago Press.

Hamilton, R. (1965), 'Skill Level and Politics', *Public Opinion Quarterly*, 31.

Hammond, J. and Mahoney, C. (1978), 'The Political Economy of Appalachian Women', *Occasional Paper*, Regional Development Center, West Virginia Wesleyan College.

Hartmann, G., Nicholas, I. and Warner, M. (1983), 'Computerized Machine Tools, Manpower Consequences and Skill Utilization', *British Journal of Industrial Relations*, XXI, 2.

Haydu, J (1983), 'Factory Politics in Britain and the United States', Department of Sociology, University of California, Berkeley.

Haydu, J. (1984), 'British and American Solutions for "the Labor Problem": Employer Strategies in the Metal Trades, 1898–1901', paper presented at the

Pacific Sociological Association Meeting in Seattle, April.

Haydu, J. (1988), *Between Craft and Class: Skilled Workers and Factory Politics in the United States and Britain, 1890-1922*, Berkeley: University of California Press.

Hinton, J. (1973), *The First Shop Stewards' Movement*, London: Allen & Unwin.

Hobsbawm, E. (1964), *Labouring Men*, London: Weidenfeld.

Hoggart, R. (1959), *The Uses of Literacy*, Harmondsworth: Penguin.

Holden, E. (1985), 'The Impact of New Technology on Work Processes: A Comparative Study', Department of Sociology, Lancaster University (mimeo).

Holley, W. and Jennings, K. (1984), *The Labor Relations Process*, Chicago: The Dryden Press.

Holmwood, J. and Stewart, A. (1983), 'The Role of Contradictions in Modern Theories of Social Stratification', *Sociology*, 17, 2, May.

Hughes, E. (1971), *The Sociological Eye*, Chicago: Aldine.

Issel, W. (1985), *Social Change in the United States, 1945-1983*, London: Macmillan.

Jackman, M.R. and Jackman, R.W. (1983), *Class Awareness in the United States*, Berkeley: University of California Press.

Jones, B. (1981), 'Destruction or Redistribution of Engineering Skills? The Case of Numerical Control', in S. Wood (ed), *The Degradation of Work*, London: Hutchinson.

Jones, B. (1982), 'Destruction or Re-Distribution of Engineering Skills? The Case of Numerical Control' in S. Wood (ed), *The Degradation of Work*, London: Hutchinson.

Jones, B. and Rose, M (1986), 'Re-dividing Labour: Factory Politics and Work Reorganization in the Current Industrial Transition', in K. Purcell et al. (eds), *The Changing Experience of Employment*, London: Macmillan.

Jones, B. and Wood, S. (1985), 'Tacit Skills, Division of Labour and New Technology', *Sociologie du Travail*.

Joyce, P. (1980), *Work, Society and Politics*, Brighton: Harvester.

Kellner, P. (1982), 'Labour and the Affluent Worker', *New Statesman*, 6 August.

Kerr, C., Dunlop, J.T., Harbison, F.H. and Myers, C.A. (1962), *Industrialism and Industrial Man*, Harmondsworth: Penguin.

Klein, J. (1965), *Samples from English Culture: Volume 1* London: Routledge & Kegan Paul.

Kleinsorge, P.L. and Kerby, W.C. (1966), 'The Pulp and Paper Rebellion: A new Pacific Coast Union', *Industrial Relations*, 6, 1, October.

Knights, D. and Willmott, H. (1988), 'Management as a Capitalist Labour Process', Paper Presented to the EIASM Workshop on the Study of Managerial Labour Processes, Brussels, May.

Knowles, K.G.J.C. and Robertson, D.J. (1951), 'Differences between the Wages of Skilled and Unskilled Workers, 1880-1950', *Oxford Bulletin of Statistics*, 13, April.

Kornblum, W. (1974), *Blue Collar Community*, Chicago: Chicago University Press.

Landry, B. (1988), *The Black Middle Class*, Berkeley: University of California Press.

Lash, S. and Urry, J. (1987), *The End of Organized Capitalism*, Cambridge: Polity Press.

Lee, D. (1972), 'Very Small Firms and the Training of Engineering Craftsmen – Some Recent Findings', *British Journal of Industrial Relations*, X.

Lee, G. and Wrench, J. (1981a), 'Where Are the Black Apprentices?', *New Society*, 24 September.

Lee, G. and Wrench, J. (1981b), *Ethnic Minority Youth and Apprentices*, London: Commission for Racial Equality.

Lee, O. (1984), 'Crisis Potential and Counteracting Tendencies in the American Polity and Culture: Understanding Ungovernability, Neo-Conservatism and the "New Right" ', Department of Sociology, University of California, Berkeley.

Leiter, J. (1982), 'Continuity and Change in the Legitimation of Authority in Southern Mill Towns', *Social Problems*, 29, 5.

Leiter, J. (1985), 'Work Alienation in the Textile Industry: Reassessing Blauner', *Work and Occupations*, 12, 4.

Leiter, J. (1986), 'Reactions to Subordination: Attitudes of Southern Textile Workers', *Social Forces*, 64, 4.

LeMasters, E.E. (1975), *Blue-Collar Aristocrats*, Madison: University of Wisconsin Press.

Lenin, V.I. (1971), *Selected Works*, Moscow: Progress Publishers.

Lloyd, P. and Shutt, J. (1983), *Industrial Change in the Greater Manchester Textiles – Clothing Complex*, North West Industry Research Unit, Manchester University.

Lockwood, D. (1960), 'The "New Working Class" ', *European Journal of Sociology*, 1, 2.

Lockwood, D. (1966), 'Sources of Variation in Working Class Images of Society', *Sociological Review*, 14, 3.

Mackenzie, G. (1970), 'The Class Situation of Manual Workers: The United States and Britain', *British Journal of Sociology*, 21.

Mackenzie, G. (1973), *The Aristocracy of Labor: The Position of Skilled Craftsmen in the American Class Structure*, Cambridge: Cambridge University Press.

Mann, M. (1973), *Consciousness and Action Amongst the Western Working Class*, London: Macmillan.

Marovelli, R.L. and Karhnak, J.M. (1982), 'The Mechanization of Mining', *Scientific American*, September.

Marshall, G., Newby, H., Rose, D. and Vogler, C. (1988), *Social Class in Modern Britain*, London: Hutchinson.

Marshall, T.H. (1963), *Sociology at the Crossroads*, London: Heinemann.

Martin, R. (1981), *New Technology and Industrial Relations in Fleet Street*, Oxford: Clarendon Press.

Mayer, K. (1956), 'Recent Changes in the Class Structure of the United States', *Transactions of the Third World Congress of Sociology*, 3, London.

Mayer, K. (1963), 'The Changing Shape of the American Class Structure', *Social Research*, 30.

Mayhew, H. (1861), *London Labour and the London Poor*, London: Cais (reprinted in 1967).

McGoldrick, J. and McEwan, T. (1986), ' "Hold the front page!": The Introduction of New Technology in the Regional Newspaper Industry', in *Business Case File in Information Technology*, London: Van Nostrand Reinhold.

McLaughlin, D.B. (1979), 'The Impact of Labor Unions on the Rate and Direction of Technological Innovation', Michigan University, Ann Arbor US Department of Commerce, PB-295 084.

McNamee, S.J. (1975), 'Skill Level and Politics', *PASS Working Paper, 1222*, Sociology Department, University of Illinois at Urbana-Champaign.

Merton, R.K. (1968), *Social Theory and Social Structure*, New York: Free Press.

Montgomery, D. (1976), 'Workers' Control of Machine Production in the Nineteenth Century', *Labor History*, Fall.

Moss, B. (1976), *The Origins of the French Labour Movement 1830–1914: The Socialism of Skilled Workers*, Berkeley: University of California Press.

Muntz, E.E. (1955), 'The Decline of Wage Differentials Based on Skill in the United States', *International Labor Review*, 71.

Nairn, T. (1964), 'The Nature of the Labour Party', *New Left Review*, 27 and 28.

Nairn, T. (1965), 'Labour Imperialism', *New Left Review*, 32.

National Graphical Association (1984), 'The Way Forward – New Technology in the Provincial Newspaper Industry – An NGA '82 Initiative', Bedford: National Graphical Association.

National Opinion Research Center (1953), 'Jobs and Occupations: A Popular Evaluation', in R. Bendix and S.M. Lipset (eds), *Class, Status and Power*, Glencoe: Free Press.

New Zealand Journal of Industrial Relations (1984), *Special Issue on the Labour Process*.

Nichols, T. and Armstrong, P. (1976), *Workers Divided: A Study in Shopfloor Politics*, Glasgow: Fontana.

Noble, D. (1977), *America By Design: Science, Technology and the Rise of Corporate Capitalism*, New York: Alfred Knopf.

Noble, D. (1984), *The Forces of Production*, New York: Alfred Knopf.

Northcott, J. (1985), *Promoting Innovation: Microelectronics Applications Projects*, London: Policy Studies Institute, Report No. 645.

Northcott, J. and Rogers, P. (1984), *Microelectronics in British Industry: The Pattern of Change*, London: Policy Studies Institute Report No. 625.

Orton, E.S. (1976), ' Changes in the Skill Differential: Union Wages in Construction, 1907–1972', *Industrial and Labor Relations Review*, 30, 1.

Ozanne, R. (1962), 'A Century of Occupational Differentials in Manufacturing', *The Review of Economics and Statistics*, XLIV.

Pelling, H. (1963), *A History of British Trade Unionism*, Harmondsworth: Penguin.

Pelling, H. (1968), *Popular Politics and Society in Late Victorian Britain*, London: Macmillan.

Penn, R.D. (1975), 'Occupational Prestige: A Great Empirical Invariant?', *Social Forces*, December.

Penn, R.D. (1982), 'Skilled Manual Workers in the Labour Process, 1856–1964', in S. Wood (ed), *The Degradation of Work*, London: Hutchinson.

Penn, R.D. (1983a), 'Trade Union Organization and Skill in the Cotton and Engineering Industries in Britain, 1850–1960', *Social History*, 8, 1.

Penn, R.D. (1983b), 'Theories of Skill and Class Structure', *Sociological Review*, 31, 1.

Penn, R.D. (1983c), 'The Course of Wage Differentials between Skilled and Non-Skilled Manual Workers in Britain between 1856 and 1964', *British Journal of Industrial Relations*, XXI, 1.

Penn, R.D. (1985a), *Skilled Workers in the Class Structure*, Cambridge: Cambridge University Press.

Penn, R.D. (1985b), '1984: A Dual Crisis for Labour?', *Berkeley Journal of Sociology*, XXX.

Penn, R.D. (1986a), 'Socialization into Skilled Identities: An Analysis of a Neglected Phenomenon', *Journal of Interdisciplinary Economics*, 1, 3.

Penn, R.D. (1986b), 'The Skills of the Welder', Department of Sociology, Lancaster University (mimeo).

Penn, R.D. (1987), 'Skilled Work and Training in Rochdale', *SCELI Working Paper 9*, Department of Sociology, Lancaster University.

Penn, R.D. (1988), 'History and Sociology in the New Economic History – A Discourse in Search of a Method', Paper Presented to the BSA Annual Conference on History and Sociology, Edinburgh University, March.

Penn, R.D. (1989), 'History and Sociology in the New Economic Sociology – A Discourse in Search of a Method', in S. Kendrick (ed), *The Significance of Historical Analysis for Contemporary Sociology*, London: Macmillan.

Penn, R.D. and Dawkins, D. (1988), 'The Development of Skilled Earnings' Differentials in the British Engineering Industry between 1962 and 1984', *SCELI Working Paper 34*, Department of Sociology, Lancaster University.

Penn, R.D., Martin, A.M. and Davies, R.D. (1988), 'Changes in the Differentials of Engineering Workers since 1979: An Analysis of Earnings Data from Rochdale', *Journal of Interdisciplinary Economics*, 2, 3.

Penn, R.D. and Scattergood, H. (1985), 'Deskilling or Enskilling? An Empirical Investigation of Recent Theories of the Labour Process', *British Journal of Sociology*, XXXVI, 4.

Penn, R.D. and Scattergood, H. (1988), 'Continuity and Change in Skilled Work', *British Journal of Sociology*, XXXIX, 1.

Penn, R.D. and Simpson, R. (1986), 'The Development of Skilled Work in the British Coal Mining Industry, 1870–1985', *Industrial Relations Journal*, 17, 4.

Penn, R.D. and Simpson, R. (1987), 'The Development of Skilled Work in the Modern British Coal Mining Industry: The Case of Maintenance Work', paper presented to the 5th Annual Conference on 'The Organization and Control of the Labour Process', Manchester University, April.

Penn, R.D. and Wigzell, B. (1987), 'The Attitudes and Responses of Trades Unions to Technical Change', *Journal of Interdisciplinary Economics*, 2.

Perkin, H. (1978), 'The Condescension of Posterity: The Recent Historiography of the English Working Class', *Social Science History*, 3, 1, Fall.

Perlman, R. (1969), *Labor Theory*, New York: Wiley.

Phelps-Brown, H. (1977), *The Inequality of Pay*, Oxford: Oxford University Press.

Reich, R.B. and Mankin, E.D. (1986), 'Joint Ventures with Japan Give Away the Future', *Harvard Business Review*, 2.

Renfield, M.F., Leab, D.J. and Swanson, D. (eds) (1984), *American Working Class History: A Representative Bibliography*, New York: R.R. Bowker.

Riemer, J. (1977), 'Becoming a Journeyman Electrician', *Sociology of Work and Occupations*, 4, 1.

Roberts, R. (1971), *The Classic Slum*, Manchester: Manchester University Press.

Rogers, T. and Friedman, N. (1980), *Printers Face Automation*, Lexington, MA: D.C. Heath.

Rose, M. (1988), *Industrial Behaviour*, Harmondsworth: Penguin.

Rothbart, R. (1981), 'It Ain't No Trade Anymore', Department of Sociology, University of California, Berkeley.

Routh, G. (1965), *Occupation and Pay in Great Britain*, Cambridge: Cambridge University Press.

Sabel, C. (1984), *Work and Politics*, Cambridge: Cambridge University Press.

Sampson, A. (1975), *The Seven Sisters*, London: Hodder and Stoughton.

Savage, M. (1982), 'Control at Work', Lancaster Regionalism Group, *Working Paper 7*, Lancaster University.

Savage, M. (1987), *The Dynamics of Working Class Politics: The Labour Movement in Preston, 1880–1940*, Cambridge: Cambridge University Press.

Scarborough, H. (1984), 'Maintenance Workers and New Technology: The Case of Longbridge', *Industrial Relations Journal*, 15, 4.

Schatz, R.W. (1984), *The Electrical Workers: A History of Labor at General Electric and Westinghouse, 1923–60*, Urbana: University of Illinois Press.

Schulman, M., Zingraff, R. and Reif, L. (1985), 'Race, Gender, Class Consciousness and Union Support: An Analysis of Southern Textile Workers', *Sociological Quarterly*, 26, 2.

Scipes, K. (1984), 'Industrial Policy: Can it Lead the US out of its Economic Malaise?', *New Labor Review*, 6, Spring.

Seltzer, C. (1985), *Fire in the Hole: Miners and Managers in the US Coal Industry*, Louisville: University of Kentucky Press.

Senker, P., Swords-Isherwood, N., Brady, T. and Huggett, C. (1981), 'Maintenance Skills in the Engineering Industry: The Influence of Technical Change', Watford: Engineering Industry Training Board.

Shapira, P. (1984), 'The Crumbling of Smokestack California: A Case Study in Industrial Restructuring and the Reorganization of Work', Institute of Urban and Regional Development, *Working Paper 437*, University of California, Berkeley.

Sinclair, U. (1965), *The Jungle*, Harmondsworth: Penguin.

Skergold, P.R. (1977), 'Wage Differentials Based on Skill in the United States, 1899–1914', *Labor History*, 18.

SOGAT '82 (1985), *New Technology: The American Experience*, Hadleigh, Essex: SOGAT '82.

Sorge, A., Hartmann, G., Warner, M. and Nicholas, I.J. (1983), *Microelectronics and Manpower in Manufacturing*, Farnborough: Gower.

Stewart, A., Prandy, K. and Blackburn, R.M. (1980), *Social Stratification and Occupations*, London: Macmillan.

Stieber, J. (1959a), *The Steel Industry Wage Structure*, Cambridge, MA: Harvard University Press.

Stieber, J. (1959b), 'Occupational Wage Differentials in the Basic Steel Industry', *Industrial and Labor Relations Review*, 12, 2.

Strauss, G. (1965), 'Apprenticeship: An Evaluation of the Need', in A.M. Ross (ed), *Employment Policy and the Labor Market*, Berkeley: University of California Press.

Strauss, G.(1973), 'Minority Membership in Apprentice Programs in the Construction Trades: A Comment', *Industrial and Labor Relations Review*, 27, 1.

Swords-Isherwood, N. and Senker, P. (1980), *Microelectronics and the Engineering Industry: The Need for Skills*, London: Frances Pinter.

Taft, P. (1964), *Organized Labor in American History*, Evanston, IL: Harper and Row.

Taplin, I. (1986a), 'Miners, Coal Operators and the State: An Examination of Strikes and Work Relations in the US Coal Industry', PhD Dissertation, Brown University, Providence, RI.

Taplin, I. (1986b), 'Strategies of Labour Force Control and the Role of the State: The Case of the US Bituminous Coal Industry', Paper presented to the 4th Annual Labour Process Conference, Aston University, Birmingham.

Technological Change Committee of the Australian Science and Technology Council (1985), *A Report on Computer-Related Technologies in the Metal Trades Industry*, Canberra: Australian Government Publishing Service.

Thomas, D. (1983), 'Will the man who put Mrs. Thatcher in do so again?', *New Society*, 26 May.

Thompson, E.P. (1963), *The Making of the English Working Class*, London: Gollancz.

Touraine, A. (1969), *The Post-Industrial Society*, New York: Random.

Turner, H.A. (1962), *Trade Union Growth, Structure and Policy*, London: George Allen & Unwin.

Turner, H.A. (1964), 'Inflation and Wage Differentials in Great Britain', in J. Dunlop (ed), *The Theory of Wage Determination*, London: Macmillan.

Vanneman, R. and Cannon, L.W. (1987), *The American Perception of Class*, Philadelphia: Temple University Press.

Walby, S. (1986), *Patriarchy at Work: Patriarchal and Capitalist Relations in Employment*, Oxford: Polity Press.

Walkowitz, D. (1981), *Worker City, Company Town: Iron and Cotton Worker Protest in Troy and Cohoes New York, 1855–1884*, Urbana: Illinois University Press.

Wallace, M. (1985), 'Technological Changes in Printing: Union Response in Three Countries', *Monthly Labor Review*, July.

Wallace, M. and Kalleberg, A. (1982), 'Industrial Transformation and the Decline of Craft: The Decomposition of Skill in the Printing Industry, 1931–1978', *American Sociological Review*, 47, 3.

Webb, S. and Webb, B. (1920), *The History of Trade Unionism* (rev. ed), New York: Longmans, Green & Co.

Weber, A. (1963), 'The Craft – Industrial Issue Revisited: A Study of Union Government', *Industrial and Labour Relations Review*, 16.

Weber, M. (1961), *General Economic History*, trans, F.H. Knight, New York: Greenberg.

Wheeler, H. and Weikle, R. (1983), 'Technical Change and Industrial Relations in the United States', *Bulletin of Comparative Labour Relations*, 12.

Whyte, W.H. (1956), *The Organisation Man*, New York: Simon and Schuster.

Wigzell, B. (1984), 'The Effects of Automation on Electricians and Instrumenters in Contemporary Manufacturing Industry in the North West of England', MA Thesis, Department of Sociology, Lancaster University.

Wilkinson, B. (1983a), *The Shopfloor Politics of New Technology*, London: Routledge & Kegan Paul.

Wilkinson, B. (1983b), 'Technical Change and Work Organisation', *Industrial Relations Journal*, 14, 2.

Williams, C. (1981), *Open-Cut*, London: George Allen & Unwin.

Willis, P. (1977), *Learning to Labour*, Farnborough: Gower.

Willmott, P. and Young, M. (1957), *Family and Kinship in East London*, London: Routledge & Kegan Paul.

Wilson, F. (1985), 'Computer Numerical Control and Constraint', Paper presented to the 3rd Annual Conference on Organisation and Control of the Labour Process, Manchester Business School (mimeo).

Work in America (1973), *Work in America: Report of a Special Task Force to the Secretary of Health, Education and Welfare*, Cambridge, MA: MIT Press.

Wrenn, R. (1982), 'Management and Work Humanization', *Insurgent Sociologist*, 11, 3, Fall.

Wrenn, R. (1984), 'The Declining Strength of Labor', Department of Sociology, University of California, Berkeley.

Wright, E.O. (1985), *Classes*, London: Verso.

Yarrow, M. (1979), 'The Labor Process in Coal Mining: Struggle for Control', in A. Zimbalist (ed), *Case Studies on the Labor Process*, New York: Monthly Review Press.

Yarrow, M. (1982), 'How Good Strong Union Men Live it Out: Explorations of the Structure and Dynamics of Coal', PhD Dissertation, State University at Rutgers.

Zimbalist, A. (ed) (1979), *Case Studies on the Labor Process*, New York: Monthly Review Press.

Index

Albright and Wilson 68–9
Amalgamated Engineering Union (AEU/ AUEW–E) 64, 65, 66, 67, 68, 69, 71, 73, 75, 76, 131, 145
American class structure 11
American Federation of Labor (AFL) 155
APEX 66
Apprenticeships 126, 134, 142–3, 150, 153
ASTMS 64, 66, 67, 68, 69, 131

Beatermen 51, 52
Bowater-Scott 64
Braverman 12, 13, 20, 26, 28, 30, 54, 88, 95, 117, 168
British Cellophane 65
British Gypsum 68
British Nuclear Fuels 69–70
British Shipbuilders (Vickers) 66, 131
'bundle of tasks' 127

car repair 45
career ladders 136–8
census data 28–47
Civil Rights Act 155
class position of skilled workers 172–4
clothing industry 113
coal industry (USA) 97–104
coal miners (Britain) 81–9
Coalition of Black Trade Unionists 155
Commission for Racial Equality 163
Compensatory Theory of Skill 23, 24, 26, 58, 74, 89, 112, 117
compositors 34, 35, 38, 41, 44, 90–5, 110–12, 131
Computer Numerically Controlled machines (CNC) 74–8, 108–10

computerization 22, 23, 49–52, 53–4, 56, 74, 81, 94, 107
computer software 91–2
Conservative Party 7
control over time 133
convergence thesis 9
Cooke, Henry Ltd 53–4
Cotton Spinners' Union 6, 7
craft unionism 140–1
craft workers (numbers) 31–44
Cropper, James plc 49–52
Cumbria 63–74

Decomposition of labour 10
deferred gratification 134
deskilling 20, 21, 22, 28, 46, 56, 73, 88, 95, 117–19, 168
differentials 170
differentiation 10–11, 129
dryerman 55
dualism 11

economic sociology 3
EESA 64, 66
EETPU 64, 65, 66, 67, 68, 69, 70, 71, 73, 131, 145, 172
electrical engineering 78–81
electricians 34, 35, 38, 41, 64–74, 106, 126
embourgeoisement 9–10
engineering industry 8, 74–81, 108–10, 146, 162
enskilling 46
Equal Employment Opportunity Act 157
ethnicity 150, 152, 153, 158–9, 161–4
Executive Order 11246 155

facework (coal) 82–3
fellow workers 127
'following the work' 74, 131
foundries 115–16

gender composition of skilled crafts 151–61
GMBATU 64, 66, 68, 71

handloom weavers 93
Hometown programmes 155
homogenization 13, 14
Honeywell 54
human capital theory 17, 18, 26

industrial unions 141–2
instrumenters 57, 64–74, 106
internal career trajectory 154
international aspects of skill changes 24
International Association of Machinists (IAM) 143
International Typographical Union (ITU) 111–12
internationalization of production 167
iron-ore mining 106–8

Knights of Labor 154–5

labour aristocracy 5, 6, 15
Lancashire coalfield 81–9

machine makers 44, 46, 79, 95, 166–7
machinemen (paper) 50, 51, 56, 105–6
machinemen (printing) 94
machinists 22, 34, 35, 38, 41, 74–8
maintenance skills 25, 40, 43, 52, 57, 81–9, 95, 117
maintenance work 52, 60–74, 84–5, 94–5, 102–3, 107
management 132
Marxism 6
Measurex Company 53
meatpacking 114–15
mechanization 52
militant craftsman 7
multi-skilling 63, 77

NGA 94, 131
NUM 86–9, 145, 147
neo-Marxism 5, 54
nonskilled workers 130
Numerically Controlled Machines (NC) 74–8, 108–10

occupational boundaries 129
occupational socialization 126–139

paper industry 49–60, 104–6, 144
Philadelphia Plan 155
Pirelli 67
printing industry 89–95, 110–12
production skills 25, 40, 43, 81–9, 95, 116–17
proletarianization 11–13

Rochdale 8, 171

sectionalism 8
seniority 135, 153–4, 157
shoe industry 114
skilled differentials 146
skilled exclusions 130
Skilled Worker Project 23, 48, 60, 74, 78
skilling thesis 18, 19, 57, 73, 88, 95, 117–19, 168
social determination of skill model 123–5
social history 6–9
SOGAT '82 64
sub-contracting (maintenance) 53

TASS 66, 76, 131
Taylorism 12
technical change 23
technicians 130
textiles 8, 30, 113
TGWU 65, 67, 71
Thames Board 54–6
theoreticism 93
theory of modern industrial capitalism 24
toolmakers 34, 35, 38, 41
trade unions 64–74, 140–9
trajectories into skilled work 125–6
'tricks of the trade' 126
tyre industry 112

UCATT 65, 66, 68
UDM 87–8, 147
United Auto Workers (UAW) 142, 164
United Steel Workers (USW) 144
US Supreme Court 157

voting patterns 168, 172

Weber *v.* Kaiser Aluminium 157
welders 34, 38, 41, 45
welding 35–7
working class 4, 5